MOUNTAINS AND OREFIELDS
METAL MINING LANDSCAPES OF MID AND NORTH-EAST WALES

MOUNTAINS AND OREFIELDS: METAL MINING LANDSCAPES OF MID AND NORTH-EAST WALES

by Nigel Jones, Mark Walters and Pat Frost

Llywodraeth Cynulliad Cymru
Welsh Assembly Government

CBA Research Report 142
Council for British Archaeology
2004

Published in 2004 by the Council for British Archaeology
St Mary's House, 66 Bootham, York YO30 7BZ

British Library Cataloguing in Publication Data
A catalogue record for his book is available from the British Library

ISBN 1-902771-47-8

Text designed and typeset by Carnegie Publishing Ltd, Lancaster
Printed in the UK by Cromwell Press, Trowbridge, Wilts

The CBA acknowledges with gratitude a grant from Cadw towards the publication of this volume.

Front cover: Dalrhiw and Nant y Car South, Llanwrthwl, Powys *(03-C-669)*
Pelton wheel at Nantiago, Llangurig, Powys *(CS92-13-05)*
Back cover: Pool Park, Minera, Wrexham *(Crown Copyright: RCAHMW 93-CS-1550)*
Cwm Elan, Rhayader, Powys *(03-C-604)*

CONTENTS

LIST OF CONVENTIONS

Conventions used in the text

Mining terms used in the text are explained in a glossary towards the end of the volume. Measurements recorded in the field or derived from modern maps are given in metric units. Measurements derived from documentary sources are quoted in the form in which they appear, which is normally in imperial units (feet and inches, yards and fathoms). The record numbers of individual mine sites and the different elements within them (eg 18186) are as listed in the regional Historic Environment Record maintained by the Clwyd-Powys Archaeological Trust, to which enquiries for further information may be addressed (7a Church Street, Welshpool, Powys, SY21 7DL, tel 01938 553670, www.cpat.org.uk).

Drawing conventions

The drawing conventions used in the small and large scale mine plans in this volume are given below.

small scale

leat	——————→
tramway	+++++++++++++++++++++++++
shafts	∘ ○ ○
building or structure	▰
building or structure (site of)	▨
platform	⌐ ¬
whim circle	(⊙) or wh.
waste tip	░
reservoir	▦

large scale

leat	——————→
rubble	⣿
waste tip	⣿

J jig waste   B buddle waste

LIST OF FIGURES

Acknowledgements

The Clwyd-Powys Archaeological Trust (CPAT) is grateful to Powys County Council who funded an initial rapid survey of mines in Powys, and to Cadw who grant-aided most of the detailed survey and interpretation presented in this volume, as well as the publication itself. All of the published plans are based on surveys carried out by CPAT. These mostly derive from the survey work grant-aided by Cadw in 1994 and 1995, the exceptions being the survey of Minera Halvans in Figure 12 which was commissioned by the former Wrexham Maelor Borough Council in 1989, the plan of Nantygarw mine in Figure 59 commissioned by Welsh Water Elan Valley Trust in 1997, and the plan of Talargoch, Clive Shaft, in Figure 130, commissioned by W S Atkins Consultants on behalf of Denbighshire County Council in 2002. All the drawings have been prepared for publication by Brian Williams.

The Trust is grateful to the Royal Commission on the Ancient and Historical Monuments of Wales (RCAHMW) for permission to reproduce the following aerial photographs which are Crown Copyright, RCAHMW: Figures 2, 6–7, 16–17, 31, 47, 71–2, 81, 83–7, 116, 123, 135, 137. These were mostly taken by Chris Musson, the exception being Figure 137 which was taken by Toby Driver (RCAHMW). The remaining photographs were taken by the authors, for which CPAT is the copyright holder.

The Trust is grateful to the many individual landowners who have granted access to their property and have provided permission to reproduce the illustrations in this volume. The authors would particularly like to thank the Welsh Water Elan Valley Trust (Cwm Elan, Dalrhiw, Nant y Car South and Nantygarw); Forest Enterprise (Nant yr Eira); Grosvenor Estates (Pool Park); Redlands (now Lafarge) Aggregates (Eisteddfod and Lower Park), and the Trustees of the estate of R W Lloyd (Belgrave).

The authors are much indebted to the many individuals and organisations that have provided help or information, including the following: Brian Hart, Glyn Owen and Wendy Owen who helped with field survey on various occasions; David Bick, John Bennett, Bill Slater, and Simon Timberlake who provided information; the staff of the County Record Office at Hawarden and the National Library of Wales, Aberystwyth who helped in tracking down documentary information. Bill and Jenny Britnell, Stephen Hughes, Chris Musson, Peter Wakelin, and Bruce Watson generously provided comments and advice during the production of this volume.

LIST OF CONTRIBUTORS

Nigel Jones is the Senior Project Archaeologist with the Clwyd-Powys Archaeological Trust, with whom he has worked for the past 20 years. He studied geography at Sheffield University before joining CPAT in 1983, subsequently studying field archaeology at Oxford University Department of Extra-Mural Studies. Among the larger projects for which he has been responsible are detailed ground surveys of metal mines in Clwyd and Powys, excavations within the medieval town of New Radnor, excavations within the Roman fort and vicus at Caersws, and detailed ground surveys of a number of deserted and shrunken settlements. His other interests include aerial photography and building recording.

Mark Walters has been the Development Control Officer with the Clwyd-Powys Archaeological Trust since 1992. A graduate in archaeology of the University of Wales Lampeter, he has more recently studied for a masters degree in industrial heritage at the Ironbridge Institute. He initiated the regional metal mining surveys in Wales included in this volume with his study of the Powys orefield. His research interests include Roman metal mining and processing, the archaeology of the gas industry in Wales, ancient and modern military archaeology and British naval history of the Second World War.

Pat Frost, is an independent archaeological consultant who established Castlering Archaeology in 1999. She previously worked for the Clwyd-Powys Archaeological Trust, with whom she was responsible for a rapid survey of the metal mines of north-east Wales, as well as assisting with the detailed ground surveys of metal mines in Clwyd and Powys. Her main research interests are in industrial archaeology and she is currently the Welsh Regional Correspondent for *Industrial Archaeology News.*

Summaries

The volume considers the physical remains of the non-ferrous metal mining industry in the historic counties of Montgomeryshire, Radnorshire and Breconshire, Flintshire, Denbighshire in mid and north-east Wales, dating from the Bronze Age to the early 20th century, but especially in the period from the early 18th century to the late 19th century.

It focuses in particular upon the meaning and interpretation of a number of more extensive mining landscapes in terms of the mining and processing techniques that are represented. It complements a number of earlier studies by mining historians that have tended to concentrate upon historical evidence, though in many cases the surviving documentary evidence is slight or difficult to relate to what is visible on the ground. The analysis of fieldwork evidence is therefore crucial to a fuller understanding of how the mining landscapes developed.

The volume provides an introduction to the field archaeology of the mining industry for those with broader interests in landscape history and archaeology, as well as providing a detailed record of the surviving field evidence for specialist readers interested in mining history, industrial archaeology and landscape management. It begins with a brief overview of the significance of metal mining landscapes and an outline history of mining and ore processing in the study area. This is followed by descriptions and interpretations of some selected and better-preserved mining landscapes in both mid and north-east Wales varying from several hundred hectares to two or three hectares in extent. The descriptions are accompanied by plans showing ground surveys, ground-level photographs of surviving structures, and aerial photographs. A final chapter considers a number of management issues relating to mining landscapes, including the question of presentation and display. The volume concludes with a glossary of mining terms and two appendices giving the location of all recorded mining sites in the study area.

Many of the mine sites considered in the volume were sited on the margins of the uplands and were often remote from centres of population. Other issues which are considered include the surviving archaeological evidence for workers' housing, the harnessing of water-power particularly in mid Wales, and developments in the use of steam power in north-east Wales where sources of coal could be more readily obtained. Consideration is also given to the impact of mining on the broader landscape in terms of leats and reservoirs which supplied water to the mines, and the means by which processed ore was transported to smelting sites, often some distance away from the mines themselves.

Crynodeb

Mae'r gyfrol yn ystyried gweddillion ffisegol y diwydiant cloddio metelau an-haearnaidd yn siroedd hanesyddol Sir Drefaldwyn, Sir Faesyfed a Sir Frycheiniog, Sir y Fflint, Sir Ddinbych yng nghanolbarth a gogledd-ddwyrain Cymru, yn dyddio o'r Oes Efydd i ddechrau'r 20fed ganrif, ond yn enwedig yn ystod y cyfnod o ddechrau'r 18fed ganrif i ddiwedd y 19eg ganrif.

Mae'n canolbwyntio yn benodol ar ystyr a dehongliad nifer o dirweddau cloddio ehangach yn nhermau technegau cloddio a phrosesu sy'n cael eu cynrychioli. Mae'n ategu nifer o astudiaethau cynharach gan haneswyr cloddio sydd wedi tueddu i ganolbwyntio ar dystiolaeth hanesyddol, er mewn llawer o achosion mae'r dystiolaeth ddogfennol sydd wedi goroesi yn brin neu mae'n anodd ei chysylltu â'r hyn sy'n weledol ar y tir. Felly, mae dadansoddi tystiolaeth gwaith maes yn hanfodol er mwyn sicrhau dealltwriaeth lawnach o sut y datblygwyd tirweddau cloddio.

Mae'r gyfrol yn darparu cyflwyniad i faes archeoleg y diwydiant cloddio ar gyfer y rhai sydd â diddordebau ehangach mewn hanes tirweddau ac archeoleg, yn ogystal â darparu cofnod manwl o dystiolaeth maes sydd wedi goroesi ar gyfer darllenwyr arbenigol sydd â diddordeb mewn hanes cloddio, archeoleg ddiwydiannol a rheoli tirweddau. Mae'n dechrau gyda throsolwg byr o bwysigrwydd tirweddau cloddio metel a braslun o hanes cloddio a phrosesu mwynau yn ardal yr astudiaeth. Yna ceir disgrifiadau a dehongliadau o rai o dirweddau cloddio detholedig a'r rhai wedi'u diogelu orau yng nghanolbarth a gogledd-ddwyrain Cymru, yn amrywio o nifer o gannoedd o hectarau i ddau neu dri hectar mewn maint. Ceir cynlluniau i gyd-fynd â'r disgrifiadau sy'n dangos arolygon tir, ffotograffau lefel y ddaear o strwythurau sydd wedi goroesi, a ffotograffau o'r awyr. Mae'r bennod olaf yn ystyried nifer o faterion rheoli sy'n ymwneud â thirweddau cloddio, yn cynnwys y mater o gyflwyno ac arddangos. Daw'r gyfrol i ben gyda rhestr eirfa o dermau cloddio a dau atodiad sy'n rhoi lleoliad pob safle cloddio sydd wedi'u cofnodi yn ardal yr astudiaeth.

Lleolwyd llawer o'r safleoedd cloddio sy'n cael eu hystyried yn y gyfrol wrth ymyl ucheldiroedd ac yn aml yn bell o ganolfannau poblogaeth. Ymhlith y materion eraill sy'n cael eu hystyried mae tystiolaeth archeolegol sydd wedi goroesi ar gyfer cartrefi gweithwyr, defnyddio pŵer dŵr yn enwedig yng nghanolbarth Cymru, a datblygiadau yn y defnydd a wnaed o bŵer stêm yng ngogledd-ddwyrain Cymru lle'r oedd ffynonellau glo yn haws cael gafael arnynt. Rhoddir ystyriaethau hefyd i effaith y cloddio ar y dirwedd ehangach yn nhermau ffrydiau a chronfeydd dŵr a oedd yn cyflenwi dŵr i'r cloddfeydd, a'r dulliau o gludo mwynau wedi'u prosesu i safleoedd mwyndoddi, a hynny gryn bellter o'r cloddfeydd eu hunain yn aml.

Zusammenfassung

Dieser Band beschäftigt sich mit den Spuren physischer Überreste des Buntmetallbergbaus in den historischen Grafschaften von Montgomeryshire, Radnorshire und Breconshire, Flintshire, Denbighshire im Mittelteil und Nordosten von Wales. Diese werden von der Bronzezeit bis ins frühe 20. Jahrhundert datiert, aber hier wird insbesondere der Zeitraum vom frühen 18. Jahrhundert bis ins späte 19. Jahrhundert behandelt.

Es wird auf die Bedeutung und die Interpretation einer Reihe von ausgedehnten Bergbaulandschaften im Detail eingegangen, vor allem was die Bergbau- und Aufbereitungstechnologien betrifft, die dort repräsentiert werden. Damit wird eine Reihe von historischen Studien über den Bergbau ergänzt, die dazu neigten sich auf historische Quellen zu konzentrieren, obwohl in vielen Fällen das überlebende Urkundenmaterial spärlich ist oder schwer auf das zugeordnet werden kann, was in der heutigen Landschaft sichtbar ist. Eine Analyse der Untersuchungen vor Ort ist deshalb unverzichtbar, um die Entwicklung der Bergbaulandschaft in ihrer Ganzheit zu verstehen.

Dieser Band bietet einen Einstieg in die Geländearbeit zum Thema Bergbauindustrie für Interessenten der allgemeinen Landschaftsgeschichte und Archäologie. Es wird aber auch eine detaillierte Übersicht der hinterbliebenen Landschaftsspuren für Spezialisten im Bereich der Bergbaugeschichte, Industriellen Archäologie und Landschaftsschutz vorgestellt. Diese wird mit einer kurzen Zusammenfassung der Bedeutsamkeit von Metallbergbaulandschaften und einer Übersicht der Geschichte von Bergbau- und Aufbereitungsprozessen im Studiengebiet eingeleitet. Es folgen Beschreibungen und Interpretationen einiger ausgesuchten und gut erhaltenen Bergbaulandschaften in Mittel- und Nordostwales, deren Umfang sich von einigen hundert Hektar bis zwei oder drei Hektar erstreckt. Die Beschreibungen werden durch Karten von Vermessungen vor Ort, Geländephotos von Strukturüberresten und Luftbildern illustriert. Das abschließende Kapitel beschäftigt sich mit einer Reihe von Maßnahmen die die Bergbaulandschaft schützen sollen, insbesondere die Frage wie diese Studien der Öffentlichkeit durch Ausstellungen näher gebracht werden können. Der Band schließt mit einem Glossar von Bergbaubegriffen und zwei Anhängen, die alle hier behandelten Bergbaulokalitäten kartieren.

Viele der Minen die in diesem Band behandelt werden befinden sich an den Rändern von Hochgebirgen und sind oft abseits von Siedelungen. Weitere Themen, die hier behandelt werden, sind die archäologische Spuren von Arbeitersiedlungen, die Nutzung von Wasserkraft, vor allem in Mittelwales, und die Fortschritte im Gebrauch von Dampfkraft in Nordostwales, wo Kohle frei verfügbar war. Es wird auch darauf eingegangen inwieweit der Bergbau das weitere

Umland beeinflußt hat, wie zum Beispiel durch die Konstruktion von Umleitungskanälen und Speicherbecken, die Wasser zu den Minen transportierten und die Methoden mit denen das Erz zu den Schmelztiegeln transportiert wurde, die sich oft weit abseits von den Minen selbst befanden.

Résumé

Le présent volume examine les vestiges matériels de l'industrie minière des métaux non ferreux dans les comtés historiques de Montgomeryshire, Radnorshire et Breconshire, Flintshire, Denbighshire, au centre et au nord-est du Pays de Galles, allant de l'âge de bronze au début du 20ème siècle, mais tout particulièrement pendant la période allant du début du 18ème siècle à la fin du 19ème siècle.

Il se concentre tout particulièrement sur la signification et sur l'interprétation de plusieurs paysages miniers plus étendus, au niveau des techniques minières et des techniques de traitement qui y sont représentées. Il s'ajoute à plusieurs études réalisées auparavant par des historiens des mines, études qui ont eu tendance à se concentrer sur les indices historiques, bien que, dans de nombreux cas, les indices documentaires restant encore soient minces ou difficiles à rattacher à ce qui reste visible sur le terrain. L'analyse des indices relevés par le travail sur le terrain est par conséquent essentielle pour comprendre comment ont été développés les paysages miniers.

Le présent volume fournit à ceux qui s'intéressent plus généralement à l'archéologie et à l'histoire du paysage une introduction à l'archéologie sur le terrain de l'industrie minière; il fournit également un registre détaillé des indices restant sur le terrain aux lecteurs spécialisés qui s'intéressent à l'histoire des mines, à l'archéologie industrielle et à l'aménagement du paysage. Il commence par une brève vue d'ensemble de la signification des paysages de mines de métaux et il brosse les grands traits de l'histoire des mines et du traitement des minerais dans la région concernée. Y font suite des descriptions et des interprétations de certains paysages miniers sélectionnés et mieux préservés, au centre ainsi qu'au nord-est du pays de Galles, dont la superficie varie entre plusieurs centaines d'hectares et deux ou trois hectares. Les descriptions sont accompagnées de plans montrant les relevés au sol, les photos au niveau du sol de structures restant encore et les photos aériennes. Le dernier chapitre se penche sur un certain nombre de problèmes de gestion liés aux paysages miniers, y compris les problèmes de présentation et d'exposition. Le volume se termine par un glossaire de termes miniers et par deux annexes qui donnent l'emplacement de tous les sites miniers notés dans la région couverte par l'étude.

De nombreux sites de mines examinés dans ce volume se situaient aux marges des hautes terres et étaient souvent éloignés de centres de population. Au nombre d'autres questions examinées se trouvent les indices archéologiques restant encore des logements des travailleurs, de l'exploitation de l'énergie hydraulique, tout particulièrement au centre du pays de Galles, et des développements dans le domaine de l'utilisation de la vapeur au nord-est du pays de Galles, où des sources de charbon étaient plus faciles à obtenir. Sont également pris en considération l'impact de l'exploitation minière sur le paysage plus large au niveau des canaux d'amenée et des réservoirs qui fournissaient l'eau aux mines, et les moyens par lesquels les minerais préparés étaient transportés aux sites d'extraction par fusion, souvent situés à une certaine distance des mines elles-mêmes.

INTRODUCTION

by Mark Walters and Nigel Jones

Background to this study

The volume has its origins in two rapid surveys of metal mines undertaken in 1993 by the Clwyd-Powys Archaeological Trust in response to concerns about the continued preservation of landscapes of this kind in Wales (cf Briggs 1992). The object of these studies was to produce an assessment of the surviving archaeological resource, to identify sensitive areas around each site, and to make recommendations about their future management. A total of 76 non-ferrous metal mines were described in Powys (Walters 1994) and 330 in the former county of Clwyd (Frost 1994). For the purpose of this volume the modern county of Powys (which includes the former historic counties of Montgomeryshire, Radnorshire and Breconshire) is termed mid Wales and the former county of Clwyd (which included the historic counties of Denbighshire and Flintshire and the present-day counties of Denbighshire, Flintshire, Wrexham and the eastern part of Conwy) is termed north-east Wales (Fig 1).

A number of mining landscapes were identified during the course of these rapid surveys where it was considered that detailed ground survey was essential for both a better understanding of the sites and for management purposes. As a result, detailed measured surveys were made of a number of sites in mid Wales during 1994 and in north-east Wales in 1995 (Jones and Frost 1995; 1996). In each case survey work was restricted to surface workings. The recording of buildings and other standing structures was limited to ground plans and a photographic record by the authors. Aerial photography was undertaken by Chris Musson of the Royal Commission on the Ancient and Historical Monuments of Wales in conjunction with ground survey. This proved to be extremely useful in the field and was also helpful in giving a clear picture of the character and landscape setting of the mining landscapes presented in this volume.

The meaning of metal mining landscapes

The extraction of natural resources has had a profound effect on the Welsh landscape. Landscapes created by the exploitation of non-ferrous metal ores, however, are generally more discrete and less well known than those created by the coal, slate and road stone industries. They were confined to the narrow veins which yielded these valuable and highly prized ores and were often hidden away on the remote upland margins where outcrops were more accessible.

The exploitation of these mineral veins in mid and north-east Wales began during the Bronze Age and was generally confined to relatively small surface workings, unlike the extensive surface and underground workings at the Great Orme in north Wales and Mount Gabriel in Ireland. The technological advances that are

known to have taken place during the Roman period probably provided greater opportunities for mineral exploitation, though it is difficult to measure the impact that this had upon the landscape. There are few sites in the study area of mid and north-east Wales where Roman extraction has been positively identified, as at the 1st-century Roman lead mines at Charterhouse, Mendip, but this is perhaps largely due to the lack of systematic archaeological fieldwork designed to locate and verify mining evidence of this date. This paucity of baseline archaeological data also holds true for the medieval period, but is somewhat redeemed by the volume of documentary evidence, for the later medieval period at least, which indicates a flourishing industry in the orefield of north-east Wales,

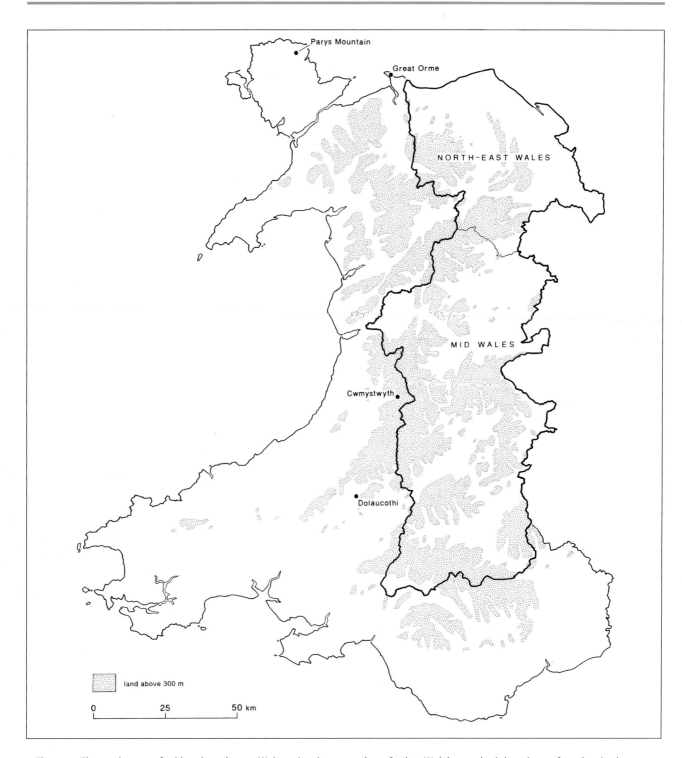

Figure 1 The study area of mid and north-east Wales, showing a number of other Welsh metal mining sites referred to in the text. The area of mid Wales shown here corresponds with the county of Powys. North-east Wales corresponds with the modern counties of Denbighshire, Flintshire, Wrexham and the eastern half of Conwy.

comparable to that in Devon and Cornwall, the Pennines, Cumbria, and Scotland. Future archaeological research could usefully integrate the documentary evidence relating to the orefield of north-east Wales with further landscape analysis of potential areas of surviving medieval mining.

It was not until the post-medieval period and the Industrial Revolution that the metal mining industry began to have a more profound and visible impact upon the landscape of mid and north-east Wales. The increasing demand for raw materials during the later 18th and 19th centuries led to rapid expansion in mining. Extensive workings initially focused upon the already known ore-bearing veins though in time the demand for new sources led to speculative ventures in increasingly remote locations. Rural communities

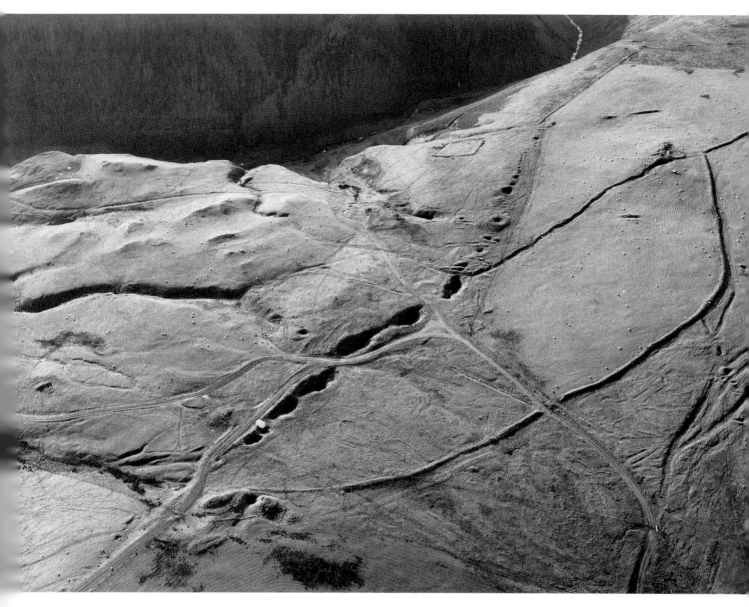

Figure 2 Aerial view of part of the complex mining landscape of the Pen Dylife to the north-west of Llanidloes in mid Wales, described in detail later in the volume. The view shows mine shafts and collapsed workings along the line of a mineral vein, with a hushing channel towards the top right and the site of the engine house towards the lower left. The engine house was the highest to be installed in Wales, a feat requiring fifty horses to haul the equipment to the site (*Crown Copyright: RCAHMW 925090–53*)

based upon dispersed farmsteads and small villages rapidly had to come to terms with an influx of miners from other parts of the United Kingdom in addition to the development of new industrial workers' housing and other essentials for the infrastructure of the industry such as roads, water-supplies and railways.

Competition for resources in a favourable economic climate resulted in the aggressive procurement of new landholdings with mineral potential, whether by lease or outright ownership, and the scars left by the extensive workings and processing areas of the largest concerns are testimony to the lucrative nature of the richest ore sources. Within the study area this is no more apparent than on the limestone plateau of Halkyn Mountain in north-east Wales where an extensive pitted moonscape was created by many hundreds of years of almost continuous lead mining, now recognised as an historic landscape of outstanding importance in Wales (Cadw 1998, 5–7).

The subsequent decline of mining from the end of the 19th century has left a rich legacy of abandoned mining landscapes often with a poignant yet bleak beauty of their own. These relict landscapes have many stories to tell which touch upon a wide range of contemporary interests and concerns – economic and social history, the history of technology, geology, ecology and vegetation history and natural resources, as well as issues relating to conservation and sustainability.

Previous studies of metal mining in mid and north-east Wales have tended to focus on the historical aspects of the industry. Following the lead given by W J Lewis's history of *Lead Mining in Wales*, published in 1967, further extensive documentary research was published by David Bick between the 1970s and 1990s in a series of volumes entitled *The Old Metal Mines of Mid-Wales* which has done much to promote a wider appreciation of the significance of metal mines in mid Wales, and which together with other of his works has provided much of the historical detail for sites described in this volume (Bick 1985; 1990; 1991). George Hall has likewise pioneered research on the southern part of areas of Wales considered in this volume (Hall 1993). Our knowledge of the early history of mining in mid Wales has been considerably enhanced by the fieldwork and excavation carried out by the Early Mines Research Group, under the direction of Simon Timberlake, at the prehistoric copper mining sites at Nant yr Eira, Ogof Wyddon, Llanymynech Ogof, and at the Craig-y-Mwyn hushing complex. Previous studies of the mines of north-east Wales have largely focused either on the geology of the area, most notably the lead and zinc ores in the Carboniferous rocks of north Wales (Smith 1921), or on the mining history and social history of particular areas, such as the Alyn Valley (Williams 1987), Minera (Pratt 1976; Bennett 1995), Halkyn Mountain (Ellis 1998), and the Milwr drainage tunnel (Ebbs 1993). These studies have been principally based upon documentary sources, as have a number of others which dealt with the mines of Flintshire and Denbighshire as a whole (Foster-Smith 1972; 1974; Burt *et al* 1992). Large-scale excavation has been largely confined to parts of the Minera mines complex, completed in the early 1990s. Other smaller-scale survey and excavation projects have been undertaken at the Gowdal lead mines at Holywell (Morgan 1994), the Pennant mine and engine house at Rhuallt (Rogers 1995), and Clive engine house (Jones 2002).

Like a number of similar studies carried out in Cornwall (Sharpe 1992; 1993), the Yorkshire Dales National Park and the Peak District National Park (White 1995) the present study sprang from a concern about the sites' future management and conservation. The focus in the present volume is therefore upon the physical remains of the industry and especially upon the interpretation of the mining landscapes which the industry created. The particular value of mining landscapes, over and above the individual structures to be found within them, is that they provide a much clearer illustration of the inter-relationship of the various structures to be found within an entire mining complex, and of the developments that were made in extraction and processing techniques over the course of time. They symbolise technologies and ways of life that are now often just out of reach of living memory. They are often poorly documented, even in the case of mines that were in operation in the 18th and 19th centuries. Frequently, the only historical reference to a mine is a note in the *Mining Journal* relating to production figures, changes in ownership or perhaps the installation of new equipment. Reports by mine agents might give details of the workings at a particular date but are frequently incomplete and difficult to relate to what is visible on the ground. Plans and section-drawings of the workings have occasionally survived, but these are often restricted to underground workings, and give little or no indication of what lay above ground. Generally, the earliest surviving surface plans are provided by the 1st edition Ordnance Survey maps of around 1880, though even this source is lacking in some of the more remote areas. The surface workings were occasionally the subject of contemporary photographs, though sadly such records are few in number.

Painstaking detective work is therefore often needed to unravel the meaning of mining landscapes, to match what is visible on the ground with the often meagre documentary evidence; to make mental associations between what might appear to be a confusing array of humps and bumps, discarded machinery, trackways and buildings scattered widely across a mountainside; to provide an interpretaton of the processes involved in the winning and processing of ores; and to assess how these may have changed through time.

Different types of mining landscapes were created in mid and north-east Wales, depending upon the natural topography, the nature of the pre-existing landscape, the disposition of the mineral veins, and the technologies that could be harnessed. Some landscapes cover many hundreds of hectares, others no more than two or three. Some landscapes were created with the aid of water power, others with horse or steam power. Some landscapes were the product of low capital ventures, reliant upon the efforts of individual miners; others were created through capital investment by multinational mining companies.

The metal mining landscapes of mid and north-east Wales represent a dialogue with the landscape and its resources that lasted for almost 5,000 years from the Bronze Age to the early 20th century but which has now been largely concluded. Above all, they are a testament to human endeavour, sometimes on an heroic scale, but often with a view to short-term gain and oblivious of its impact upon the natural environment. Nonetheless, these landscapes have now become valued in their own right, cherished for the human stories they have to tell and the lessons they have to teach.

Recording methodology and presentation of survey results

Most of the ground surveys published in this volume were made using EDM total station survey equipment and PenMap version 1.27 for Windows, running on a Compaq Concerto portable computer. Processed survey data was subsequently imported into AutoCAD release 12 and integrated with some ancillary detail digitised from early editions of the Ordnance Survey (OS) maps, in some instances including detail from beyond the areas surveyed on the ground. Because of the general level of complexity, the published plans of individual mine sites were subsequently drawn by hand from plots generated by AutoCAD. The contours in the accompanying illustrations are those generated by PenMap from survey data and are expressed in metres above Ordnance Datum by means of best fit with spot-heights and contours published by the OS.

Because of the scale and complexity of the Halkyn Mountain mining landscape a different strategy was adopted. The mining activity shown in Figures 88–90 is partly derived from a survey published by the British Geological Survey (Campbell and Haines 1988) and partly from original plotting and rectification from the vertical monochrome air photographic coverage commissioned by the former Clwyd County Council

in 1984. To this have been added selected details of other mining evidence, including some leats, reservoirs, tramways, whim circles and buildings from both documentary evidence and field recording, particularly in the area to the south-east of Halkyn. The resulting plans of Halkyn Mountain show over 4,000 shafts, but are by no means comprehensive, and do not include all the linear quarries, smaller trials and ancillary structures that are visible on the ground and on aerial photographs.

For the sake of consistency, the descriptions of individual mine sites in this volume are normally accompanied by two scales of drawings, a smaller scale interpretative plan at 1:4,000 which generally also acts as a key for one or more larger scale drawings at 1:1,000. In view of the different methodology adopted in the case of Halkyn Mountain, these plans are presented at a scale of 1:10,000.

The historical outline given in the following chapter draws attention to a number of differences between the mining landscapes of mid Wales and those of north-east Wales. To highlight these differences the descriptions of the landscapes in these two areas are given in different chapters.

Access and safety considerations

Note that all of the mine sites described in this publication are in private ownership. Permission should always be sought from the landowner before visiting a site. Mine sites are notoriously dangerous and often present hazards which may not be immediately obvious. Extreme care should therefore be taken at all

times to avoid open workings or areas of collapse, as well as many of the structures, which are liable to be in an unstable condition. Children visiting mining sites should remain under the supervision of a responsible adult at all times.

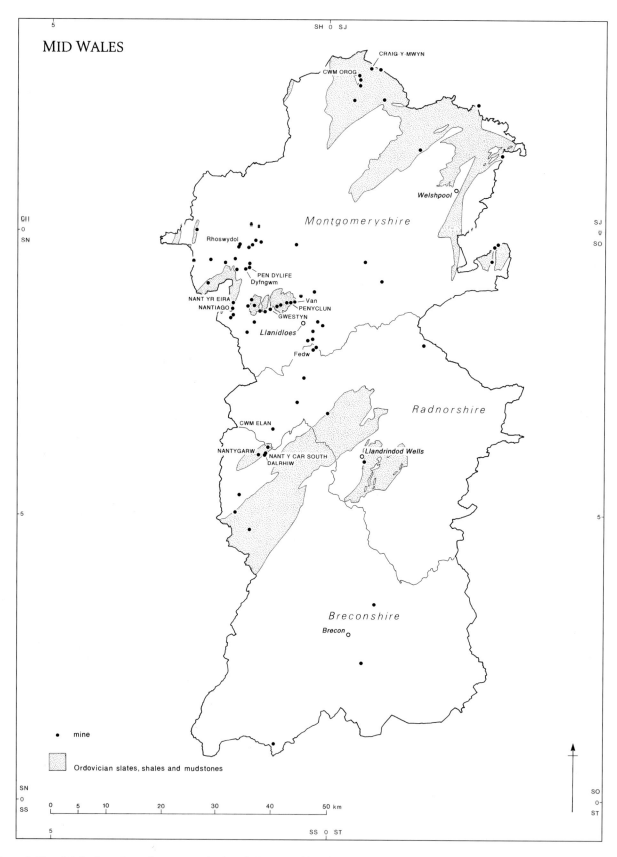

Figure 3 The distribution of non-ferrous metal mines in Powys, mid Wales. Detailed descriptions of the mines named in capital letters are given later in this volume. The gazetteer in Appendix 1 provides details of the principal metals that were obtained

1 Geological and historical background

by Mark Walters

Where the metal ores are to be found

Most sources of metal ores in mid and north-east Wales were initially discovered at the surface, in rock outcrops, or exposed in the beds of streams, where the weathered minerals often displayed bright colour changes that were easily recognisable. Many veins were first discovered by chance. The Llangynog vein in mid Wales, for example, was discovered in 1692, 'by a shepherd running after his flock, and treading upon the slippery surface of a flake of ore; the moss giving way under his wooden shoe, the glossy ore appeared' (Davies 1810). Stories with a similar Arcadian resonance were chronicled elsewhere in the late 17th and 18th centuries, and no doubt have a certain kernel of truth: shepherds would certainly have had more opportunity than anyone else to make discoveries in the mountains of mid and north Wales at this period, before the professional prospector arrived upon the scene.

To the geologist, the upland areas of mid Wales where metal ores were found, are seen to be dominated by slates, shales and mudstones of Ordovician and Silurian age (Fig 3; Jones 1922). The older Ordovician mudstones and grits belong to the Van formation, which forms the solid geology of the Plynlimon (Pumlumon) dome and west Montgomeryshire and is further divided into the Upper and Lower Van formations. The Upper Van formation consists of soft black mudstones, which readily weather on exposure to a clay like deposit, while the Lower Van formation consists of thick beds of hard grit which are divided by shale beds of varying thickness. The whole formation is about 730 metres in depth with approximately 300 metres belonging to each of the Upper and Lower Van formations. The Silurian Gwestyn formation is found above the Ordovician formations and consists of pyritic black shales and thin beds of sandstone. Exposed shales readily weather to an orange/yellow colour due to the iron sulphide content. The Gwestyn beds surround the outcropping Ordovician rocks and decrease in thickness to the north-west from 400 metres at Van to 100 metres at Machynlleth. The Gwestyn rocks are well exposed in the Clywedog Valley and around Dylife. The Silurian Frongoch formation lies above the Gwestyn rocks and covers the rest of the area, being made up of grey shales, flags and hard greenish-grey mudstones. Most of the west Montgomeryshire mines are located in this formation.

A period of earth movement known as the Caledonian orogeny caused the Silurian and Ordovician rocks to be uplifted and folded and a number of north–south and east–west faults subsequently developed across the area. The east–west faults in particular attracted mineralisation which filled the fault and fracture voids with economically viable minerals such as galena, sphalerite and chalcopyrite that are commonly associated with the less valuable gangue minerals such as quartz, calcite and barite. The mineral veins are typically enriched on the western limbs of anticlinal folds and the actual rock type also seems to play a part in the zoning of minerals: lead and zinc lodes are commonly located within turbidite sequences of the Van and Frongoch formation, while copper deposits are confined to the pyritic shales of the Gwestyn formation. The mineral lodes themselves can display zoning through enrichment in a particular direction: west of Plynlimon, for example, lodes are rich in zinc to the east, but get richer in lead towards the west. To the east of Plynlimon this enrichment is reversed in direction. The mineral veins vary in thickness from a few centimetres to a maximum at Van of 15 metres in width. The veins are typically inclined along a steeply dipping fault plane which necessitated extraction by stoping (see p 179 for definition) above and below an access level in most cases.

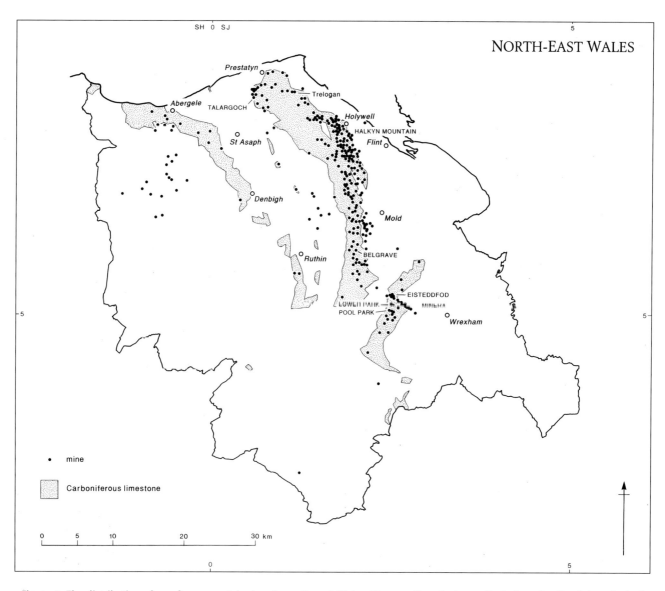

Figure 4 The distribution of non-ferrous metal mines in north-east Wales. The gazetteer in Appendix 2 gives details of the principal metals that were obtained. The richest veins and thus the main concentration of mining sites lay in the Carboniferous limestone formations which run south from Prestatyn to Llandegla, to the south-west of Mold. Interrupted by the Bala Fault, the veins continued south to Minera and Eglwyseg Rocks, to the west of Wrexham. Mineralisation produced mainly galena or lead ore, which outcropped particularly in the area of Halkyn and Holywell, with smaller amounts of silver, zinc, gold, barytes, cobalt, copper, manganese and nickel ore.

The mineral veins in the north-east Wales orefield are found within the Carboniferous limestone formations which extend in an arc from Prestatyn on the coast to Minera and the mines on Esclusham Mountain near Wrexham (Fig 4; Smith 1921). This eastern outcrop is more enriched than the western outcrop which can be traced from the coast at the Great Orme near Llandudno to a point in the south-east close to the Llanelidan, south of Ruthin. While lead, silver and zinc predominate in the eastern outcrop, copper minerals are more common to the west at locations such as Ffos-y-Bleiddiaid near Abergele and at the Great Orme. The veins generally follow east–west

trending fault lines in the limestone, but south of Mold the trend changes to a NW–SE direction in the Maeshafn and Minera mines. A later north–south strike fault system cuts across the common vein trend in the Halkyn area and rich deposits have also been located in formations known as 'flats' which appear to have filled cavities formed along the limestone joints. Mineralisation occurred at some time during the Triassic period as a result of the leaching of minerals from both surrounding and deeper Carboniferous deposits and their deposition in cavities as a hydrothermal fluid. The principal minerals extracted were galena (lead sulphide), sphalerite (zinc sulphide) and chalcopyrite (copper sulphide). Lead carbonate (cerussite) and zinc carbonate (calamine) were formed as secondary minerals in the veins and tend to be located near the weathered surface outcrops. The waste or 'gangue' minerals found in common association with the ores include calcite, quartz, barytes and fluorspar.

A brief history of mining in mid and north-east Wales

The way in which the non-ferrous metal veins are disposed in the country rock had a profound effect upon the amount of effort required to extract the ore. Veins exposed in rock natural outcrops were clearly the most accessible, and though these were often not the richest deposits which existed they were invariably the first to be exploited. Pursuing veins extending down into the bedrock or simply buried beneath layers of overburden presented miners with various challenges which could only be readily overcome by technological innovation.

Prehistoric mining

Evidence of prehistoric mining activity was first recognised in the study area of mid and north-east Wales in the mid-19th century. Reworking of long-abandoned mining sites during a revival of the lead mining industry in Wales at this time brought to light many ancient stone, metal and bone tools. The re-working of Llanymynech Ogof in 1823, Machynlleth Park in 1856, Newtown in 1856, Nant yr Eira in 1859, and Nantyricket in 1872–79, for example, all produced evidence for earlier mining. At that time, these finds were assumed to be evidence of Roman activity, and were reported as such in contemporary mining and antiquarian reports. Prehistoric mining had left relatively little trace within the present-day landscape of Wales, however, despite the fact that it sometimes appears to have been carried out over fairly extensive areas. This is perhaps largely due to the subsequent burial of many of the original surface workings and their later underground development below later tips of mine waste, particularly those resulting from more extensive 19th-century mining activities.

Occasionally, early opencast workings still remain visible within the landscape. The best examples within the study area of mid and north-east Wales are probably those at Nant yr Eira, Montgomeryshire, made much clearer by recent woodland clearance, where a deep gash is visible in the hillside, accompanied by grassed over waste tips to either side (Fig 5). Where the potential ore source was buried the overburden could be cleared in a number of ways and as in later periods, one of the most basic of these involved excavating a series of short linear or circular trial-pits, sometimes known as costeaning pits, where it was anticipated that the mineral vein extended. The exploitation of metal ores during the prehistoric period is most frequently represented by deep, linear opencast workings of the kind evident at Nant yr Eira, where mineral veins would have been most easily recognised and recovered. Workings of this kind are often associated with evidence of firesetting, in the form of charcoal fragments together with burnt stone and broken hammerstones in the spoil tips. At greater depth, if drainage problems were not encountered, narrow galleries followed the vein below ground. Early workings of this kind were highly efficient and characteristically adopted working areas generally no larger than the ore body itself. With the exception of Llanymynech, stone tools have been found in stratified contexts and as residual finds in later spoil tips. In all cases the metal sought was copper, most frequently in the form of chalcopyrite. There has been some debate as to whether galena (lead ore) was mined in the later Bronze Age. When alloyed with copper and tin this gives a more malleable metal in the smithing process and bronze tools of this date have been found to have a significant lead constituent in their make-up. However, no certain evidence for the mining of lead in the late Bronze Age has yet been identified.

The most detailed archaeological research has been undertaken at Nant yr Eira, starting with the pioneering excavations of Oliver Davies in 1937 (Davies 1938, 56–8), and followed by the more detailed examination undertaken by Simon Timberlake in 1988 (Crew and Crew 1990, 18–21). Radiocarbon dating of charcoal samples recovered from spoil tips during the 1988 excavations has produced an early Bronze Age date, suggesting that the assemblage of early mining tools from the site are of comparable date to those which have been excavated more recently in other areas of Wales, most notably at Cwmystwyth, Ceredigion (Crew and Crew 1990, 22–30), Parys Mountain, Anglesey (Crew and Crew 1990, 15–18) and the Great Orme, Llandudno, Gwynedd (Lewis 1994, 31–6) (see location in Fig 1). Excavations by the Early Mines Research Group at Cwmystwyth in

Figure 5
Nant yr Eira mine, Llan-
gurig, Powys, showing the
Bronze Age open-cut,
viewed from the south. Two
excavations along the
western side of the open-
cut have produced stone
tools and evidence of firesetting (Davies 1938;
Timberlake 1990). The early
workings were reworked
between 1860 and 1887.
(*CPAT 331–17*)

1989–91 and again in 1993–94 revealed opencast workings of early to mid Bronze Age date which had clear evidence of working by hammerstones on the battered faces of the opencast wall. Radiocarbon dates from the material backfilling the opencast provided dates ranging from 1900 to 1400 cal BC. The earliest date, of about 2000–1900 cal BC, came from a wooden launder found in the base of the opencast which was probably used to draw water away from the lowest working area.

At the Great Orme, Gwynedd, systematic archaeo-logical survey and recording since 1988 have revealed the largest complex of Bronze Age workings in the United Kingdom. Here, initial surface opencasting developed into deep underground workings where narrow, sinuous workings followed the ore vein in restricted horizontal or shallowly dipping passages that frequently opened out into larger chambers where ore concentration was particularly rich. Many stone and bone artefacts have been found, as well as some Bronze Age metal items, which may represent mining tools. Radiocarbon dates from the Great Orme mines span the years from 1880–600 cal BC and suggest mining activity throughout the Bronze Age. There are a cluster of dates around 1400–1300 cal BC, however, which point to the period of greatest expansion at the site (Lewis 1994, 31–6).

Archaeological work at Parys Mountain, Anglesey, has been less extensive, the small-scale trial trenches excavated by the Early Mines Research Group in 1988 focusing on the relocation of a trench dug by Oliver Davies in 1937 on the north edge of the Oxen Quarry. The excavations produced about 30 hammerstones, probably derived from beach cobble deposits near Amlwch, together with much charcoal and waste material. The ore mined at this site was probably chalcopyrite. Radiocarbon dates again matched those obtained from other prehistoric mines in Wales and fall within the early to mid Bronze Age date range.

Exploratory excavations by the Early Mines Research Group in 1997 (Timberlake 1997, 62–5) at Ogof Wyddon (also known as Witches Cave), near Machynlleth, produced hundreds of fragments of broken stone hammers in spoil tips at the rim of the deep open-cut. A charcoal sample possibly derived from firesetting activity has been dated to 1890–1630 cal BC, suggesting an early Bronze Age date. Petrological analysis of the hammerstone flakes suggests a potential source for the stones some 20 kilometres away at Tonfannau beach, north of Tywyn (Timberlake and Mason 1997; Timberlake 1998; Craddock and Lang 2003).

The early mines on Llanymynech Hill in northern Powys have received relatively little attention. Finds from the underground workings inside the hillfort, known as Llanymynech Ogof, have suggested that the earliest mining activity here took place before the 2nd century AD (Adams 1992, 47). Rescue excavations close to the hillfort defences have produced evidence of metalworking debris dating from the Iron Age in the 2nd to 1st centuries BC (Musson and Northover 1989, 20) whilst survey work by the Early Mines Research Group in 1996 (Timberlake 1996, 68–70) have raised the possibility that mining may have begun here during the Bronze Age.

Prehistoric workings are also suspected within the study area at Pen Dylife, Nant Gyrnant and possibly Siglenlas, where early copper extraction is documented and there are workings characteristic of the period. Chronologically distinctive stone tools have not as yet been recorded at any of these sites, but extensive later workings may have buried the earliest tips. The proximity of Craig Rhiwarth hillfort to the workings at Cwm Orog might also suggest a prehistoric connection there, although no physical evidence has been revealed so far.

Although little archaeological work has been undertaken at possible prehistoric mining sites in north-east Wales, there are promising sites such as Ffos-y-Bleiddiaid near Abergele worthy of further investigation. Here, a deep and impressive linear open-cut bisects the limestone promontory with further workings beyond the base of the open-cut. Some indication of the antiquity of Ffos-y-Bleiddiaid workings may be given by the stone hammers and the hilt of a so-called Roman sword found here during the 19th century (Smith 1921, 1). The 19th-century descriptions of the underground working (North 1962, 26) suggest small passages opening into chambers, all of which demonstrated highly efficient ore removal. This would seem to mirror the type of workings at the Great Orme, though the ore visible in the waste material at Ffos-y-Bleiddiaid is predominantly galena rather than chalcopyrite or malachite. The workings here again lie close to the earthworks of the hillfort known as Castell Cawr (SH93807660) which raised the possibility of a further association between hillforts and early mine workings. A number of other later prehistoric hillforts within the region, such as Moel Hiraddug (SJ06307870) and Moel y Gaer (SJ21156910), also lie near metal-bearing veins which may have been discovered and worked before the Roman period.

Few studies of prehistoric mines in their contemporary landscape have been undertaken in Wales. The most detailed work so far has been carried out at Cwmystwyth, Ceredigion, where the peat deposits on the hillside above the Bronze Age opencast have been sampled for palaeoenvironmental information and compared with samples from the opencast excavation (Crew and Crew 1990, 65–9). A good correlation appears to have been established here between the initiation of mining in the early Bronze Age and woodland clearance and seasonal agricultural use of the resulting upland pastures. That sources of local wood were available is evidenced by the charcoal in the excavations and the presence of the wooden launders in the opencast and this information is backed up by the pollen analysis.

No certain links have been established between Bronze Age settlements and mines: the relationship between prehistoric mines and other contemporary sites is yet to be explored fully. Specialised mining settlements where ore smelting and smithing were carried out might be expected within the immediate hinterland of a Bronze Age mine. Evidence of this kind must await a more holistic approach to prehistoric mining landscape studies, but some progress of this kind is being made on the Great Orme, where recent survey of the headland has revealed smelting waste close to the ore sources.

Roman mining

The impact of mining on the landscape of mid and north-east Wales is likely to have become more pronounced during the Roman period. Exploitation in the Roman world often appears to have been begun under military supervision, being subsequently carried out by civilian companies or guilds that operated according to a codified system of mining laws. The scale of working and the enhanced processing techniques known to have been adopted elsewhere in the Roman world were certainly capable of drastically changing the topography immediately around the extraction area. There is now good evidence from locations such as Rio Tinto in Spain that great advances in extractive technology were made during this period, including deep shafts, long levels, de-watering adits, power for pumping and winding. Together these represent a level of technology that was not to be superseded in western Europe until the 16th century.

In Wales, evidence of this kind of technological sophistication and complexity has so far only been demonstrated in the case of the Roman gold mines as Dolaucothi in south-west Wales (Fig 1). Deep opencast workings and waste tips scarred the hillsides at Allt Cwmhenog and Allt Ogofau above the Cothi Valley and leats were dug over great distances to provide water for power and hushing at the main extraction site. Hushing was an ancient technique used by Roman miners both for prospecting and clearing overburden and was especially useful if the overburden was deep or there were potentially a series of veins trending across the slope of a steep hillside. One or more dams were built at the top of the slope which were fed by a leat system. Once the ground had been prepared by light digging, the sluice on the filled dam would be opened and a torrent of water would cascade downhill, stripping the overburden from the bedrock below and exposing any mineral veins. The technique

continued to be employed up to the 19th century in some areas of Britain, most notably in the northern Pennines. Good examples perhaps of post-medieval date are to be seen at Pen Dylife (Fig 2) and Craig-y-Mwyn (Figs 7 and 9) in mid Wales, though other examples elsewhere in the region might be much earlier.

The need to provide access, accommodation, processing and manufacturing facilities, and military supervision, is also likely to have left its mark on the broader landscape of the region, though here as elsewhere we still know very little about how roads, settlements and forts may have interacted with the extraction sites. The Roman fort and bath house at Pumsaint lie under a kilometre from the mine workings at Dolaucothi. Survey and excavation at Dolaucothi have shown that the Roman workings include surface prospecting by hushing, extensive surface opencasting and trenching, and by stoping with adit access. The largest of the opencast workings here, known as Ogofau pit, is up to about 150 metres across and 36 metres deep (Lewis and Jones 1969; Burnham 1997; Bird 2001). Beneath the pit are a series of underground workings which extend to 45 metres in depth. It was in these lower workings that a substantial fragment of a Roman drainage waterwheel was found. The hushing tank earthworks are well preserved and were probably used both for initial prospecting of the hillside outcrops and early development of the extraction area by firesetting and quenching. While these remains are all related to the extraction of gold, the methods of extraction and processing that were employed here give an indication of the scale and technological sophistication that might be expected on Roman lead and copper mines in Wales.

A large number of mines in mid and north-east Wales have been claimed to be of Roman origin (Davies 1935; Jones 1922), but so far the only unequivocal evidence comes from the underground workings at Llanymynech Ogof, Powys. A coin hoard deposited in the 2nd century AD was found here concealed within a pile of stacked and calcited waste material (Adams 1992, 47), suggesting that parts of the mine had been worked out by this date. Numerous other finds elsewhere in the workings, including human remains and pottery and metal finds of Roman date, suggest that the disused mine workings were used as a place of burial, probably from the 2nd century onwards. The workings show at least three clear phases of extraction with narrow, sinuous galleries, possibly of Iron Age date, later widened into squarer-cut and more deeply penetrating galleries which may be of 1st-century Roman origin. The latest phase of working is represented by a shaft cut in 1823, with subsequent minor extraction or trial workings evidenced by shot holes in the rock face.

Ore reserves elsewhere in the study area would have been of considerable economic importance during the Roman period, particularly in western Mont-gomeryshire and Flintshire where large sources of lead were to be found close to the surface in many places, occasionally containing significant quantities of silver that could be extracted by cupellation. The remoteness of many of these sources combined with the disruptions of the conquest period in Wales during the 70s AD probably inhibited the development of mines during the early Roman period. It seems unlikely that these sources were ignored for long, however, and the lack of certain sites in mid Wales, as elsewhere in Wales, is probably largely a reflection of the relatively limited amount of research that has been undertaken on the Roman mining industry.

On current evidence, there are suggestions of Roman workings at Dylife/Pen Dylife, Dyfngwm, Llanymynech, Newtown, Llandrindod, Tyisaf, Allt-y-Main, Nantyricket, Siglenlas, Craig-y-Mwyn and Cefn-Pawl in mid Wales, and at Ffos-y-Bleiddiaid, Halkyn Mountain, Graig Fawr and Nant-y-ffrith in north-east Wales. Only the large group of mine workings at Pen Dylife lie directly on the supposed course of a Roman road. This passes the Roman fortlet at Penycrocbren (Fig 76), sited just above the oldest open-cuts and shafts. Associated smelting complexes seem to have been sited well to the east of the mines, represented by concentrations of slag associated with Roman finds from neighbouring sites at Caersws, Trefeglwys and Llanfyllin.

Further significant evidence of metal processing during the Roman period has been identified in north-east Wales. A Roman pig of lead was found at Carmel, near Holywell, and three similar pigs have been found near the Roman legionary fortress at Chester, about 20 kilometres further east. Two of the pigs are inscribed with the letters DECEANGL from the name Deceangli – the tribe which inhabited north-east Wales, and provide unequivocal evidence of an active lead extraction and exporting industry in the region in the late 1st century AD onwards (Webster 1953; Whittick 1982; Tomlin *et al* 1990). Excavations in the Pentre Oakenholt area of Flint, again near the shores of the Dee estuary, have provided evidence of lead smelting, most probably based on ores brought down

from Halkyn Mountain, several kilometres away (Atkinson and Taylor 1924). The remains of Roman domestic buildings and a bath house at Pentre Farm, Flint, are thought to be the dwelling of a Roman official responsible for supervising this industry, which probably exported lead along the Dee estuary and coastal road to Chester and beyond (O'Leary *et al* 1989).

A number of other finds suggest that mining was more widespread in north-east Wales during the Roman period. A coin of Gordian III (AD 243–44) was found in 1887 under an old washing floor at Talargoch Mine, Dyserth (Webster 1953, 15–16). Bronze Age and Romano-British finds have been found in the natural cave near Big Covert, Maeshafn, where galena ore was mined extensively (Hesketh 1955, 141–8). A small Roman settlement which may have sprung up in the wake of the lead mining industry has been identified at Ffrith, 5 kilometres north-west of Wrexham (Blockley 1989a, 135–65), where a military connection is suggested by the presence of stamped tiles of the twentieth legion and a number of other finds (Frere 1989, 258–9). Undated lead workings are known along the north side of the Nant-y-ffrith valley, just 2 kilometres to the west. Near Abergele, close to the site of the workings at Ffos-y-Bleiddiaid, a number of Roman period finds have been reported within and around the periphery of the modern town. These may suggest a Roman settlement on the lower-lying ground below the workings involved in the processing and manufacture of products from the ore. This is mirrored at Prestatyn where a late Iron Age and Roman settlement lies at the foot Graig Fawr, a hill with substantial traces of early lead workings (Blockley 1989b).

Medieval mining

Documentary evidence provides a principal source of information about mining within the study area of mid and north-east Wales during the medieval period. In 1187, for example, lead ore was being transported down the River Severn from mines probably located on Llanymynech Hill (Lewis 1967, 26). In 1194 the Carreghofa (Carreghwfa) mine at Llanymynech was being reworked, supposedly to produce silver for the Shrewsbury mint (Adams 1992, 3). One of the charters granting the territory of Cwmllwyd above the head of what is today Llyn Clywedog, to the Cistercian monastery of Ystrad Marchell (Strata Marcella) in 1198, adds to the customary grant of rights the unusual wording 'above and below the land', suggesting that the monks hoped to find lead ore within the holding (Thomas 1997; Williams 1997, 129). Rhoswydol mine lies within another of the land-holdings listed in the charters and although a local tradition linking the mine to the monastery should be treated with caution, the oldest stope and open-cut workings on the top of the hill may well date to this period, if not earlier.

The conquest of Wales by Edward I in the late 13th century led to a surge in the demand for lead for new building projects associated with the newly founded English planted towns and castles. Fifteen cartloads of lead were required to roof Flint Castle (Lewis 1967, 29), for example, and lead was urgently needed to re-roof churches damaged in the hostilities throughout Flintshire and Denbighshire. This expansion declined in the years prior to the outbreak of the Black Death and the chamberlain of Chester recorded in 1347–48 that no income from mining was available in the cantref of Englefield, which included the important Halkyn orefield (Evans 1929, 19 and 45). The plague passed through the mining communities of north Wales in 1349 and devastated the already dwindling workforce to such an extent that the Halkyn mines were still largely inactive two years later (Evans 1929, 68).

Considerable information about the principal areas of lead mining in north-east Wales in the medieval period and of their administrative and legal framework is to be found in documents relating to the medieval mining laws of Flintshire and Denbighshire in the 14th century. The earliest references to these mining laws can be found in the Register of Edward the Black Prince during the years 1351–65 and the records kept by his officials in Chester. Mining laws for Hopedale are recorded in 1351 and refer to mines north of Minera, probably in the Nant-y-ffrith Valley, while a separate set of laws are recorded for the Holywell mines in 1352 which were probably located south-west of the town. The third area for which mining laws are recorded is at Minera, near Wrexham, where the importance of the lead industry was reflected in the creation of a separate township. In common with the other lead mining areas of north-east Wales, Minera was actively being mined shortly after the Edwardian conquest and the mines were worked continuously between 1301 and 1315 (Pratt 1976, 118–19). The lack of documentary references to mining at Minera after the Black Death and up to about 1388 has been taken to reflect the decline of the industry as a conse-quence of that outbreak, similar to that which affected

the Halkyn area, mentioned above. A survey of the lordships of Bromfield and Yale in 1391 on behalf of the earl of Arundel describes the workings of mines in the area (Pratt 1962, 28–36) and records the mining laws, which bear a strong resemblance to those recorded in the Register of Edward the Black Prince in 1352. In the Minera and Eryrys mining districts each miner was granted a plot of land sufficient for his house and curtilage, and enough wood to repair his house or fences and to make props for his pits. The miners were freemen and could pasture their stock on common land and sell their ore on the free market providing they paid their dues to the lord, who owned the mineral rights. Mining techniques recorded in the laws suggest that veins were traced and extracted from the surface, shallow underground working being evidenced by the mention of the use of windlasses and stows. The authority of the medieval mining laws appears to have declined throughout the 15th and 16th centuries, perhaps partly as a consequence of the Glyndŵr rebellion in the first decade of the 15th century, which drove many of the English tenant miners out of mining districts like Minera. In the early 17th century the Grosvenor family was successful in suppressing the mining laws applying to the Halkyn mining district, instituting in their place a system of annual bargains with royalties being paid to the estate for ore extracted from a closely defined area measured in meres of fixed length and width. The bargain system finally disappeared after the 1850s and was replaced in a few instances by the takenote system of mining leases.

For the most part, medieval mining was probably carried out with broadly the same techniques as those employed during the Roman period, as indicated in the Georgius Agricola's treatise, *De re metallica*, published in 1556. Having located a source of ore a mine would be initially developed through surface extraction and opencasting along an open-cut. In north-east Wales it seems likely that bell-pits and shallow shafts, usually of no more than 30 metres in depth, were dug for the removal of ore down to the level of the water table. A series of these shallow shafts might subsequently be linked underground to create a long lateral working area. Removal of ore from the deeper workings was at first achieved by a hand winch or windlass, to which a bucket or series of buckets was attached.

The use of the horse whim to raise and lower buckets in the shaft appears to have been one of the few innovations in mining technique that were intro

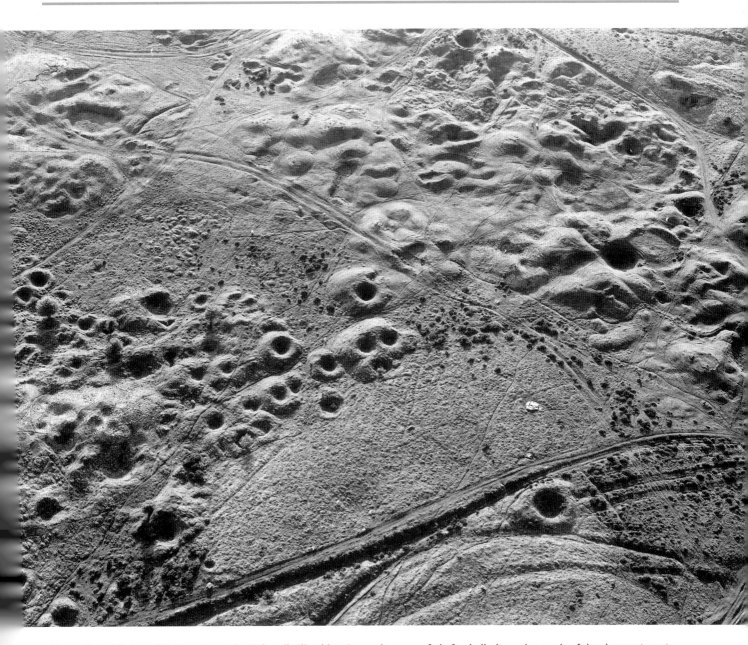

Figure 6 Aerial view of Halkyn Mountain, Holywell, Flintshire. A complex area of shafts, bell-pits and mounds of development waste to the north-east of Rhes-y-cae, probably resulting from mining over a period of six or seven hundred years between the Middle Ages and the early 20th centuries. The ore from the smaller, shallower pits was raised by hand. In the case of the later, larger shafts horse-power or steam-power was generally used. A horse whim circle is visible next to one of the large shafts towards the top right-hand corner of the photograph. An overhead winding drum within a wooden frame, powered by one or two horses, was used here to raise ore from the shaft by means of a pulley set on an A-frame above the head of the shaft. The extensive waste heaps around the shaft suggest that ore may also have been processed in this area. (*Crown Copyright: RCAHMW 935136–48*)

duced during this period. The remains of post-medieval horse whim circles are fairly common and usually consist of a flat circular area of grass or crushed stone, sometimes with a stone kerb around the periphery, and often with a posthole or shallow depression at the centre that marked the position of the upright pivot post. A horizontal winding wheel was placed on top of the pivot pole and was rotated by a horse linked to the pivot pole by a wooden arm. The winding wheel carried rope or cable that ran up to a simple wooden headframe above the shaft. Good

examples of post-medieval horse whim circles can be seen at Pen Dylife, on Halkyn Mountain and at the Esclusham Mountain mines of Lower Park and Pool Park. These early forms of haulage were later replaced by dedicated winding wheels with an attached cable winding drum and rotative steam engines with the dual role capability of pumping and winding through gearing linkage to an externally mounted winding wheel on a loading base.

Field evidence of medieval mining is poor in the mid Wales orefield, though little or no archaeological excavation has taken place to determine whether remains of this date survive. Many of the mines that may have developed in the medieval period are likely to have been extensively reworked in the 18th and 19th centuries and many features may now lie buried below later waste heaps. In mid Wales there are suggestions of medieval mining remains at Dylife (including Esgairgaled), Pen Dylife, Rhoswydol, Llanymynech, Craig-y-Mwyn, Allt-y-Main, Dyfngwm/Castle Rock, Gwestyn, Siglenlas, Llandrindod and Nant y Blaidd. The situation is similar in north-east Wales, though there are firmer grounds for supposing that the extensive mining landscapes on Halkyn Mountain (Fig 6) and at Eisteddfod (Fig 99) had their origin in this period. Here, the available mining technology, combined with the proliferation of small mining ventures encouraged by the mining laws and the leasing systems in use at the time, gave rise to extensively pitted landscapes. Eisteddfod in particular possesses exceptionally well-preserved remains of linear surface workings, hushing, shallow shaft workings and processing features, matching the description of mining techniques given in the 14th-century mining laws that applied in the Minera district.

The impact of mining on the landscape was already being commented upon in certain areas of Wales by the earlier 16th century. In the 1530s, for example, the king's antiquary, John Leland, noted its effects upon the natural woodland in the Cwmystwyth area of mid Wales 'wher hath bene great digging for leade, the melting wherof hath destoid the wooddes that sumtime grew plantifulli therabout' (Smith 1907–10, quoted by Linnard 2000, 67).

Post-medieval mining
From the 17th and 18th centuries, mining landscapes within our study area became much more extensive and for the first time there is good surviving evidence of a wide range of ancillary structures associated with the industry, including dressing floors, wheelpits, engine houses, mine offices and smelteries. Aggressive expansion of earlier workings in search of new minerals at greater and greater depths led to a vast increase in the volume of waste tips at the surface, in many instances masking earlier mining landscapes. This period also saw the emergence of the first clearly recognisable mining communities, such as the small villages on Halkyn Mountain and those near Minera. The development of the road network through the turnpike trusts in the late 18th and early 19th centuries allowed products to be delivered more efficiently to the smelters and by facilitating the transport of newly-developed machinery also assisted in the development of a number of the more remotely sited mines.

Rapid advances in mining technology at Welsh mines becomes evident from the 17th century onwards and it is at this time that we see the rise of the wealthy industrialists and engineers who played such a key role in the industrial revolution. The creation of the Society of Mines Royal led to a brief expansion of the industry, particularly in Cardiganshire and west Montgomeryshire, during the 17th century. Hugh Myddleton actively developed a number of previously abandoned mines between 1617 and 1631 (Lewis 1967, 42). He absorbed ideas from the continent and applied them to the Welsh terrain with limited success, his most significant innovation being the sinking of deep shafts in conjunction pumping engines driven by waterwheels above ground.

As the shaft descended through unstable ground it would be securely shored up with timber bratticing or a stone or brick collar, though where hard, stable rock was encountered this shoring was often dispensed with. The digging of the shaft would progress in stages, with lateral levels or cross-cuts being excavated which branched off the shaft and pursued the mineral vein. Where the vein continued above and below these lateral access levels a technique known as stoping was adopted. This involved the widening out of the side walls, roof and floor of a level to the full width of the ore body. As work progressed above or below the level, wooden platforms would be erected which bridged the stope on stemples, which were commonly complete tree trunks wedged into the side walls or fitted into notches cut in the rock. The platforms could be used to stack waste material or 'deads' as the workface progressed.

The use of ventilation shafts, usually 80–100 metres apart, further improved underground conditions and enabled mines to be dug to even greater depths. By the introduction of these techniques Myddleton was to show that Welsh ore sources were winnable from greater depths than previously attempted and also led to the discovery that ores were often more enriched and thus more valuable at depth. A number of simple but primitive mining techniques continued to be employed despite various technological advancements of this kind, however. At Craig-y-Mwyn, for example, extensive traces of hushing leats and reservoirs can be seen above the deeply gashed hush on the hillside (Figs 7–8) which probably developed from the mid-17th century onwards.

Figure 7   Aerial view of Craig-y-Mwyn mine, Llanrhaeadr-ym-Mochnant, Powys, showing the open-cast with associated hushing channels, leats and reservoirs. (*Crown Copyright: RCAHMW 935097–52*)

Figure 8 Hushing channel at Craig-y-Mwyn mine, Llanrhaeadr-ym-Mochnant, Powys. Hushing was used as a means of prospecting and extraction. Water collected in reservoirs and was released to remove overburden, exposing the ore-bearing rocks. This view from the valley bottom shows the broad fan of material washed out from the hushing channel on the hillside above. (*CPAT 279–16A*)

In the first half of the 17th century lessees worked Craig-y-Mwyn, Dylife, Ceulan, Gwaith y Mwyn and the unlocated 'Robindor' mine. Following the death of Myddleton in 1631, Thomas Bushell became the chief lessee in 1636 (Lewis 1967, 46). Like Myddleton, he was keen to develop new techniques and is often quoted as being responsible for the revival in use of deep levels and inclined de-watering adits. The first adit of this kind is believed to have been dug in Cardiganshire in 1637–38 (Lewis 1967, 47) and deep adits were soon a commonplace feature elsewhere. Good ventilation was essential in these deeper mines and Bushell pioneered the use of bellows-driven pumping engines feeding air through lead pipes placed in the floor of the adit.

Advances in the processing of the mined ore, by contrast, were slow, the initiative often only being taken on the larger mine sites where there was a greater incentive to ensure that the vastly increased quantities of ore reaching the surface were efficiently reduced to fine concentrate for smelting. Water-powered stamp mills first appeared in the 1780s and were effectively the precursors of the roll crushers and rock breakers introduced in the 19th century. The stamp mill was powered by a waterwheel operating a camshaft that drove vertical crushing hammers which pounded the ore on stone anvils or mortars. No early stamp mills have yet been identified in mid or north-east Wales, but remains are suspected at Dylife where multiple hollowed mortar stones have been found in Nant Dropyns at Esgairgaled (Walters 1994).

Towards the end of the 17th century lead mining was again in general decline. In 1678 the situation at Y Garreg Wen, Llanymynech, was perhaps typical, with only two miners engaged on the newly developed workings (Lewis 1967, 69). In 1692 the rich veins at Llangynog were first discovered and rapidly developed (Williams 1985). Llanymynech was again being worked in the same year and is believed to be the first place in Wales where gunpowder was used (Lewis 1967, 77). Explosives were still relatively expensive at this time and there was a widespread distrust and fear of their use by miners until the mid-18th century.

In 1698 a group of wealthy speculators set up the Company of Mine Adventurers under the joint governorship of William Waller and Humphrey Mackworth (Lewis 1967, 81). This company developed a number of mines in Cardiganshire and west Montgomeryshire and remained in existence for 60 years, during which time most of the larger mines in these counties had seen some activity. The first 30 years of the 18th

century saw little activity in the mid Wales orefield, but from 1730 exploration was rapid as the mining of both copper and lead became economically viable once more. By the 1770s most of the mines in the western part of the mid Wales study area had either been reopened or were being worked for the first time.

Technology altered little at this time and despite the introduction of steam engines in mines elsewhere during the 18th century, the cost of installing and running them in mines in the mid-Wales study area was considered prohibitive before the middle of the 19th century. Winding continued to be powered by whim engines, while waterwheels drove all of the pumping and processing operations. Most of the main mineral veins in mid Wales had been worked at some point by the end of the 18th century and exploration in the 19th century, which was to lead to some of the richest ore discoveries, concentrated on locating deep extensions of the main lodes by cutting deeper shafts, levels and connecting cross-cuts, as at Pen Dylife (Fig 9).

In north-east Wales, by contrast, technological advancements were adopted earlier and gave rise to much larger-scale mining in this area by the end of the 18th century. Until the invention of the steam engine by Thomas Savery at the end of the 17th century, and the improvements introduced by Newcomen by 1712, the raising of ore had always been by simple mechanical methods such as rope and bucket, windlasses and horse whims.

The Grosvenor Estate, which owned the whole of Halkyn Mountain, was the largest mining district landowner in the area in the 17th and 18th centuries and the estate continued to derive considerable revenue from renting out plots or 'bargains' to miners on an annual lease. The early 18th century in particular brought large profits and a great expansion in the industry in Flintshire. The abundance of coal in Flintshire and the discovery that it could replace the use of charcoal in smelting lead ore, led to the establishment and expansion of operations by the London Lead Company, which later became the Quaker Company. This company worked the richest mines on Halkyn Mountain and northwards to Dyserth and Trelogan. In 1703, the company began to build its own smeltery at Gadlys, near Bagillt.

The Quaker Company was a pioneer of the lead mining industry and was active in Flintshire until 1792; its records are valuable in documenting the technological advances which took place during the 18th century (Bevan-Evans 1960; 1961; 1962). The company installed the first of many Newcomen

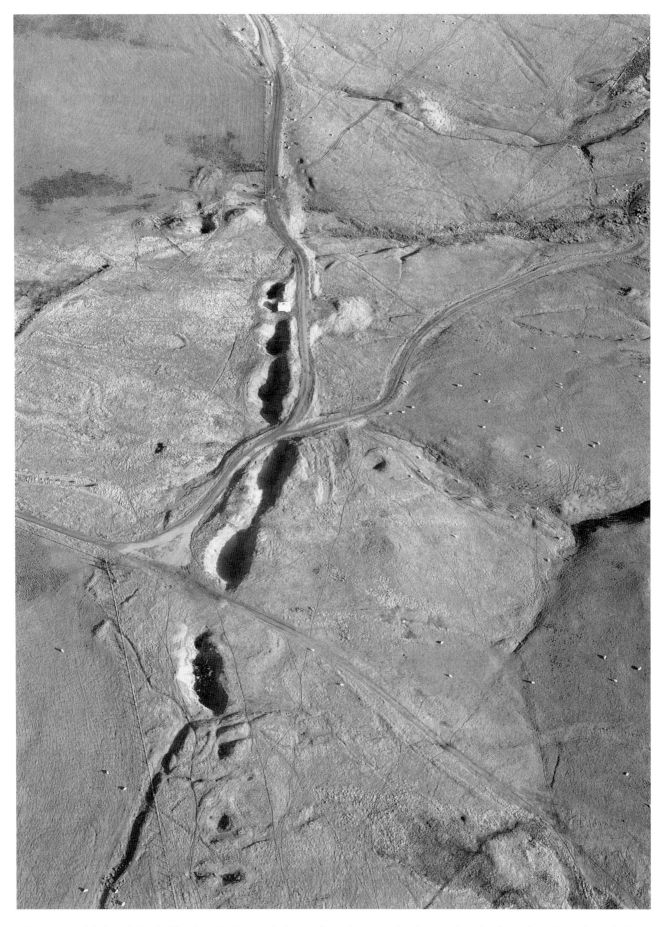

Figure 9 Aerial view of Pen Dylife mine, Llanbrynmair, Powys, from the west, showing a series of collapsed workings along the Pen Dylife vein. Many of these shafts have associated whim circles providing evidence for winding. (*Crown Copyright: RCAHMW 925091–44*)

engines at Trelogan in 1732 in an attempt to pump the deeper shafts free of water. This engine replaced a windmill which had previously performed this function, a technique also pioneered by the Quaker Company. Another of the company's innovations was the use of adits which served as both drainage and access levels. Previously, the majority of mines would have been under water and unworkable during the winter months. These improvements enabled mining to take place all year round, and facilitated the exploitation of deeper and richer veins. By the end of the 18th century most of the richest veins in north-east Wales were already being worked, and further expansion necessitated deeper workings along these lodes. The adjoining Coal Measures provided ample fuel for the steam engines and the proximity of the River Dee assisted with the shipment of ore to manufacturing industries and large smelteries elsewhere along the coast. With a healthy demand for lead on the home and international markets the Welsh lead mining industry was full of confidence in the late 18th century and more than ready to meet the demands of the new century.

Mining in the industrial era

A zest for developing new or improved mining and processing techniques completely revolutionized the industry during the course of the 19th century, and had a profound effect upon the development of mining landscapes. Fed by an economic boom in the metals industry and a demand for materials from the expanding building and manufacturing industries, virtually every mine in the study area of mid and north-east Wales was affected by renewed extraction and processing activity at this time. Waste tips, processing tips and even reprocessing tips expanded to even greater volumes, burying elements of earlier mining landscapes in the process. Permanent buildings of varying function were erected to cover a higher proportion of the intervening ground between the shaft and the dressing floor tips, and over the course of time often followed a common pattern as processing techniques became increasingly standardized. Mining communities reached their zenith during this period and many completely new settlements sprang up to house the mining families, such as those at Dylife, Halkyn and Van. The development of the railway network from the 1840s onwards helped many mines to transport their product more profitably and receive the latest equipment from distant manufacturers. Some of the mineral railways later developed into

passenger services and were the forerunners of the more developed railway network of the 1860s.

Steam engines were first used in the mid Wales study area during the 1850s at Dyfngwm and Abergwesyn (Bick 1990, Part 4, 17). Vertical Cornish engines were in use pumping the main 'engine' shafts while smaller horizontal engines were put to many uses including winding, stamping and crushing. By the 1870s they were a common feature, but only on the largest and most modern mines. The small Cornish engine house at Penyclun, near Llanidloes (Figs 78–9), probably installed in the 1860s, is one of the few such structures to survive in mid Wales. The cost of installation and supplying fuel were critical factors and in general, given the high rainfall and the distance from the coalfields, water power remained supreme in mid Wales until the decline of the mining industry.

The problem of draining deep mines continued to be tackled in a number of ways and often more than one technique was used at the same mine. Where the underground workings were above a river valley it was often possible to excavate a slightly inclined drainage level or adit at the lowest level of the mine which would de-water all of the workings above it and deposit the water directly into a natural watercourse, or supply that water to power machinery at the processing area. Where the underground workings descended below ground that could be drained by an adit the mine would need to be continuously pumped from a sump at the base of the main shaft. The pump would either bring the water up to the surface or up to the level of a drainage adit where it could be drawn off in pipes or wooden launders. Pumping machinery developed from simple water-powered 'rag and chain' or continuous bucket systems to more efficient rising main systems powered by waterwheels or steam driven pumping engines in the late 18th and 19th centuries. Cwm Elan mine has a particularly well-preserved example of the water-powered pumping system, typical of a kind used throughout the mid Wales orefield and in those areas of north-east Wales where steam power was not adopted. The wheelpit at Cwm Elan contained a cast-iron waterwheel with a side armature that rotated with the wheel. This armature in turn was linked to a series of reciprocating horizontal rods that were carried on vertical posts to the top of a pivoting wooden angle bob set in a square pit on the edge of the shaft. The end of the A-framed angle bob which extended out over the shaft collar was attached to a vertical wooden pumping rod and this would be moved up and down by the action of the horizontal reciprocating rods being moved forwards and backward on the surface. The pumping rod was encased by a cast-iron rising main pipe and supported a long cast-iron linkage which extended down to the sump at the bottom of the shaft and a pumping valve and rose which sucked water up the rising main as the pumping rod was lifted. The cast-iron fittings from the reciprocating surface linkage can be seen on the ground close to the shaft at Cwm Elan and the vertical pumping rod still resides in the top of the shaft.

In the case of steam-powered pumping machinery the job of the reciprocating rods and waterwheel was replaced by a beam engine which powered a mounted cast-iron rocking beam, linked at one end to the pumping rod in the shaft and to the steam engine's cylinder rod at the other. The use of steam engines for both winding and pumping was more common in Flintshire and Denbighshire where coal was readily available and where deeper mines could not be drained by adits alone. The earliest engine was installed at Talargoch, near Prestatyn, around 1716 and the London Lead Company had installed a Newcomen engine at Trelogan by 1732. By the 19th century the Cornish beam engine had become the most commonly installed type and well-preserved examples of the substantial stone-built structures which housed engines of this kind can be seen at Talargoch in north-east Wales and at the Minera Mines Museum, Wrexham.

Having been brought to the surface in a kibble or skip the ore was moved around the surface of the mine by use of additional skips mounted on horse-drawn or manually handled tram lines, or by barrowing. Material brought to the surface was either waste, in which case it was trammed out on 'finger' spoil heaps and dumped at the edge of the expanding spoil tips, or it consisted of mixed ore and gangue minerals embedded in country rock which would be taken to the dressing floor to be sorted and broken down to a fine lead, copper or zinc-rich concentrate which would be taken to the smeltery.

From the shaft the ore was first taken to be stored in ore-bins. These were stone-built hoppers consisting commonly of a half cone or three-sided slope with a small opening at the front through which ore could be raked over a grill and washed. Ore-bins became common from the late 18th century but are often poorly preserved because of their rough, drystone construction. Well-preserved and reconstructed examples can be seen at the Minera Mines Museum, Wrexham, while the lead mine at Cwm Orog in Montgomeryshire includes a variety of types on the hillside above the dressing floor. In north-east Wales there was a tendency to build the ore-bins into the shaft-mound waste material itself, as at Lower Park, and there are sometimes shelters, or recesses for storage or carts next to the ore-bin. The ore was sorted according to size on the stone-surfaced picking floor in front of the ore-bins, the more manageable pieces being broken down by hammers in a process called bucking or hand-cobbing. Waste gangue minerals were separated as far as possible and dumped while the broken down ore was then taken either to a stone breaker for further reduction or directly to the crushing house. The sorting and bucking process was frequently carried out by women and children that were too young to enter the mines, as well as by the men.

Dressing floors underwent extensive developments during the course of the 19th century in which virtually all the former manual stages of processing gradually became mechanised. Crusher houses probably first appeared in Wales in the 1820s (Lewis 1967, 347) and are frequently the most impressive structures which survive on the dressing floor. In Powys all of the larger mines had a crusher house by the 1850s. The ore received at the crushing house was taken to the upper floor via a rear entrance and tipped into a hopper which fed the ore down onto two counter-rotating smooth or fluted crusher rolls made of cast-iron and powered by a waterwheel. The space between the crusher rolls was controlled by a counter-weighted lever mechanism, which governed the fineness of the material produced. The crushed ore passed onto a slide which carried the ore into a rotating sieve or trommel screen which further graded the size of the ore. Material which did not pass through the sieve was returned to the head of the crushers for further reduction via a raff-wheel, which acted like a waterwheel in reverse. From the trommel screens the finely graded ore was dropped into a barrow or skip and trammed out to the jig platforms. Crusher houses tend to consist of the substantial walls which housed and supported the crusher rolls along with an adjacent waterwheel pit. Like the ore-bins, the walls were often made of poor-quality stonework and many have collapsed through weathering and erosion. Cwm Elan has an outstanding example with the beams of the removed crusher rolls still stacked inside the building and a deep wheelpit which can be accessed via the tailrace arch at ground level (Fig 23).

The jig or jigger platforms were generally located next to the crusher house and consisted of a levelled stone platform on which a series of jiggers were placed.

A jigger was a water-filled wooden tub, also known as a hotching tub, within which a mesh-bottomed box containing ore-bearing material was raised and lowered manually by means of a long lever operated by hand. The agitation caused the heavier ore to settle in the bottom of the box where it could be scraped out once jigging was complete. The fine gravely waste material would be thrown out of the mesh box onto tips nearby. The invention is attributed to a Captain Barrett of Grassinton Moor Mine, who in 1810 hung a sieve on the end of a lever which supported it in a tub to make it easier to operate. Reconstructed examples of working jigs can be found at the Minera Mines Museum near Wrexham. From the mid 19th century large mechanised processing mills were constructed to house mechanised jiggers powered by steam engines or waterwheels (some to the design patented by George Green of Aberystwyth and produced at his Cambrian Foundry), the remains of which are to be seen in mid Wales at Greens Mill, Rhoswydol, Nantiago (Fig 10), Dyfngwm and Nantygarw.

Jigging produced fine metal-rich particles and some fine waste material which could be further separated and refined by means of buddles. Early buddles to the form of slightly inclined troughs or flat buddles. Ore was put onto the trough and raked up and down, the fine particles of waste being washed away by a constant stream of water while the heavier particles of ore collected at the bottom. Circular buddles were developed from the mid-19th century consisting of a cone set within a circular pit, often about about 7 metres in diameter, with rotating brushes generally powered by a small waterwheel. The crushed ore was loaded into a constant flow of water to form a slurry, which was fed via a launder onto the central cone of the buddle. The rotating brushes swept the slurry around on the buddle surface, separating the lighter waste from the heavier, metal-rich particles. The latter was scraped off the buddle surface and loaded into sacks for transport. The distinctive, fine-grained silty waste material was usually dumped on waste heaps near the buddle. Buddles are normally recognised in the field by their

Figure 10 Iron Pelton-wheel and its timber supporting frame within the late dressing mill of about 1900 at Nantiago mine, Llangurig, Powys. Nantiago characterises the mining sites of the Industrial era in mid Wales, where large-scale processing mills were installed (CPAT 144–3)

Figure 11
Remains of timber launders at Nantiago mine, Llangurig,
Powys. The launders were used to carry slimes from the
dressing floors to the settling pits (*CPAT 144–31*)

circular bases and are often accompanied by a wheelpit for a small waterwheel which drove the rotating brushes. Occasionally, timber supports for the buddle superstructure survive at the centre and sides of the buddle circle and by stone-lined or wooden launders embedded in the ground which carried off the waste slimes. Well-preserved buddles can be seen at the Cwm Elan and Fedw mine in mid Wales and a reconstructed working example can be seen at the Minera Mines Museum near Wrexham.

As in the case of the Nantiago mine (Fig 11) the fine slurry of waste slimes was generally carried away from the buddles in wooden launders or stone-lined open drains to the settling or slime pits. These were often sited next to an existing watercourse and consisted of rectangular stone- or wood-lined tanks or reservoirs. In this final process of separation, the heavier, metal-rich sediment could be separated from the lighter waste material once it had settled out on the bottom of the tank. The overflow and residues could be washed into the adjacent watercourse, often causing contamination downstream. Well-preserved slime pit earthworks can be seen at Cwm Elan and Dyfngwm.

By the mid to late 19th century all of the above processes were being automated and gathered under one roof. These large gravity-fed processing mills were powered either by a waterwheel or horizontal steam engine that drove hoppers, crushers, sieves, jigs and buddles. Mills of this type, known as halvans plants, were also used to reprocess earlier waste tips, a good example of which was excavated in 1988 at the Minera mines complex near Wrexham (Fig 12; see Silvester 1993). All that usually survives of these complex structures are the solid tiered concrete foundations and various concrete mountings with metal rod fixing points. The superstructure was often clad in light prefabricated materials such as wood or corrugated sheeting which has generally since been removed. One of the last surviving examples of one of this type of structure in mid Wales survived at Cwmystwyth until the 1970s, but this has now been dismantled. Good examples of the massive concrete or stone bases of these mills can be seen at Dyfngwm, Dylife, Nantiago and Rhoswydol in Montgomeryshire and Nantygarw in Radnorshire.

The increase in processing speed, performance and quality of product, combined with more mechanised means of extraction through drilling and improved explosive techniques, contributed to the spread of huge areas of waste tips around the periphery of mine dressing floors. These tips spread their fingers out across the surrounding fields and are often one of the most prominent and enduring features of the relict mining landscapes of the modern age, and as well as being a testimony of the labours of men, women and children employed in the mining industry over the last two centuries are often valued for their geological and nature conservation interests.

The most productive period in the mid Wales study area covered the three decades between 1845 and 1875, during which time the Van and Dylife mines were the pre-eminent suppliers of lead in the county

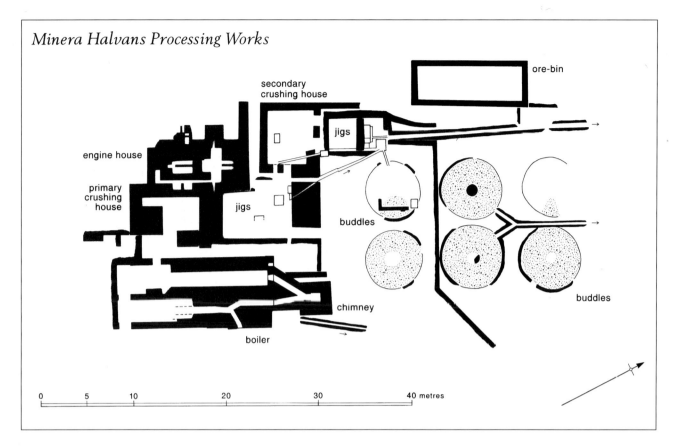

Minera Halvans Processing Works

Figure 12 Plan of the Minera Halvans processing works, Wrexham, revealed by archaeological excavation.
This plant, erected in 1873, is a good example of a late 19th-century investment for reprocessing low grade mine waste or 'halvans'
to recover additional metals. All of the ore-dressing processes, including crushing, jigging and buddling, were placed under one roof
and the machinery powered by a steam engine. The excavated remains have been reburied and are no longer visible.

– Van even being distinguished as the most productive lead mine in Western Europe during the 1870s. However, a rapid drop in the price of lead during this decade due to competition from abroad resulted in the closure of many mines. The market never really recovered after this decade; some mines survived on the secondary production of zinc and the reworking of old waste tips up to the First World War, while others, such as Van and Nantiago, struggled through to final collapse in the 1920s.

In north-east Wales the gradual expansion of the industry and the need for higher levels of capital investment led to the replacement of small mining ventures by large-scale mining companies during the course of the 19th century. By the late 19th century Flintshire had become the most productive mining area in Wales, second only in importance to the Pennines in Britain as a whole.

The large capital investments that were being made are evident in the reports given in contemporary mining journals. Although the industry was affected by general fluctuations in the market during the 19th century, companies continually invested in new plant and machinery. Unlike some other mining areas, the main orefields of north-east Wales were located in upland limestone areas where there was a general lack of surface water which could be used as a source of power. The steam engine, fired with coal, became the major power source for most mines in the region during the 19th century. Cooperative schemes were undertaken to overcome drainage problems. The Halkyn Deep Level Tunnel was started in 1818 from Nant-y-flint and extended from 1875 by the Halkyn District Mines Drainage Company. In 1896, the Holywell-Halkyn Mining and Tunnel Company began the Sea Level or Milwr Tunnel from Bagillt. These tunnels drained the Halkyn Mountain and Holywell Mines and eventually reached the Mold Mines.

The end of the 19th century saw a dramatic decline in the fortunes of the north-east Wales mining industry due to competition from abroad. During the First World War, the Ministry of Munitions provided loans to stimulate the industry. In 1913 the Holywell-Halkyn Mining and Tunnel Company began to extend the Sea Level Tunnel (Ebbs 1993, 8). Drainage and mining interests were amalgamated in 1928 when the

Figure 13 Remains of the stone-built smithy at Cwm Elan mine, Rhayader, Powys. (*CPAT 284–09*)

Halkyn District United Mines extended the Sea Level Tunnel southwards and opened up new veins. The tunnel served an underground railway system using battery locomotives for the carriage of ore and personnel. The 20th-century surface operations were powered by electricity.

Mining was suspended during the Second World War, but subsequently recommenced with a number of concerns that combined the mining of lead ore with the quarrying of limestone for agricultural purposes. The large-scale operations of the Halkyn District United Mines (the amalgamation of nine former mining companies) were centred on the Pen-y-bryn Shaft on Halkyn Mountain and the Olwyn Goch Shaft at Hendre, which continued to be worked intermittently for limestone and lead until 1977. Maintenance work continued until the final closure of this last metal mine in north-east Wales in 1987.

A number of other building types can be found on mine sites in addition to the engine houses and mills described above. There are rarely any surviving plans which indicate their purpose, and many buildings are in a ruinous condition, there are sometimes clues to their original function. Dynamite or gunpowder were normally stored in a separate magazine, generally in a remote location outside the main complex so that an accidental explosion would not result in loss of life and machinery. Magazines are sometimes round in plan and built of two or more concentric thick stone walls with internal concrete or stone partitions. The multiple walls were designed to minimize the radius of blast damage if an accidental explosion occurred. Rectangular magazines were also used and tend to be more common in north Wales while the round magazine dominates in mid Wales. A number of well-preserved examples of round magazines can be seen at Llangynog and a roofed example has been restored at the Mid Wales Lead Mining Museum at Llywernog, Ceredigion. Small rectangular magazines are to be seen at Cwm Elan and Nantygarw.

The smithy and carpenter's shop were essential on a mine where tools and machinery constantly needed repair and maintenance. The smithy is often readily recognizable by the presence of a smithing hearth against a wall. The floor of these buildings is sometimes still littered with cast off broken tools and

Figure 14 Row of miners' cottages known as Rhanc-y-mynydd ('Mountain Rank'), near Dylife, Llanbrynmair, Powys (*CPAT 154.03*)

smithing hearth debris. The smithy at Dylife, for example, can still be readily identified in this way. Well-preserved examples of smithies can be seen at Cwm Elan (Fig 13) and Nantygarw. Many mines also had a single building which provided accommodation for the manager and also acted as a mine office. Later buildings of this kind often took the form of a stone built house with several rooms on the ground floor and first floor, and can often be seen to have been accompanied by a number of small outbuildings and a garden area or paddock marked by a low stone wall or bank, of which a characteristic example survives at the Cwm Elan mine.

Due to the remoteness of many of the mines in mid Wales the miners themselves often either journeyed to the site each day or were in some instances housed during the working week in purpose-built barracks at or near the mines. At the Cwm Elan mine, for example, there is no clear indication of where the workforce lived, and it is likely that they were accommodated in neighbouring farms, whilst at Nant yr Eira, Nantygarw and Nantiago there is evidence that

accommodation was provided on site. Because of the unpredictable and often seasonal nature of employment many of the miners and those engaged in ore processing often supplemented their incomes by working on farms or in other rural industries. 19th-century census records in the area around the Van mine near Llanidloes, for example, show that miners either stayed in Llanidloes itself and travelled in each day, or lived in farms scattered around the neighbourhood. These records also show many of the miner's families in this area had sons and daughters who also worked in the industry or were employed in the local flannel mills at Llanidloes. It was only during the latest and most productive phases in the late 19th century that workers' housing was provided, Van Terrace being a surviving example of the simple two-up, two-down dwellings that were erected at this period. The mine manager and engineers were also housed in the village at this time and chapels and a shop were erected to service the local community. The chapel at Van included a miners' library, a feature commonly provided through the educating zeal of the independent ministers. Dylife is a further example of what was once a small but thriving mining community in mid Wales, consisting of a church, several nonconformist chapels, a public house, smithy, miners' cottages and a number of scattered smallholdings typified by the short row of former miners' cottages at Rhanc-y-mynydd (SN854939) near Dylife (Fig 14), each with a vegetable allotment and adjacent paddocks for stock.

In north-east Wales a number of larger communities became established in the most productive mining districts. At Minera the workforce was housed both in the village and in the surrounding hillside terraces above the mines. On Halkyn Mountain a number of small mining communities sprang up, as at Rhes-y-cae, Moel-y-crio and Halkyn and here, as in mid Wales, a number of workers combined mining with the running of farms and smallholdings.

As in earlier periods the smelting of ores was carried out in furnaces at smelting mills which were often at some distance from the mines, in places where the fuel for smelting was more readily obtained and which were better placed to market the refined metals. In mid Wales the ores often transported considerable distances for smelting. Throughout the 18th and 19th centuries much of the output of the mines in western Montgomeryshire, Radnorshire and Breconshire was carried westwards up to 40 kilometres across the mountains to the harbour at Aberystwyth, to be shipped by sea to smelting mills at Bristol, Swansea or on the Dee Estuary, or to the furnaces later established in the Aberystwyth area. In eastern Montgomeryshire, smelting was undertaken from at least the first decade of the 18th century within several kilometres of the mines at Llangynog, Cwm Orog and Craig-y-Mwyn at what was known as the Cubil smelting house, described in 1751 as a by then disused 'cupola and bell' (Williams 1985, 69). Early smelting was carried out with charcoal, the supply of which is likely to have put increasing pressure on local supplies of timber. By the 1720s ore was being transported to a bank of furnaces at Pool Quay at the head of the Severn navigation, about 3 kilometres north of Welshpool and over 30 kilometres by road from the Llangynog mines (Lewis 2000). Coal had come into general use for smelting lead ore by the 1690s and could be more readily transported here by water. By the 1730s some ore from the Llangynog mines was also being taken downstream to the smeltery at Benthall in Coalbrookdale in Shropshire (Williams 1985, 74).

The mines of north-east Wales generally had better access to sources of coal and consequently transport costs to the smelteries were less. From early times many of the lead smelting mills were clustered within easy reach of the coalfields at a number of inland sites and along the shores of the Dee Estuary, including Greenfield, Mostyn (Llannerch-y-mor), Bagillt, Flint, Mold, Gadlys, and Minera, and often within 5 to 10 kilometres of the mines themselves.

Until almost the end of the 19th century many mines relied almost exclusively on horse-drawn transport and packhorses for transport of men and equipment to the mines and taking the processed ores to the smelteries. Distinctive features of many of the mining landscapes in both mid and north-east Wales are consequently the 'miners' tracks' which wind their way between mining setts and the places where the miners lived, and providing a link with the outside world. The mine at Nantygarw in mid Wales, for example, lay at the end of a narrow, 3-kilometre mountain track. The neighbouring mine at Dalrhiw depended for its existence upon a wooden footbridge across the Rhiwnant stream. These lines of communication were often quite tenuous and vulnerable to the exigencies of the weather.

Few of the mines in rural upland areas could afford to develop a private mineral railway and many of the mines in mid Wales had become exhausted by the 1860s when the Cambrian Railway became more accessible. One of the exceptions was the Van mine near Llanidloes which had become one of the most productive and profitable lead mines in Western Europe by the 1870s. This benefited from private railway venture by Earl Vane who leased the mine to the mining company and was at the same time the chairman of the Cambrian Railway. The Van Railway Company was formed in 1871 and a standard gauge railway line branch was opened in that year from the Cambrian Railway at Caersws to the mine dressing floor sidings in Van where an impressive underground railway portal still exists. Manning Wardle locomotives were used on the line which finally closed in 1940. Much of the line survives amidst the rural agricultural landscape today where the original embankments, cuttings and track bed can still be traced. The underground railway portal is unique amongst lead mines in the United Kingdom and has been restored and gated at the mine site. The Tanat Valley Light Railway which joined the main line at Llanymynech in 1904 briefly helped to revive the mines at Cwm Orog and Craig-y-Mywn, but both mines had become largely exhausted by this time and were both closed by 1912.

The railway helped to revive the slate quarrying industry and the hard rock quarrying in the Llangynog area, however, and like the Van Railway much of this disused line can still be traced along the floor of the Tanat valley.

Similar problems of accessibility affected mines in north-east Wales, where collieries were better served by the valley and coastline railway links than the lead mines. A mixture of narrow gauge and broad gauge railways were developed at the Minera mines from the 1850s onward and were eventually linked to the main line railway network at Wrexham which brought coal into the mines to feed the engine boilers. A branch line from the coastline railway network similarly enabled the Talargoch mines to export lead and receive coal.

2 Interpreting the mining landscapes of mid Wales

by Nigel Jones and Pat Frost

Craig-y-Mwyn, Llanrhaeadr-ym-Mochnant, Powys (Figs 7–8, 15–19)

Craig-y-Mwyn mine (SJ07422852) (Fig 15) lies at a height of about 500 metres on the steep, north-facing slopes of Y Clogydd on the eastern edge of the Berwyn mountains in north-west Powys, overlooking the valley of the Afon Rhaeadr river. The mine is aptly named, having the meaning in Welsh of 'mine/ore cliff'. It lies some five kilometres to the north-west of village of Llanrhaeadr-ym-Mochnant and practically in sight of the famous waterfall at Pistyll Rhaeadr – one of the so-called 'Seven Wonders of Wales' – where the river cascades down an even steeper slope than that occupied by the mine workings. Altogether, the mine workings and processing area occupied over ten hectares. Today, the mine forms part of the Tanat Valley landscape of outstanding historic interest in Wales (Cadw 1998; Britnell and Martin 1999).

The mine produced lead ore which occurred in four main veins, two aligned ENE–WSW and two E–W, with the mineralisation including galena and sphalerite in a dominantly calcite, quartz and barytes gangue. The solid geology is of Ordovician Llangynog-formation shales, slates and tuffs (Williams 1985, 75).

The workings extend from the valley floor up the steep slope and onto the open moorland above. One of the main points of interest is the large opencast workings, clearly visible on the aerial photographs (Figs 16–17), associated with an extensive hushing system dating from the mid-17th century and earlier. It was this hushing system, with its leats, reservoirs and hushing channels, which formed the focus of the ground survey and analysis presented in Figures 18 and 19. The workings within the opencast and the ore processing areas a few hundred yards further east on the lower slopes of the hill lay beyond the scope of the present survey but are described below. The workings have been abandoned for almost a century, but the opencast workings in particular still

form a dramatic feature within the landscape.

The impact of the earliest workings appears to have been relatively muted, with small-scale trials and perhaps prospective hushing taking place along the upper edge of the valley side. By the mid-19th century, hushing operations had created an enormous opencast area (18355) on the crest of the hill, almost a 100 metres across, with a corresponding fan of mining waste spilling out onto the valley floor below (see Fig 8). A number of levels were also driven into the hillside on either side of the opencast, and these too have left their mark. A network of tracks traverse the slopes, linking the levels with the dressing area on the lower slopes of the hill, and providing access to the upper area containing the hushing remains. The moorland above the mine is crossed by a system of leats and reservoirs, providing water for the hushing operations. The surviving features in the dressing area date from the mid- to late 19th century and include an incline, crusher and wheelpit, although the nature and extent of spoil tips suggests that other processing was also undertaken.

The earliest phase of mining is undated but predates the 18th century and may be medieval, Roman or even prehistoric in date. The area formed part of Powis estate, owned by the Herbert family, who leased the mining interests to a variety of parties. The earliest recorded workings date from the 17th century (Lewis 1966). In 1656 John Arthur of Northampton was granted a lease of lead mines in an area which included Craig-y-Mwyn (Williams 1985, 75). During the mid-18th century the mine was explored by the German mine manager Henry Henning (Heinrich Henninck) who sank a shaft and level (Williams 1985, 77). Thereafter, the history of the mine is poorly documented until 1851, when reports indicate more extensive workings and new machinery. Despite this investment,

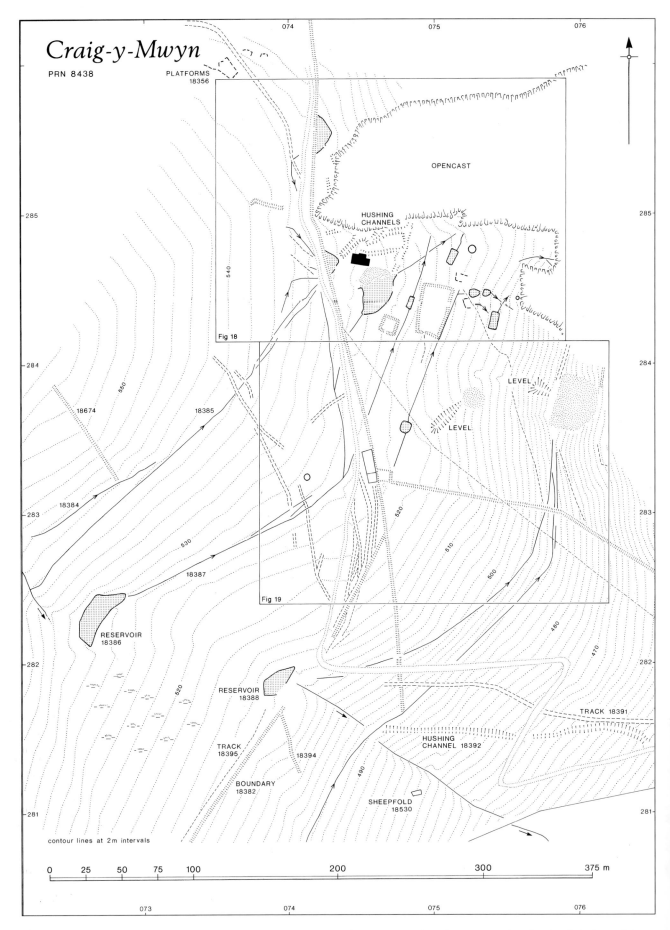

Figure 15 General plan of Craig-y-Mwyn mine, Llanrhaeadr-ym-Mochnant, Powys. See Figures 18 and 19 for detailed plans of the inset areas.

however, the venture failed and the mine was put up for sale in 1856.

In 1868 the Craig-y-Mwyn Lead Mining Company was formed, but this was short-lived, the mine being taken over by the newly formed East Llangynog Company in 1870, under the new name of East Llangynog Mine (Williams 1985, 81). A mine plan of 1871 shows six levels, a newly-constructed incline, a crusher and waterwheel, a powder house, smithy, workshops, stables, coaching house and carpenter's shop (Williams 1985, 83, Fig 24). The company went into voluntary liquidation in 1874 and was sold by public auction to Joseph Taylor, who established the Llanrhaeadr Mining Company in 1875. This venture met with little success, however, and after three years of little activity went into liquidation in 1880. Between 1899 and 1900 the mine was worked by a Belgian concern, the Vieille Montagne Company, and later by Robert Owen, between 1901–07. It was worked by Joseph Matthews between 1908–10 and was probably finally abandoned in 1911 (Williams 1985, 85).

The remote location of the mine meant that the transportation of ore to the smelteries was always a crucial factor in the economic viability of the mine. Although small-scale smelting appears to have been undertaken in nearby Llangynog in the first half of the 18th century (Williams 1985, 31), most of the ore was smelted at either Pool Quay, near Welshpool, or Benthall in Coalbrookdale. The opening of the Tanat Valley Light Railway in 1904 appears to have given a brief lease of life before working ceased a few years later.

It seems likely that throughout much of its history, labour was provided by workers drawn from the local agricultural community. The presence of a row of miners' cottages on the lower slopes of the hill (to the east of the survey area) suggests that by at least the late 19th century the mine had attracted a more permanent workforce.

The earliest workings are thought to have been associated with hushing, and a report of 1755 records working dating back to at least 1706, describing the

Figure 16 Aerial view of Craig-y-Mwyn mine from the east, showing the large opencast workings (right of centre) with surrounding hushing channels, reservoirs and leats. (*Crown Copyright: RCAHMW 935097–53*)

Figure 17 Aerial view of Craig-y-Mwyn mine from the south-east, showing the opencast workings, hushing channels, reservoirs and leats, with Level No 1 at bottom right. (Crown Copyright: RCAHMW 935097–51)

site as 'an old torn place rent to pieces by hushing in former times' (*Montgomeryshire Collections* 45, 1937–38, 49). The evidence for hushing consists of a series of leats drawn from a boggy valley about 300 metres to the south-west of the opencast workings, which fed a system of reservoirs from which a complex of hushing channels can be traced. A mine plan of 1855 (Williams 1985, 76) depicts three 'miners' pools' as sources for part of the leat system, two of which were identified during the course of the recent ground survey (reservoirs 18386 and 18388, shown on Fig 15).

Water was drawn from these two reservoirs as well as from a number of other neighbouring springs to be stored in a series of smaller reservoirs nearer the edge of the large opencast, the two principal leats for the hushing system associated with the main opencast workings being 18385 and 18387 (see Fig 15). These and the reservoirs' associated hushing channels around the edge of the opencast are clearly visible on the aerial views shown in Figures 16 and 17. Once sufficient

water had been gathered in one or other of the reservoirs the outlet sluice would be opened, releasing a torrent of water along one of the hushing channels, the force of which would have revealed mineral veins within the exposed rock surface. The technique may have been employed initially as a means of prospecting, but the extent of the opencast, which has a large fan of water-washed spoil at its base, suggests that the hushing system was used primarily for ore extraction.

The remains of three main hushing reservoirs can be discerned amongst the palimpsest of earthworks along the western and southern edges of the opencast (Fig. 18). The northernmost reservoir (18357) is defined by a large bank, about 1.3 metres high and 3.8 metres wide, enclosing an area of 365 square metres, with a sluice to the south-east. The reservoir has been partly filled in by the modern track and there is no clear indication of the leat system that must once have fed into it. A second reservoir (18358) to the south-west of the opencast has been largely obscured by the

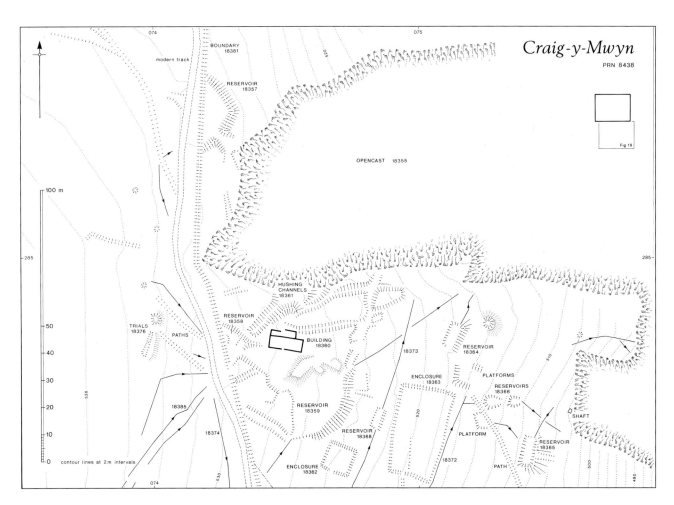

Figure 18 Craig-y-Mwyn mine: detailed plan of the northern inset area shown in Figure 15.

modern track, but there is still clear evidence of the associated leat system and hushing channels leading towards the opencast. A third reservoir (18359), to the south of the opencast, seems to be partly hidden beneath spoil tips built up along its northern side, but remains clearly defined along the southern side by a bank up to 1.3 metres high and 4 metres wide, with the hushing sluice at its north-eastern corner. Traces of the leat which fed the reservoir are visible at its south-western corner. A separate system of leats and smaller reservoirs (18364–6, 18368, Fig 18) fed ancillary hushing operations to the south of the main opencast.

Two rectangular earthwork enclosures lie within the hushing complex. The larger one (18363), about 32 metres by 19 metres across, contains a possible building platform in the south-west corner. The smaller enclosure (18362) is roughly square and about 10 metres across, with an entrance on the south-west side. It is unclear whether either enclosure is associated with mining activity, although similar enclosures have been identified on mine sites elsewhere in mid Wales, as for example at Cwm Elan, Dalrhiw and Pen Dylife,

and may represent pounds for horses employed at the mine.

The remains of a rectangular stone building (18360) near the hushing channels towards the southern edge of the opencast is likely to mark the site of the house and smithy recorded in 1751 (National Library of Wales, Powis MS 21712). The building, which has traces of an additional outbuilding against its northern wall, measures about 12 by 4 metres across and has dry-stone walls about half a metre thick of which generally only the basal courses survive. A number of possible platforms about 80 metres to the north-west of the opencast (18356, Fig 15) may represent other building structures associated with mining activity at one period or another. An enclosure and possible building platform (18378) about 150 metres to the south of the hushing complex is associated with a system of boundaries which overlie structures associated with the mine workings and are therefore likely to be associated with later agricultural activity.

The veins exposed within the opencast were further exploited by a series of levels and shallow trial

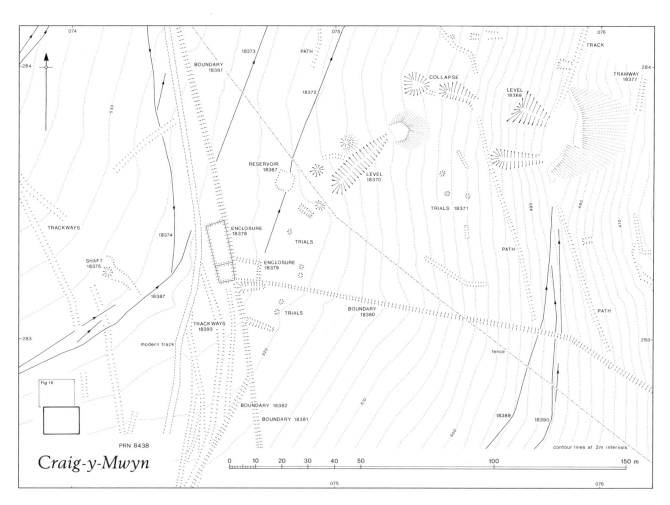

Figure 19 Craig-y-Mwyn mine: detailed plan of the southern inset area shown in Figure 15.

workings driven into the hillside, mostly to the south of the opencast (Fig 19). Only one shaft (18375) has been identified, about 150 metres to the south of the opencast. A possible platform for winding gear is visible on the north side of the shaft, although there is no evidence to suggest that ore was raised here. This, together with the lack of development waste, suggests that the shaft was linked underground with the level (18369, Fig 19) about 150 metres to the north-east associated with a large fan of debris spilling out onto the hillside. The level is identified as Level No 1 on the mine plan of 1855 (Williams 1985, 89). The shaft and level appear to have been those said to have been dug in 1747 by Henry Henning who was then in charge of the mine (Williams 1985, 77), one of the functions of the level probably being to drain the mine from below, rather than pumping from above (Murphy 1997, 93). Ore was transported from the level via a short track or tramway leading northwards to the bottom of the large opencast. Another level can be seen to the north of the opencast outside the survey area, with the ruins of a small building at its entrance.

Lead ore was transported down to the dressing floors lower down the hill by means of an incline which runs from within the large opencast, again outside the area surveyed. The mine plan of 1855 describes a 'trough to drop ore down to crushers',

presumably an ore-chute, in the same position as the incline. The remains of a winding house lie at the head of the incline, still with iron fixing bolts *in situ*. Much of the dressing floor area has unfortunately now been levelled, obscuring much of the evidence relating to ore processing but which probably included jig platforms, buddles and settling pits. The remains of the crusher house still survive, however, at the base of the incline. A new crusher is known to have been constructed in 1851, replacing an earlier structure, and was powered by a waterwheel 20 feet in diameter, although a larger 30-foot wheel had been installed by 1855 (Williams 1985, 79). The wheelpit survives, but is in a poor condition. The main water source to drive the waterwheel was originally drawn from the Cwm yr Ast stream. The leat was extended in 1872 to take water directly from the Afon Rhacadr stream at the head of the Pistyll Rhaeadr waterfall, which fed a large reservoir to the north-west of the crusher. Other structures which it is still possible to discern at the foot of the opencast are the ruins of the explosives magazine near the reservoir to the north-west of the crusher, and the site of the stables and coach house south of the main dressing area. A row of four miners' cottages stands in ruins further south, with what appears to be a block of privies to the rear.

Cwm Elan, Rhayader, Powys (Figs 13, 20–8)

Cwm Elan mine lies on the western slopes of the Nant Methan Valley (SN90006510), 1 kilometre west of the Garreg-ddu Reservoir and 7 kilometres south-west of the town of Rhayader, high on the western edge of the Elan Valley, at a height of about 300 metres (Fig 20). The solid geology is composed of Silurian Llandovery-series rocks which contains at least two lodes striking E–W, with galena and sphalerite mineralisation. These yielded lead and zinc ores which were transported elsewhere for smelting.

This relatively small and compact mine occupied an area of less than 5 hectares at the head of an upland valley on the fringes of the remote and desolate moorland of Elenydd. The landscape had previously been occupied by little other than a number of small, scattered and seasonally-occupied farmsteads from at least the medieval period, falling within the extensive monastic grange of Cwmteuddwr granted to the Cistercian monastery of Strata Florida in the later 12th century. Mining operations began in the late 18th

century, but most of the surviving remains belong to a single phase of operation dating to the late 19th century, and represent one of the most intact examples of late 19th-century mining technology and planning in mid Wales. Its remote location, combined with its management as part of the Elan Valley estate during the last hundred years has contributed to its remarkable state of preservation. All mining activity in the Elan Valley came to an abrupt halt when the extensive watershed of the Elan and Claerwen rivers was purchased by Birmingham corporation in the late 19th century for the construction of the Elan Valley Reservoirs, in order to preserve the purity of the city's water supply (Mansergh 1894). Today, the mine forms part of the Elan Valley landscape of special historic interest in Wales (Cadw 2001; Britnell 2004).

Lead ore was first discovered during the cutting of a drainage leat in about 1796. The early workings were at first carried out under the supervision of the landowner, Thomas Grove, 'a Wiltshire gentleman,

Figure 20 General plan of Cwm Elan mine. See Figures 27 and 28 for detailed plans of the inset areas.

Figure 21 Cwm Elan mine: engine shaft (18467) viewed from the east, showing timber pumping rod surviving *in situ*. *(CPAT 283–23)*

Figure 22 Cwm Elan mine: wheelpit (18469) for pumping and winding the engine shaft. It once once held a waterwheel 36 feet in diameter and 4 feet wide (Hall 1993, 80–1). Supporting walls for the winding drum adjoin the west (left) side of the wheelpit. Iron pumping rods and supports lie scattered around the immediate area. (*CPAT 283–35*)

Figure 23 Cwm Elan mine: crusher house (18478), viewed from west. The walls survive to more or less their full height. Inside the building the large support beams which would have held two sets of crushing rolls are now partly collapsed, along with the axle for the waterwheel. The wheelpit (18477), 14 metres long and 4 metres deep on the south (right) side of the crusher, survives to its full height. The waterwheel appears to have been driven by water reused from the pumping wheelpit (18469) via a system of launders, possibly supplemented by additional water drawn from the stream to the south where two leats can be traced. (*CPAT 283–14*)

Figure 24 Cwm Elan mine: remains of circular buddle (18480) showing traces of the timber centre post and two supports for a launder. The buddle was powered by a small wheelpit to the west (18479), measuring 6 metres by 1 metre, driven by water emitting from the crusher wheelpit. A slight channel to the south of the wheelpit suggests that when the buddle was not in operation the water would have been diverted directly into the stream. *(CPAT 283–04)*

Figure 25 Cwm Elan mine: remains of explosives' magazine (18466) on the hillside to the south of the mine. *(CPAT 283–30)*

Figure 26 Cwm Elan Mine: mine manager's house and office (18455, left), with the later red brick house (18456) built in the 1890s by the Birmingham Corporation Waterworks beyond. (*CPAT 284–15*)

who purchased 10,000 almost worthless acres' of the Grange of Cwmteuddwr in 1792. Grove eagerly set about improving his new Welsh estate, building a new summer residence and introducing modern farming practices (Williams 1905; Hawkins 1985). He clearly also seized the opportunity of gaining additional revenue from lead mining which was already proving profitable at Cwmystwyth, just a few miles across the hills to the west. The new country house, known also as 'Cwm-Elan', occupied a picturesque setting on the floor of the Elan Valley, about a kilometre to the south-east, on a site now submerged below the Garreg-ddu Reservoir. The mine was subsequently leased to a firm headed by Sir Thomas Bonsall that was responsible for cutting a drainage adit. Operations were later taken over by a Cornish company before working was temporarily abandoned (Hall 1993, 80).

The main phase of working, and that responsible for the majority of surviving structures, began in 1871 with the formation of the Cwm Elan Mining Company. Two main lodes were explored, with the Main or South Lode close to the Engine Shaft, and the North Lode 14 fathoms away in a cross-cut. By November 1872 workings included shallow and deep adits as well as a 10 fathom level. In April 1873 a processing mill began operation which included a Blake's stone-crusher, crushing rolls, Collom's patent jiggers and round buddles, all supplied by William Thomas of Llanidloes Foundry. Power was generated by three waterwheels, the largest of which was 36 feet in diameter by 4 feet wide (Hall 1993, 80). The workings had extended to 20 fathoms by 1874 but drought and lack of funds forced the company into voluntary liquidation. Work restarted the following year under

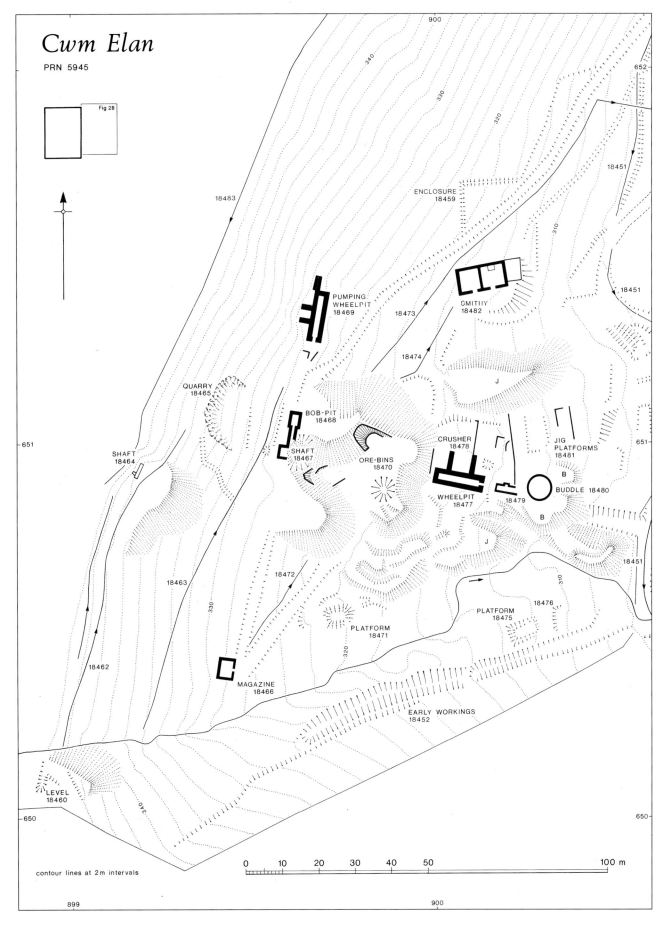

Figure 27 Cwm Elan mine: detailed plan of the western inset area shown in Figure 20.

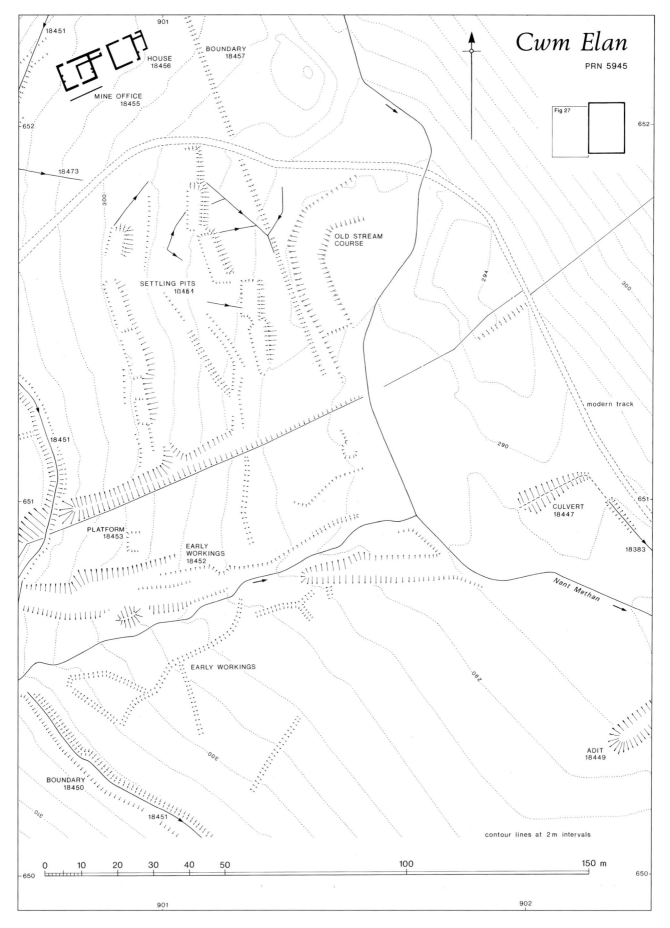

Figure 28 Cwm Elan mine: detailed plan of the eastern inset area shown in Figure 20.

the auspices of the New Cwm Elan Mine. The shaft was eventually extended to 40 fathoms by the time that mining operations finally came to an end in 1877 (Hall 1993, 80).

The later 18th- and early 19th-century workings are probably represented by a series of open-cuts (18452, Figs 27–8) to either side of the un-named stream which runs along the southern boundary of the mine and forms a tributary to the Nant Methan. These early workings are possibly to be associated with a group of four building platforms, two (18471, 18453) to the north of the stream, and two (18475–6) to the south. The two southern platforms are surrounded by small tips suggesting ore processing. Other evidence of this early phase of mining may have been buried beneath the larger-scale 19th-century workings to the north.

The main shaft, the engine shaft (18467, Fig 27), has partly collapsed, but still retains the pumping beam *in situ* (see Fig 21), with a stone-lined bob-pit to the north. A level runs in westwards for a short distance from the top of the shaft. Power for pumping and winding was provided by a waterwheel about 30 metres to the north of the shaft (18469, Fig 22). A second shaft (18464) is perched on the hillside about 40 metres to the west of the engine shaft, associated with a level cut into the hillside from the top of the shaft. Other workings consist of a trial level (18460, Fig 27) on the southern side of the stream, now collapsed at the entrance, and a collapsed drainage adit (18449, Fig 28) on the banks of the Nant Methan, with the remains of a building platform on its southern side (18448, Fig 20).

Ore raised from the engine shaft was loaded into a bank of three ore-bins (18470, Fig 27) to the east of the shaft head. Only one of the ore-bins is now clearly identifiable, the two others having been lost in an area of collapse around the shaft. Once it had been sorted, the ore would probably have been carried by means of a tramway to the crusher house (18478, Fig 23), just downhill. Timbers visible within the spoil tip below the ore-bins may be the remains of supports for a tramway for loading the crusher. A large levelled area to the north of the crusher may have housed the Blake's stone-crusher which the mine once possessed (Hall 1993, 80). A series of stone-revetted platforms just to the east of the crusher represent bases for jiggers (18481). Large heaps of jigger waste are to be seen between the crusher house and the smithy. To the south of the jig platforms are the remains of a circular buddle (18480, Fig 24), with areas of fine buddle tailings to the east and south, where the crushed ore

would have been further refined. A final stage in the recovery of lead ore is represented by a series of large rectangular settling pits (18454, Fig 28) about 80 metres to the north-east of the buddle. The slimes produced by the buddle would probably have been laundered to the pits, fine material suitable for smelting being recovered once it had settled out. At least ten pits can be identified, set out in three rows, with interconnecting channels, though most are now silted-up and some have been disturbed by agricultural activity.

The mine also possesses a good and well-preserved complement of ancillary buildings which like the wheelpits were constructed of local stone, probably provided by the small stone quarry (18465, Fig 27) cut into the hillside to the west of the mine. The remains of a rectangular, stone-built explosives' magazine (18466, Fig 25), about 5 by 6 metres across, are dug into the hillside about 50 metres to the south of the main shaft, approached by a track. On the north side of the site are the ruins of the smithy (18482, Fig 13), superimposed upon traces of an earlier rectangular enclosure of unknown purpose. The smithy was a two-roomed, single-storey building, 14 by 7 metres across. The base of a smithing hearth survives in the room to the east; the room to the west was probably a store-room, and a lean-to on the eastern end may have been a coal store. On the valley floor to the north-east of the main workings are two substantial houses (Fig 26). The western one is the stone-built former mine manager's house and office (18455). The eastern one is a red brick house built in the 1890s by the Birmingham Corporation Waterworks, some years after the abandonment of the mine, to house one of their estate workers. There is no indication of workers' housing contemporary with the later 19th-century workings and it seems likely that the workforce journeyed to the mine each day from the neighbouring farms and cottages.

Water was vital for both power and for ore processing throughout the lifetime of the mine. A complex pattern of leats has been recorded which clearly belong to different periods, though not all are fully explained. A number of leats taken from the un-named stream to the south of the mine appear to belong to early workings. The lowest one (18472, Fig 27) was partly buried below the powder magazine and later spoil tips. Two other leats (18473–4) similarly emerge from a spoil tip, the latter being partly overlain by the smithy. The purpose of the two higher leats taken from this stream (18462–3) is equally speculative, though they may have provided additional water for the later waterwheels. The principal source of water for the later workings was taken from the Nant Methan stream whose flow was supplemented by a leat dug over a period of three months in 1876. This meandered across the moorland for the extraordinary distance of 16 kilometres, bearing water from the natural lake known as Llyn Cerrigllwydion Isaf (SN844700), 170 metres higher up and just 7 kilometres away as the crow flies. An upper leat taken from the Nant Methan stream (18483) ran along the contour of the steep hillside to the west of the mine and most probably fed the pumping and winding waterwheel by means of a wooden launder, of which no trace survives. On emerging from the pumping wheelpit the water would have been laundered to the crusher waterwheel, then laundered on again to the smaller waterwheel which powered the buddle.

The purpose of the two small reservoirs (18675, Fig 20) on the bank of the Nant Methan to the north of the mine is unexplained but they may represent a domestic water supply for the mine office or later house. A leat (18451, Figs 27–8) carrying water from the Nant Methan across the eastern side of the mine and onwards to the south-east may likewise represent a water supply for Cwm Elan house at the foot of the hill, bearing clean water uncontaminated by the mine waste which must once have polluted the natural watercourse. A lower leat (18363, Fig 28) which probably also represented a domestic water supply, emerges from a stone culvert on the east side of the mine.

Cwm Orog, Llangynog, Powys (Figs 29–37)

The Cwm Orog mine (SJ05202730) lies 2 kilometres north-west of Llangynog on the steep northern slopes of Craig Rhiwarth. The mine is dramatically sited below the rampart of the large prehistoric hillfort (see Fig 30) which crowns this prominent hill on the southern edge of the Berwyns, dominating the Tanat Valley. The workings occupy a zone up to 100 metres wide, stretching for a distance of over 700 metres from the dressing floor and settling pits at the foot of the hill, at a height of about 265 metres, up to a series of trials, levels and stopes at 460 metres and within a stone's throw of the hillfort defences. The solid geology is dominated by Ordovician shales, slates and felsites. The main vein runs ENE–WSW with galena and sphalerite mineralisation and N–S barytes crosscourses which yielded lead, silver and zinc ores, together with barytes.

The mine occupies an exposed, north-facing moorland landscape overshadowed by screes and rocky outcrops, whose economic value before the coming of the mine was limited to upland grazing. Several phases of activity are represented, but the primary interest in terms of landscape history is the evidence of the different methods that were used to transport the ore from the levels at the upper end of the site down to the dressing floor below. Three successive systems of transporting ore can be identified at Cwm Orog – tramways, followed by the use of an incline, followed by an aerial ropeway – reflecting technological advances during the course of the 18th, 19th and early 20th centuries. Cwm Orog is but one part of a more extensive mining and quarrying landscape centred on the small village of Llangynog, including the Llangynog lead mine itself. Like the Craig-y-Mwyn mine described above, Cwm Orog forms part of the Tanat Valley landscape of outstanding historic interest in Wales (Cadw 1998; Britnell and Martin 1999).

For a short period in the 1730s it was one of the largest lead producing operations in Europe (Murphy 1997, 93), though production fluctuated wildly and in the early 1740s Llangynog was described as 'like a dying man' (Murphy 1998, 67). The village of Llangynog largely owes its existence to these extractive industries, which had a significant impact not only on the landscape but also on the livelihood of the local population. The wives and children of the miners were engaged in processing the ore. Local tenant farmers were forced to transport the ore by road to smelteries at Pool Quay and elsewhere, or face eviction (Williams 1985, 29, 38). The workforce was housed in rows of stone-built cottages in the village, which still survive, and an influx of English-speaking mine workers in the early 18th century gave rise to a number of social problems.

The history of mining at Cwm Orog dates back to at least 1656, when all of the lead mines in the township of Rhiwarth were leased to John Arthur of Northamptonshire (Williams 1985, 96). Working was certainly under way by 1706, several trials being recorded prior to 1751. However, the close proximity of the hillfort raises the possibility that lead was being extracted in the area during later prehistoric times. The earliest workings appear as a series of linear cuts and small depressions at the top of the site (18396, see Fig 29 inset), close to the hillfort, which may either

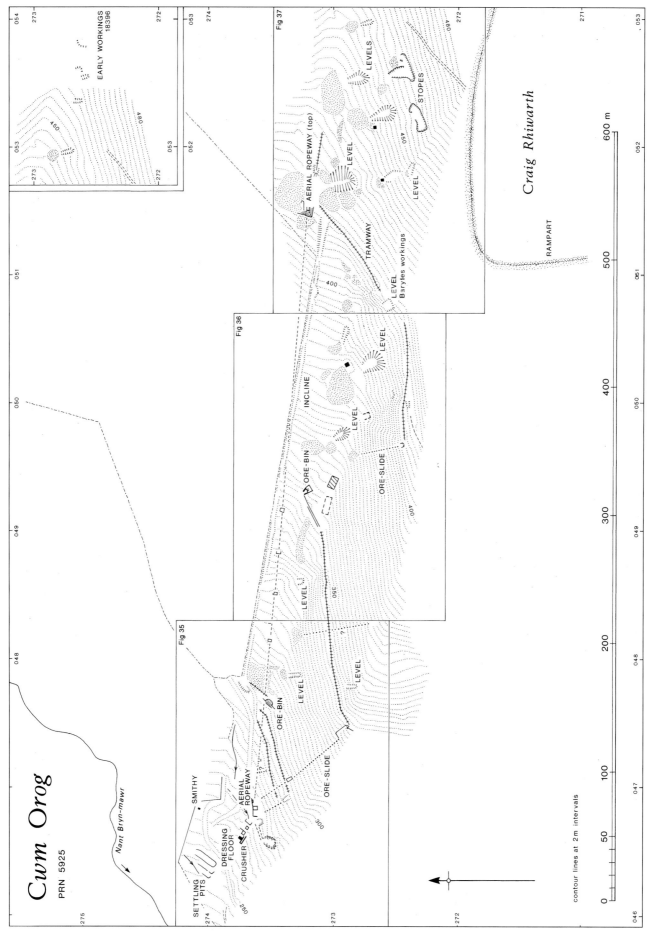

Figure 29 General plan of Cwm Orog mine. See Figures 35–7 for detailed plans of the inset areas. The inset area at the top right shows early workings just to the east.

Figure 30 Aerial view from the north-west showing location of Cwm Orog mine under snow, below the ramparts of Craig Rhiwarth hillfort. The levels and the top of the incline at the upper end of the Cwm Orog mine are visible in the lower left corner. (*CPAT 86–4–11*)

represent prehistoric workings or trials dating to the 17th or 18th century.

The Cwm Orog mine is listed in 1845 and in the period between 1861 and 1865, but no production figures are recorded. By 1870 significant quantities of ore appear to have been discovered whose exploitation was awaiting the erection of a dressing plant (Williams 1985, 96). In December 1871 the mine was leased by the Earl of Powis to William Sadler and William Sennett of London and the following year saw the formation of the Cwm Orog Silver-Lead Mining Company. This venture met with little success, however, and was formally wound up in 1886. By 1912 the mine had changed hands a further four times, including ownership by the Vieille Montagne Company (1898–1900) and Cwm Orog Mines Ltd (1908–12), and was subsequently worked for barytes in 1915 (Williams 1985, 97). A smeltery was in operation in Llangynog for a period, though most of the ore was smelted some distance away. Ore was also transported by road for smelting at Pool Quay, at the head of the Severn navigation and was also transported to Ironbridge and Bristol via the River Vyrnwy and River Severn (Hughes 1988, 111). As in the case of the Craig-y-Mwyn mine, the opening of the Tanat Valley Light Railway in 1904 with a railhead at Llangynog appears to have briefly revived production.

A series of fourteen levels with a spoil tip below can be identified driven into the hillside, dispersed along the entire length of the mine (Figs 29, 35–7). These workings are mostly undated, but there are indications that some of the larger workings above the upper aerial ropeway terminal and head of the incline are the latest. By implication, some of the smaller workings lower down may possibly be earlier in the sequence. Five levels can be identified towards the top (18397–400, 18402, Fig 37), not all of which are likely to have been contemporary. The two largest levels, which both have stone-lined entrances, have been identified as Level No 1 (18398) and Level No 2 (18399), documented from perhaps the 1870s (Williams 1985, 97). On the slopes above the levels is an area of collapsed stopes

Figure 31 Aerial view of the lower end of the Cwm Orog mine, viewed from the north-east with the Llangynog to Bala turnpike road beyond. The line of the incline down to the dressing floor is visible to the left. (*Crown Copyright: RCAHMW 935098–64*)

Figure 32 The lower end of the Cwm Orog mine, viewed from the west, with Craig Rhiwarth hillfort in the background. The dressing floor (18444) and crusher (18443) are visible towards the centre and the line of the incline (18409) is visible behind the building on the left. (*CPAT 427–10*)

Figure 33
Cwm Orog mine:
crusher house
wheelpit (18442)
with remains of cast-
iron waterwheel lying
amongst the
collapsed masonry.
(*CPAT 275–03A*)

(18401, Fig 37) including an open collapse that has previously been misinterpreted as a shaft, together with a number of trials (18406).

As noted above, the remains of three successive transport systems can be readily identified at Cwm Orog which were used to transport the ore to processing areas further downhill. The earliest system is represented by four tramways which contour the side of the hill for up to several hundred metres, and which fed a series of ore-slides and ore-bins towards the western end of the mine. The ore-slides would have been constructed of timber, and only faint traces of them now survive. Differences in the construction of the slides and bins suggests that not all the tramways were built at the same time.

The upper tramway (18410, Figs 36–7) had been disturbed by an open-cut or collapsed level (18676) on a barytes vein, probably representing workings that are known to have commenced in 1915 to meet the exigencies of the First World War. The tramway terminates in a well-built, semi-circular stone ore-chute (18644) leading to a platform at the head of the ore-slide (18421). The base of the ore-slide, which has a pronounced debris fan, lies 20 metres east of foundations for a rectangular building and adjacent platform (18420, 18423) which possibly represents an early processing area. A second tramway (18411, Figs 35–6) has a sub-rectangular ore-bin (18422) at its eastern end which was probably supplied by ore from the level (18419) about 40 metres further to the southeast. At the western end of the tramway the ore was tipped into a stone-lined chute (18645) constructed on exposed bedrock, then down to a platform enclosed by a low stone wall before being loaded onto the ore-slide (18429) which carried it down to the processing area towards the foot of the hill. A stone pier base (18583) midway down the ore-slide would have supported a bridge over a third tramway running along the contour, suggesting that the two were contemporary. The third tramway (18412) also had an ore-bin

Figure 34 Cwm Orog mine: dressing floor (18444) in foreground and crusher (18443) beyond, at the lower end of the mine, viewed from the north-west. (*CPAT 427–22*)

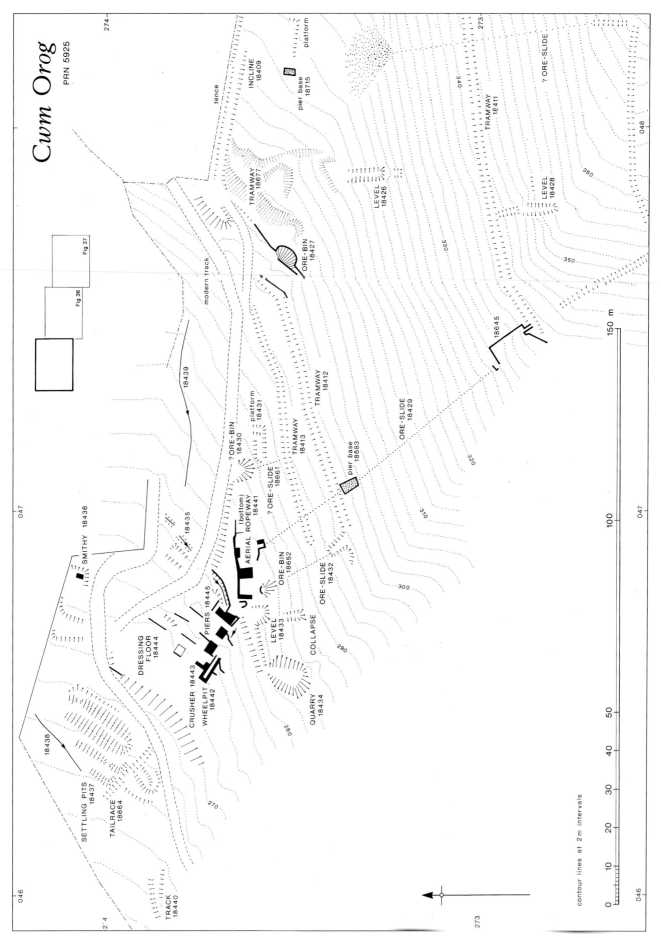

Cwm Orog

PRN 5925

...wing detailed plan of the western inset area shown in Figure 29.

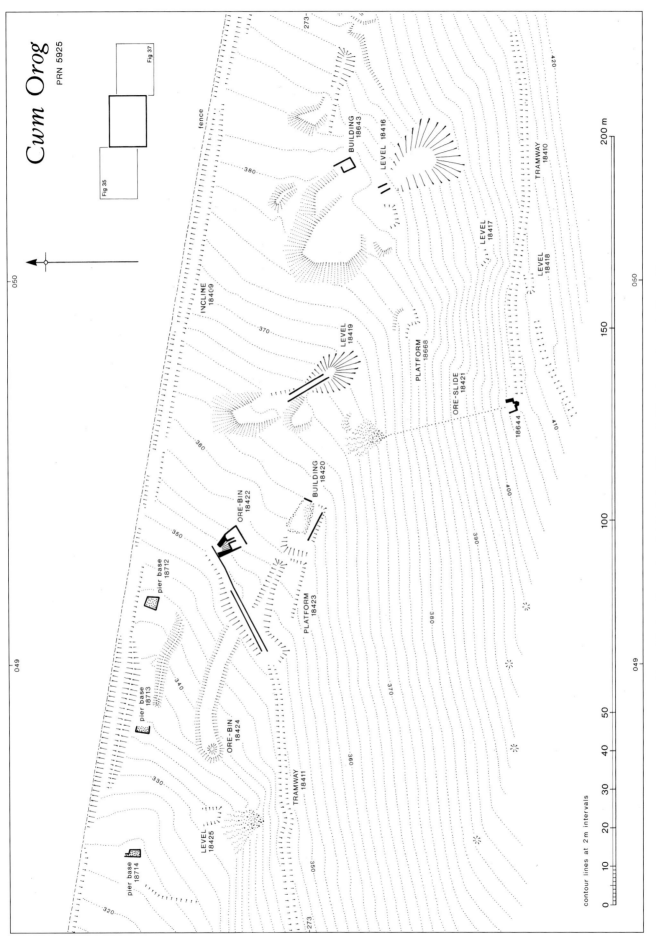

Figure 36 Cwm Orog mine: detailed plan of the central inset area shown in Figure 29.

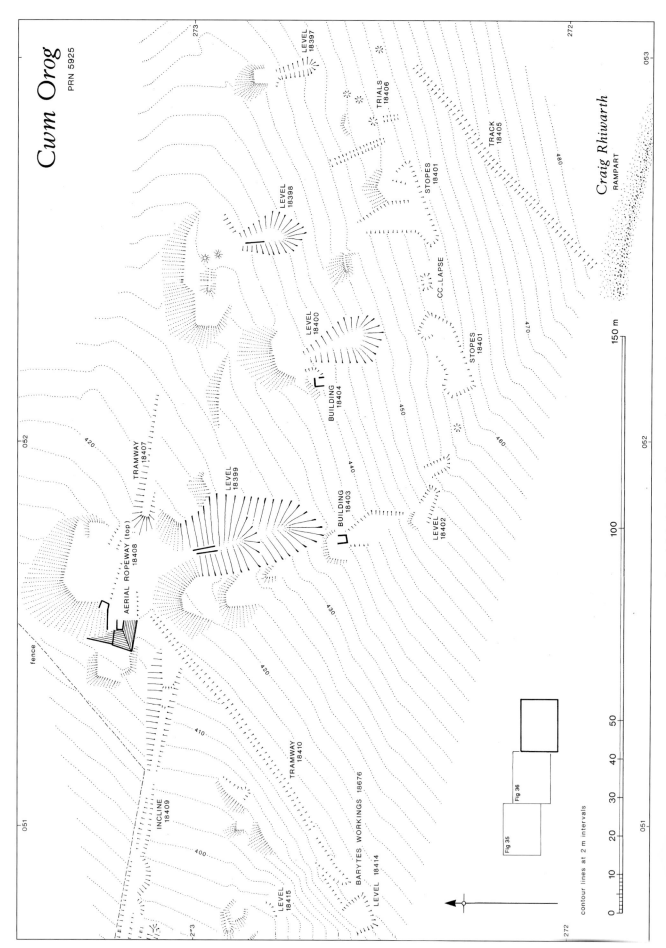

Cwm Orog

PRN 5925

LEVEL 18397

TRIALS 18406

LEVEL 18398

TRACK 18405

STOPES 18401

CC. LAPSE

LEVEL 18400

STOPES 18401

BUILDING 18404

LEVEL 18399

TRAMWAY 18407

AERIAL ROPEWAY (top) 18408

BUILDING 18403

LEVEL 18402

Craig Rhiwarth

RAMPART

fence

INCLINE 18409

TRAMWAY 18410

BARYTES WORKINGS 18676

LEVEL 18414

LEVEL 18415

Fig 35

Fig 36

contour lines at 2 m intervals

0   10   20   30   40   50   100   150 m

...iled plan of the eastern inset area shown in Figure 29.

(18427) at its eastern end, which is semi-circular with a stone-revetted sorting area in front. Unlike the two higher tramways, the western end of the tramway has an earthwork ramp at the head of the ore-slide rather than an ore-chute. The slide (18432) fed a small ore-bin (18652) at its base. A fourth tramway (18413), just below the third, is much less distinct than the others, suggesting that it was the earliest and associated with a possible ore-slide (18661), ore-bin (18430) and building platform (18431).

The two upper tramways and ore-slides appear to have been superseded by the construction of the incline (18409) from the upper workings represented by a steep track just over 2 metres wide and 350 metres long. At some point the incline was replaced by an aerial ropeway running from the head of the incline down to the crusher. It seems likely that the ropeway was installed as part of the investments made by Cwm Orog Mines Ltd who worked the site during the second decade of the 20th century. Mining returns record that 42 people were employed at the mine in 1908, which represents a significant increase on previous years (Bick 1990, 55–6). The line of the ropeway is represented by four surviving stone-built pier bases (18712–15, Figs 35–6), spaced at intervals of about 35 metres. These would have supported stanchions carrying the steel cables which carried tubs filled with ore. A substantial platform (18408) at the top of the ropeway probably housed a winch. The lower end of the ropeway ended above the dressing floor, at a substantial stone-revetted platform built against the hillside.

The dressing floors at the bottom end of the mine workings have suffered considerably from levelling in recent years, though substantial remains associated with the crusher still survive (see Fig 32). Three large masonry piers (18445) once supported a tramway leading from the aerial ropeway terminal to the top of the crusher (18443), which was powered by a water-wheel on the south-west side. The wheelpit (18442), which measures about 8 by 2.5 metres externally, still has the remains of a cast-iron pitchback waterwheel lying amongst the collapsed masonry (see Fig 33). The waterwheel was fed by a leat (18435) drawing water from the Cwm Orog stream to the north-east, possibly supplemented by a second leat (18439). The *Mining Journal* for 1870 refers to the stream being diverted to power the waterwheel and also records that the dressing floors were then under construction. The waterwheel may also have powered a buddle which is shown on a photograph of 1908 (Williams 1985, 98, Pl 23) but no trace of which survives today.

The remainder of the dressing floor (18444) is poorly preserved, and although it would have been a hive of activity in its heyday during the late 19th and early 20th centuries, all that now remains visible are two concrete bases and several lengths of retaining wall (see Fig 34). The foundations of the smithy (18436), which includes a standing fireplace, lie in the corner of the boundary wall to the north. Below the dressing floor to the west are the earthwork remains of several settling pits (18437), the tailrace leading from the waterwheel (18664), and part of an earlier track (18440) leading to the mine.

Dalrhiw and Nant y Car South, Llanwrthwl, Powys (Figs 38–45)

The two mines of Dalrhiw (SN88566070) and Nant y Car South (SN88676090) lie on opposite banks of the Rhiwnant stream, a tributary of the River Claerwen, about 2 kilometres south-west of the Caban-côch Reservoir in the Elan Valley. The solid geology is composed of Silurian rocks of the Trannon and Llandovery series. Dalrhiw mine exploited a N–S vein with chalcopyrite and galena mineralisation which produced copper and lead ores. Nant y Car South exploited three parallel N–S striking lodes in the valley bottom, with chalcopyrite and galena mineralisation which produced copper, lead and zinc ores. One of the primary interests in the Dalrhiw and Nant y Car South mines is that they represent a relatively compact and well-preserved mining landscape resulting from a short but intense period of operations

over a period of only 30 years in the second half of the 19th century.

The mines occupy a remote and imposing glaciated valley on the northern edge of the historic county of Breconshire, close to its boundary with Radnorshire, at just over 300 metres above sea level, amidst some of the most desolate scenery in Wales. Together, the two mines cover an area of about 3 hectares of gently sloping ground, the valley sides rising steeply to rocky outcrops above. To the south and west lie the remote moorland of Elenydd and Abergwesyn Common. The only access is to the north and east by way of a narrow miners' track leading towards the Claerwen Valley. A second miners' track, to the north of Nant y Car South, leads on westwards to the Nantygarw mine (Fig 54), described in a later section of this volume.

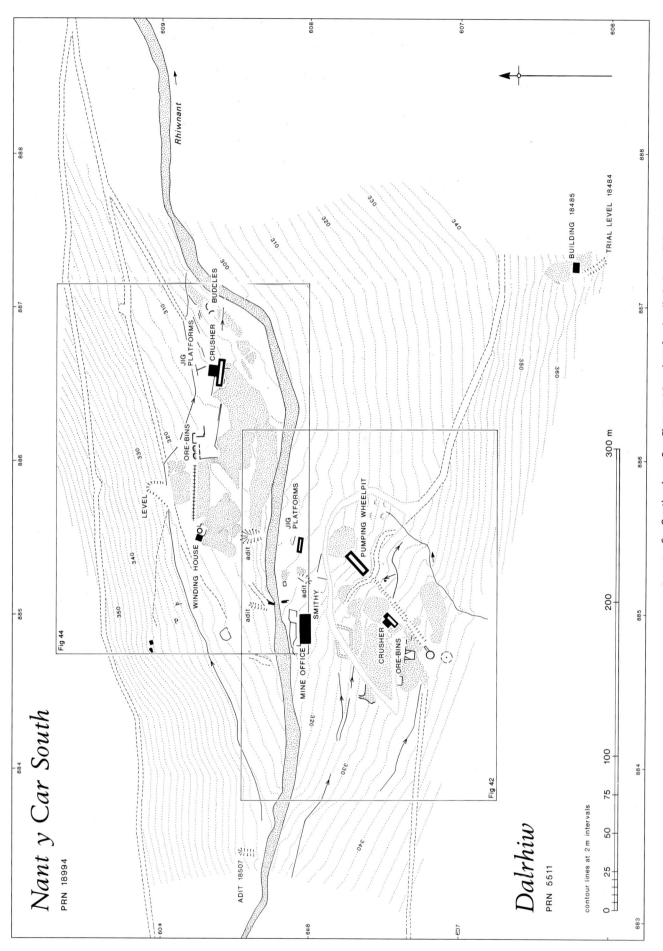

Nant y Car South

PRN 18994

Dalrhiw

PRN 5511

contour lines at 2 m intervals

South mines. See Figures 42 and 44 for detailed plans of the inset areas.

Figure 39 Dalrhiw mine: pumping wheelpit (18502) from the south, looking towards the Rhiwnant stream. The waterwheel drove pumping rods via a system of flat-rods, for which part of the track-bed (18506) is visible in the foreground. (*CPAT 285–10*).

Few earlier traces of settlement or land use are to be identified in these upland valleys apart from a number of abandoned farmsteads and *hafodydd* 'summer houses' dating from the medieval period. The only other sites to be found in the immediate vicinity of the mines are four small stone-built shelters and a sheep-fold to the west of Nant y Car South (see Fig 44). Like Cwm Elan mine, described above, the land formed part of the extensive watershed of Elan and Claerwen rivers acquired by Birmingham Corporation for the construction of the Elan Valley Reservoirs between 1893–1910 (Mansergh 1894). The mines lie on the edge of the Elan Valley landscape of special historic interest in Wales (Cadw 2001; Britnell 2004).

Documentary evidence records that the earliest workings of the Dalrhiw Company consisted of an adit (18503, Fig 42) driven south from the banks of the Rhiwnant stream in 1850, followed a year later by the sinking of the shaft to meet this level, along with the construction of a waterwheel (Hall 1993, 85–6). A trial level (18484, Fig 38) and the remains of a building are also to be seen on the hillside about 300 metres to the south-east, which may represent early exploratory workings. By 1853 the shaft had reached a depth of 27 fathoms, but would not appear to have

been operating with great efficiency: the report of an inspection by Captain James Skimming in 1854 noted that a good copper lode was evident in the roof of the adit but condemned the lack of enterprise. The report had the effect of revitalising the mine, including the breaking and dressing of ore on site (Hall 1993, 86). Between 1862 and 1867 the mine was worked by Parry and Company. Production continued until 1881. Processed ore would have been transported down to the Claerwen Valley and then over the mountains via the turnpike road towards Aberystwyth, to be smelted either in west Wales or carried by sea to be smelted in Swansea. From 1864, however, rail transport was available from Rhayader, 12 kilometres to the east, following the opening of the Mid-Wales Railway (Kidner 2003).

The engine shaft and connecting drainage adit dug in 1850–51 are still clearly visible (18487, 18503, Fig 42). Ore was raised from the shaft by a horse whim, the circle for which (18489) is sited next to the south side of the shaft. A substantial pumping wheelpit which housed a 52-foot by 5-foot wheel (Hall 1993, 85) was aligned upon the shaft (18502, Fig 39). This was connected to the shaft by a system of flat-rods whose track-bed (18506) can be traced running uphill

Figure 40 Dalrhiw mine: bank of three ore-bins (18490) built into the tip of development rock north of the engine shaft, viewed from the north-east. (*CPAT 285–16*)

for a distance of over 60 metres to the bob-pit (18488), the stonework for which survives on the edge of the shaft.

Ore raised from the shaft was loaded into the tops of the three square stone-built ore-bins (18490, Fig 40) a few metres to the north, one of which survives in a more or less intact condition. The ore would subsequently have been sorted on the platform or picking floor in front of the ore-bins before being taken to the crusher house (18493) just to the north. There are the remains of a stone building (18491) next to the west end of the ore-bins and an additional platform (18680) to the east, both of unknown function. The small crusher house, which measures about 3.75 by 3 metres across internally, was powered by a small waterwheel. A stone-slabbed floor along the northern wall of the crusher house may belong to an adjoining building, or possibly represents an ore washing area.

Water for both the pumping and crushing waterwheels was drawn from the Rhiwnant stream by two

leats several hundred metres upstream. The upper leat (18495, Fig 42) was probably culverted to the crusher wheelpit beneath the area containing the ore-bins, and may also have fed a small reservoir (18496) slightly downhill, now partly obscured below a modern track. Water issuing from the crusher wheelpit probably fed the overshot pumping waterwheel a further 30 metres downhill, via a wooden launder. An additional leat (18681) to the east of the crusher house probably redirected water into a stream to the east when not required by the pumping waterwheel. The purpose of a lower leat (18497) from the Rhiwnant is unclear, though it may have supplemented the flow of water to the pumping waterwheel.

Further ore processing was carried out on the valley floor, below the pumping wheelpit next to the Rhiwnant stream. There is a third wheelpit (18504) here, about 10 by 2.5 metres across, which seems likely to have been powered by water from the tailrace of the pumping wheelpit. The waterwheel appears to have

Figure 41 Dalrhiw mine: north side of the small wheelpit (18504) which probably to have powered jiggers on the platform just to the north. Against the east wall of the wheelpit are the remains of a trough built of stone slabs which probably acted as a settling tank. (*CPAT 285–06*)

powered jiggers set on a platform (18505) just to the north. The platform is covered with jig tailings, which also extend to the banks of the stream. A trough constructed of stone slabs lies on the floor, and a second one against the east wall of the wheelpit (Fig 41), both of which contain fine jig tailings. Unlike the adjacent mine at Nant y Car South there is no indication that buddles were ever employed here.

The ruins of the stone-built mine office or manager's house (18500) lie on the banks of the stream to the west of the adit. The main building, 12.3 by 7 metres across, had two rooms with a central chimney and two doorways on the north side. Attached to the east end is a later structure, possibly a smithy (18501), with a hearth against the eastern gable wall. Between the building and the stream is a small walled enclosure, probably representing a garden. The remains of a small stone-built shelter or store (18682) lie to the east, on the far side of the parapets of a footbridge across the Rhiwnant, the principal access to the mine,

linking the Dalrhiw with Nant y Car South mines. To the south of the mine office are the low earthworks of an enclosure (18498) which may represent a pound for horses employed at the whim or for transporting processed ore away from the mine. A second enclosure, of unknown function (18499), partly surrounds the pumping wheelpit.

The Nant y Car South mine occupies a steeper and even more restricted area on the opposite bank of the Rhiwnant stream. Nant y Car mine (Nant y Car North) had been in operation at a site on the south side of the Claerwen Valley (SN89086192), about a kilometre to the north, before the mid-19th century. The workings there had developed on a much larger scale by 1844 and by the 1850s a rich vein of copper ore was being exploited, though by 1854 this had proved disappointing (Hall 1993, 84). Prospecting elsewhere in the sett in 1855 revealed a promising lead lode in an adit on the north side of the Rhiwnant stream (Nant y Car South). The following year

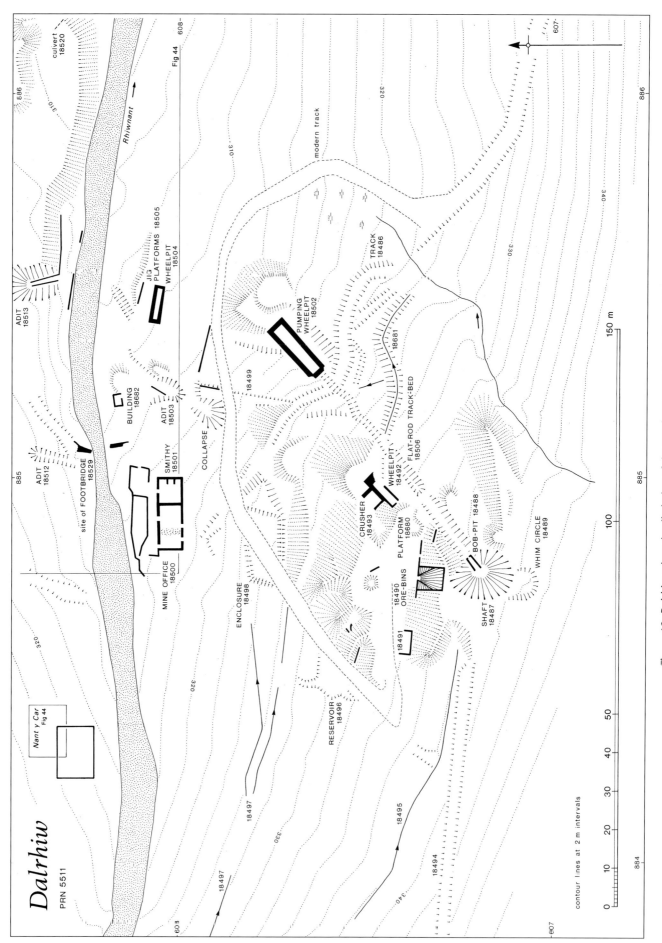

Dalrhiw

PRN 5511

Figure 43 Dalrhiw mine: detailed plan of the southern inset area in Figure 38.

contour lines at 2 m intervals

Figure 43 Aerial view of the Dalrhiw and Nant y Car South mines, to the left and right of the Rhiwnant stream respectively, viewed from the east. (*CPAT 03-C–0669*)

additional machinery was brought in to deepen the workings, although this lode too proved disappointing and the company was wound up in 1859. In 1863 the mine was taken over by B B Popplewell, and then successively by George Tetley in 1872, Mrs Tetley in 1875 and finally by C W Seccombe in 1878. Around 1883 a new and richer lode was discovered at the head of the valley, which was developed by Seccombe as Nantygarw mine, described elsewhere in this volume, as a consequence of which Nant y Car South was abandoned (Hall 1993, 84–5).

The earliest workings at Nant y Car South appear to be represented by two smaller adits (18507, Fig 38, and 18512, Fig 44) driven into the hillside close to the stream, both of which were probably early trials prospecting for ore. The main phase of development during the 1860s and 1870s saw a number of dramatic changes including the sinking of a main shaft and level

and the installation of ore processing equipment. The large spoil tips of development and processing waste spreading out like the fingers of a hand to the south of the shaft and the ore-bins represent a particularly characteristic feature of mining landscapes of this period.

The workings consist of a single engine shaft (18515) and a collapsed level (18527) which together with two large areas of collapse extend for about 75 metres into the hillside. The shaft was pumped via a system of flat-rods driven by the large wheelpit (18522) about 100 metres to the east. Part of the track-bed (18521) for the flat-rods survives between the wheelpit and shaft. The engine shaft remains open, but is flooded to within about 2 metres of the surface. The dry-stone lining rests on timber lintels. A wooden ladder is still visible towards the top of the shaft, below the water level. The foundations of a

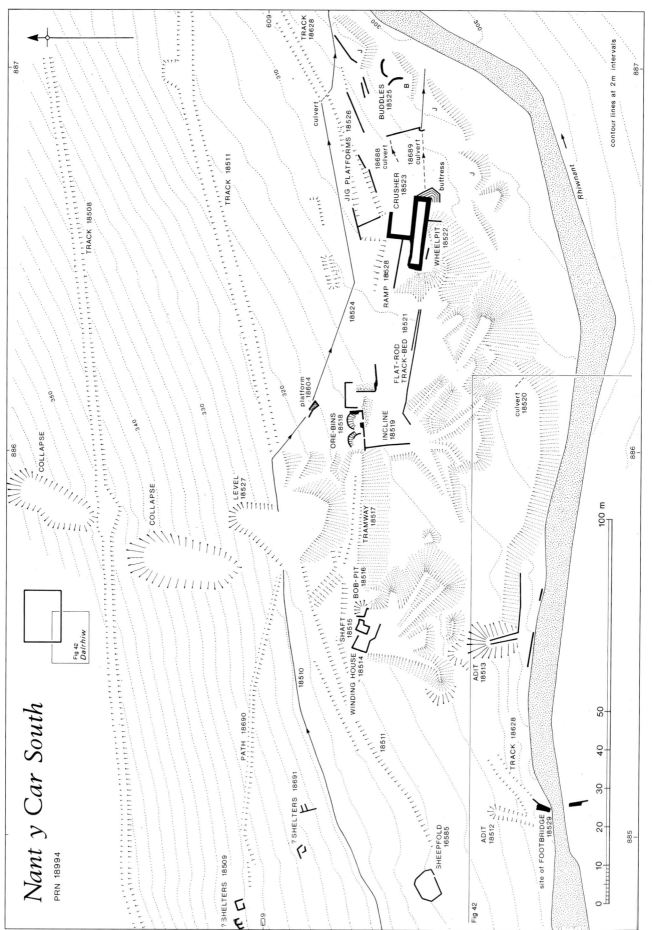

Figure 44. Nant y Car South mine: detailed plan of the northern inset area shown in Figure 38.

Figure 45 Nant y Car South mine: remains of the substantial crusher house (18523) viewed from the east. There are four remaining beam ends *in situ* in the far wall, indicating that two sets of crusher rolls were in operation. The crusher was powered by a water-wheel which was also pumping and winding the engine shaft, the wheelpit of which (18522) adjoins the south wall of the crusher. (*CPAT 330–04*)

winding house (18514) lie to the west of the shaft, together with a partly collapsed bob-pit (18516) to the east. Ore was raised from the shaft and taken along a tramway (18517) and loaded into a bank of two or possibly three ore-bins (18518), which presumably also received the ore mined in the collapsed level to the north-west. In front of the ore-bins is a level picking floor where the ore would have been sorted. A short incline along the western side of the ore-bins took waste material to the tips just to the south.

The sorted ore from the picking floor was loaded into the stone-built crusher (18523, Fig 45) via a loading ramp (18528). A possible flywheel pit, now collapsed, lies along the southern wall of the large wheelpit (18522), about 18 metres long, and

buttressed on the downhill side. Water to drive the crusher waterwheel was drawn from Rhiwnant about 300 metres upstream, being carried by a stone-lined leat (18510) to a stone platform which would have supported a wooden launder leading to the wheelpit. A sluice near the platform would have diverted water into a second leat (18524) which bypassed the wheelpit when power was not required for pumping or crushing.

To the north-east of the crusher are a number of stone-revetted platforms (18526). These were probably for jiggers, the waste from which covers a large area between the crusher and the stream. The remains of two circular buddles (18525) lie between the jig platforms and the stream.

...plan of Gwestyn mine. See Figures 48 and 49 for detailed plans of the inset areas.

Gwestyn, Llanidloes, Powys (Figs 46–9)

Gwestyn mine (SN89408610) (Fig 46) lies on the broad upland ridge between the Nant Gwestyn brook to the north and the upper reaches of the River Severn to the south, about 6 kilometres to the west of the small market town of Llanidloes. The solid geology comprises part of the Lower Silurian Gwestyn formation (Jones 1922, 47). The Van lode has been exploited on a vein running ENE. Mineralisation includes a calcite gangue with chalcopyrite and rare galena, sphalerite and chalybite, from which copper and lead were extracted.

The workings occupy an area of about 3 hectares of gently sloping semi-improved pasture running along the mineral vein and are superimposed upon a palimpsest of earlier trackways which present a striking picture from the air (Fig 47). Former mine buildings have now largely been levelled but are still recognisable as earthworks. One of the attractions of the site is the challenge it poses in distinguishing the mining remains from the pattern of grass-covered earthworks that underlie it. There are hidden dangers, however: parts of the site were actively subsiding when survey work was being undertaken and are clearly extremely hazardous. The mine falls within the Clywedog Valley landscape of special historic interest in Wales (Cadw 2001) which also encompasses the Bryntail lead mine

Figure 47 Aerial view of Gwestyn mine from the north-west, showing the mine earthworks overlying a palimpsest of trackways.
(*Crown Copyright: RCAHMW 925089–68*)

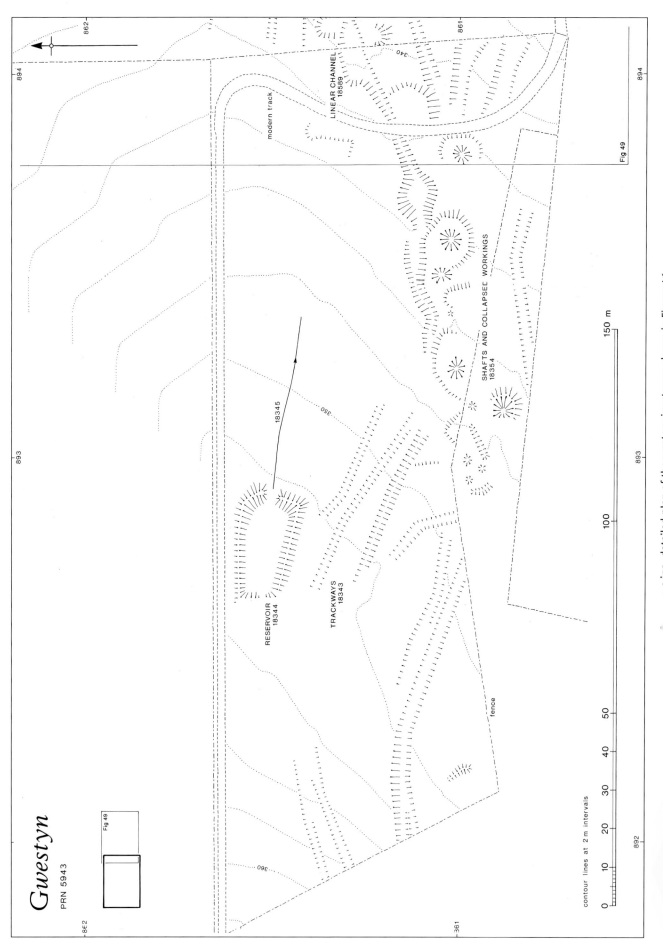

Gwestyn

PRN 5943

RESERVOIR 18344

TRACKWAYS 18343

LINEAR CHANNEL 18589

SHAFTS AND COLLAPSED WORKINGS 18354

18345

modern track

fence

Fig 49

contour lines at 2 m intervals

0 10 20 30 40 50   100   150 m

... detailed plan of the western inset area shown in Figure 46.

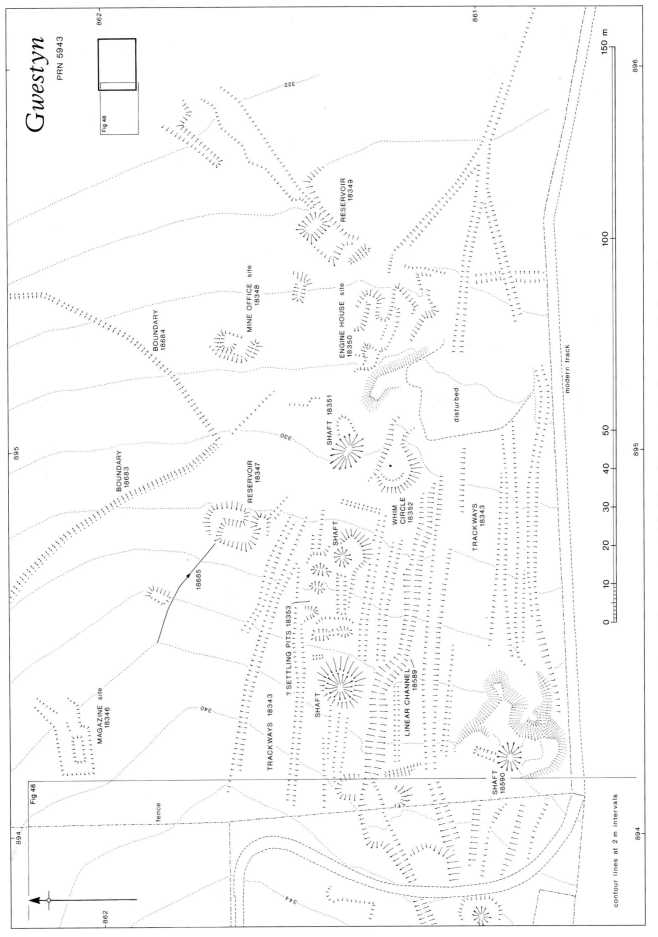

Figure 49 Gwestyn mine: detailed plan of the eastern inset area shown in Figure 46.

museum, at the foot of the Llyn Clywedog dam, about 2 kilometres to the north-west, the Van lead mines north of Llanidloes, as well as the Pen Dylife and Penyclun mines described later in this volume.

The history of the trackways underlying the mine (18343) is poorly documented, though it seems likely that they mark the course of an old drovers' road to Llanidloes, an important staging point between west Wales and the English markets during their heyday in the late 18th and early 19th centuries (Moore-Colyer 2002). The origins of mining activity at Gwestyn are equally obscure but certainly predate the early 19th century when a Cornishman known as 'Old Brown' reworked old workings both here and at the neighbouring Geufron mine, a kilometre to the south-west (SN88588570). Two main shafts were sunk after 1852, the earlier Young's Shaft followed by Pearce's Shaft, both of which were drained from 1855 by a waterwheel powered by water drawn from the Nant Gwestyn brook (Bick 1990, Part 4, 34). A letter of 1860 from Captain James Paull to John Taylor gives details of an inspection of the mine, and lists a 36-foot wheel with good 9-inch rods, a carpenter's workshop, a smithy and offices. By the late 1850s the mine was unprofitable and up for sale. Following a period of inactivity, the mine reopened in 1872 as Gwestyn Consols under the direction of Captain Pearce, who had also managed the Geufron mine, and began driving adits from the Nant Gwestyn brook to meet the lode. This again proved unsuccessful, however, and the venture soon failed (Bick 1990, Part 4, 34). The destination of the ore obtained from the mine is uncertain, but is likely to have either been transported eastwards towards the Clywedog Valley and Llanidloes, or alternatively westwards to the harbour at Aberystwyth where it could be shipped by sea to more distant smelting mills at Bristol, Swansea or on the Dee Estuary.

The surface workings consist of a run of shafts, trials and collapsed workings along the vein, several of which show signs of significant recent collapse. Two main shafts can be tentatively identified. Shaft 18590 (Fig 49), surrounded by a large spoil tip and with a possible capstan circle on its northern side, may be Young's Shaft, which in the 1950s is recorded as having been open to a depth of about 100 feet down to water (Bick 1990, Part 4, 34). A larger shaft, just under a hundred metres to the north-east (18351, Fig 49), is probably the one sunk by Captain Pearce in the 1850s, and may have been later drained by the stone-lined adit (18673, Fig 46) near the Nant Gwestyn brook about 250 metres to the north.

Just to the south of the shaft are the earthwork remains of a whim circle about 10 metres in diameter, set on a raised platform, which probably originally powered the shaft or may have supplemented the use of water power when this was not available. Paull's letter of 1860 mentions that he was unable to visit the underground workings because the waterwheel was idle, though the site of the wheelpit is now lost. The use of water power is indicated by a number of reservoirs and leats. A large reservoir (18344, Fig 48), about 32 by 14 metres across, is defined by low earthwork banks to the east of the workings. No trace remains of the leat which fed it from the Nant Gwestyn brook, although the position of the inlet and outlet sluices can still be determined, together with a short section of leat (18345) flowing from the reservoir to the east. A second reservoir (18349), falling in two levels, lies further to the east. A third reservoir (18347), depicted on the 1st edition Ordnance Survey map of 1886, survives as a substantial earthwork, with banks up to 1.3 metres high. The feeding leat and outlet sluice are still visible. It is possible that this supplied water to a steam engine housed in the engine house (18350), also depicted on the map of 1886, which is represented by slight earthworks about 20–30 metres to the east of shaft 18351. The engine, probably installed due to the unpredictability of water power, probably pumped the shaft by means of a system of flat-rods. Other building remains are likewise indicated by earthwork evidence, including the site of the explosives' magazine (18346) and the mine office (18348), slight stone foundations still being evident in the case of the mine office.

The surviving earthworks provide no clear evidence for the processing of ores at the site, though a series of shallow depressions (18353) to the west of the main shaft may possibly represent settling pits.

Nant yr Eira, Llangurig, Powys (Figs 5, 50–3, 135)

Nant yr Eira is one of the remotest mine sites in mid Wales, lying on the eastern slopes of Plynlimon (SN82708730), on the edge of the post-war Hafren Forest, within several kilometres of the source of both the River Severn and River Wye. The solid geology is composed of Ordovician Lower Van formation grits. The vein strikes N–S and E–W, with mineralisation including chalcopyrite and lead, with quartz gangue which yielded lead, copper and silver ores.

This relatively small mine occupies of area of under a hectare, hidden away towards the head of the Nant yr Eira stream, a small tributary which ultimately feeds the uppermost reaches of the River Severn. The main workings occupy steeply sloping ground on the eastern bank of the stream, with a number of outlying features further upstream, beyond the survey area. Recent forestry plantation has tended to obscure the landscape setting of the mine, though it is heartening to note that recent felling by the Forestry Commission has significantly improved the situation (see Fig 135). A number of additional structures have also come to light as a result of felling operations, after the survey was undertaken, including the ruins of a two-room bunkhouse about 70 metres east of the main complex.

Nant yr Eira is of particular significance as one of a small number of sites in Wales where Bronze Age mining has been recognised. The early workings are represented by an impressive open-cut (18531, Figs 5, 50) towards the top of the site, through which the stream now runs, metal ore in all probability having been first identified where it had been exposed in the natural streambed. There is documentary evidence that the open-cut was reworked during the 19th century (see below), which has probably destroyed some of the evidence for earlier working, but excavations of potentially early spoil tips by Oliver Davies in 1937 led to the recovery of hammerstones and muller-querns, as well as evidence for firesetting (Davies 1938). The site was further examined by the Early Mines Research Group in 1988, when two trenches were excavated. Radiocarbon dates obtained from charcoal recovered during excavation suggests that mining was being undertaken in the period between about 2000–1500 BC (Timberlake 1990, 20). The early workings take the form of a large open-cut about 95 metres long, 6 metres wide, and up to 7 metres deep, with spoil tips to either side. There is evidence of possible firesetting at several points along the sides of the open-cut, as well as a number of rock-cut niches along the eastern side,

of unknown date or function (Timberlake 1990, 19).

The mining remains which lie slightly further downstream all date from the mid-19th century. The spoil tips spread along and down the slope below the open-cut and these, together with the crusher wheelpit and other structures now dominate the immediate landscape. Given its extreme remoteness, mining activity must in it heyday have appeared quite at odds with its surroundings. Land use in preceding centuries had been limited to summer grazing and it is significant that there are few indications of earlier activity other than a possible sheepfold (18545) partly buried below a later waste tip.

The mine was worked by the Snowbrook Mining Company ('Snowbrook' being a translation of the Welsh *Nant yr Eira*) between 1858–87, following the rediscovery of the workings by Captain Reynolds of Llanidloes. The southern end of the old open-cut was explored in 1860 under Captain Goldsworthy, when a winze was put down below the base of the open-cut (Bick 1990, Part 4, 29). There appear to have been two routes of access to the site. Ore could have been transported either eastwards to the Llanidloes in the Severn Valley or southwards via the Nantiago mine, about a kilometre away, and from thence into the Wye Valley.

Apart from reworking the open-cut, 19th-century activity was focused on a single main shaft (18546), now hidden within forestry. A second shaft, possibly a trial, lies about 450 metres to the north-west, on the banks of the Nant yr Eira. A spoil tip on the opposite bank of the stream from the main mine site may be evidence of a further collapsed trial level (18640).

Raised tramways (18642, 18534) carried ore from both the main shaft and the later workings at the southern end of the open-cut to two ore-bins (18535) where it was stored. The ore would have been sorted on a platform here before being loaded into the crusher. The crusher is fairly well preserved, and has substantial stone walls still standing to almost their full height (18537, Figs 51–2). Timber posts still visible just above the crusher possibly formed supports for a wooden chute leading to a platform at the top of the crusher. Power was supplied by a waterwheel on the west side of the crusher, driven by water drawn from the Nant yr Eira stream. Records of the 1860s indicate that a 38-foot by 3-foot waterwheel was employed at that time (Bick 1990, Part 4). In order to drain the upper workings a channel (18694) had been dug

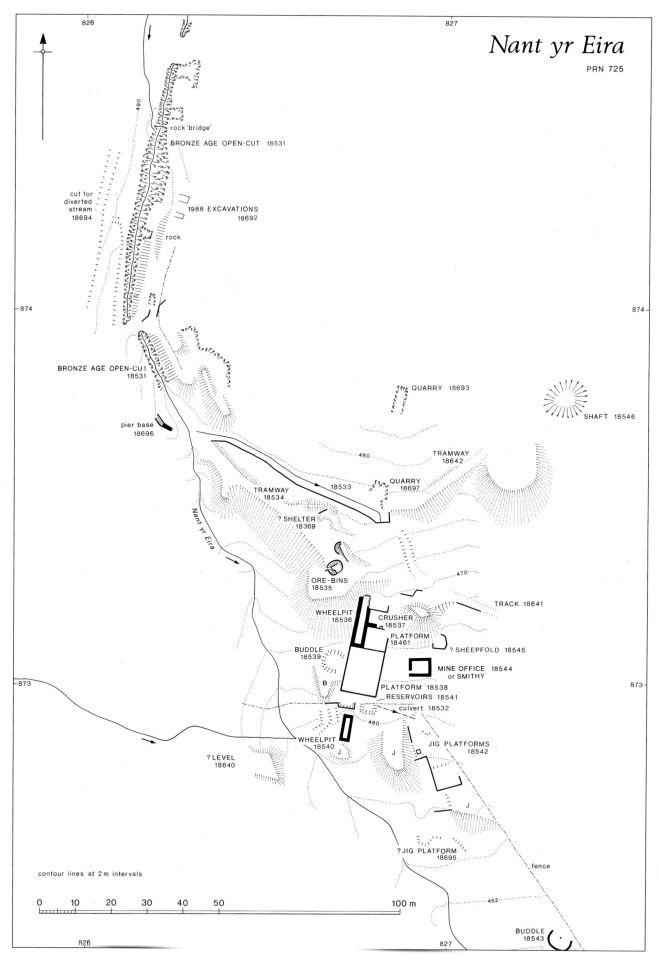

Figure 50 Plan of Nant yr Eira mine.

Figure 51 Nant yr Eira mine: crusher house (18537) to the left and wheelpit (18536) to the right, viewed from the north. (*CPAT 331–06*)

Figure 52 Nant yr Eira mine: crusher wheelpit (18536) and stone-revetted platform (18538) viewed from the south-west. Part of a second wheelpit (18540) visible to the right probably powered jiggers on the jig platform (18542) to the east. (*CPAT 330–23*)

Figure 53 Nant yr Eira mine: ruins of a small rectangular building (18544), possibly a smithy or mine office. (*CPAT 146–26*)

which diverted to the west of the open-cut. The water was then bridged over the stream via a pier base (18696) and thence by a stone-revetted leat (18533) and launder to the crusher waterwheel. A tributary of the Nant yr Eira was dammed to create a reservoir about 200 metres to the north of the open-cut, outside the survey area.

Further separation and sorting of the ore appears to have been carried out on a platform (18461) in the angle between the crusher and wheelpit, fed by a small chute in the crusher house wall. A larger stone-revetted platform below this (18461, Fig 52), about 12 by 10 metres across, has an area of fuel ash slag and two iron tie-rods on its surface, suggesting the use of a small portable steam engine, probably to power further crushing or sorting machinery. To the east of the lower platform are the ruins of a small rectangular stone building, possibly the smithy or mine office (Fig 53). This and other stone-built structures on the site were probably built of material obtained from the two small quarries (18693, 18697) to the west of the main shaft.

The tailrace from the wheelpit appears to have fed two small reservoirs (18541) against the south side of the raised platform. A culvert can be seen issuing from the east side towards the jigging area. A second wheelpit, 5.2 by 1.3 metres across internally, lies just to the south of these reservoirs. It most probably powered jiggers set on the platforms (18542) surrounded by jigger waste further to the east. It is uncertain whether the reservoirs were the water source for the second waterwheel or whether this was fed directly from the crusher wheelpit tailrace. Several other slight platforms (18695) within the waste tips further to the south may represent the site of further jiggers. Further downhill, beyond the jigging area, are the remains of a buddle, about 4 metres in diameter, which still retains its central support. A second and possibly earlier buddle (18539) is possibly represented by a circular earthwork, about 4.6 metres in diameter, just to the south-west of the crusher house wheelpit.

Nantygarw, Llanwrthwl, Powys (Figs 54–9)

Nantygarw mine (SN87436060) (Fig 54) lies at the head of a remote upland valley on the north bank of the Nant y Carw just over a kilometre upstream from the Dalrhiw and Nant y Car South mines described above, encircled by unimproved moorland. The solid geology comprises Silurian rocks of the Trannon and Llandovery series, with mineralisation in the form of galena with chalybite gangue located in a N–S striking vein.

The mine is dramatically sited at a height of about 400 metres above sea level, and has spectacular views to the east, looking down the Rhiwnant Valley to Dalrhiw, Nant y Car South and beyond. The predominant land use now as in the past has been limited to upland grazing and there are few other indications of human activity to be seen in the vicinity. The mine workings cover an area of less than 3 hectares and occupy the only available ground on a natural terrace at the mouth of a hanging valley which drops down precipitously to the valley of the Rhiwnant stream a hundred metres or so to the east. The valley sides just above the mine are precipitous and rocky, gradually giving way to more gentle slopes as the ground rises to the surrounding moorland plateau. The only access to the mine was by means of a track leading northeastwards along the Rhiwnant Valley, via the Nant y Car South mine. The surviving remains belong to more than one period of tenure but are dominated by the latest phase of activity which saw the installation of the processing mill which constitutes one of its major points of interest. Other substantial structural remains survive, including the shaft, wheelpit, and smithy. Extensive spoil tips of processing waste spread outwards from the processing mill, while at the bottom end of the site spoil tumbles down the steep valley sides to the Rhiwnant below. Like the Dalrhiw and Nant y Car South mines, it lies on the edge of the Elan Valley landscape of special historic interest in Wales (Cadw 2001; Britnell 2004).

Ore deposits may have first been discovered here in 1877, but the earliest documentary reference dates to 1883, when is appeared in a list of mines in the *Mining Journal*. At this time, it appears to have been leased by C W Seccombe, who also mined at Nant y Car. In September 1886 he sold his lease to the Builth Lead Mining Company and reports in 1888 refer to an adit and a level being worked, with the dressing of ore commencing in November of that year. The company was wound up in 1893. The property then appears to

have been in the possession of George Green for a short time. Green owned the Cambrian Foundry at Aberystwyth which supplied equipment to mines in mid Wales and further afield, including his patented 'self-acting dressing machinery'. This included crusher rolls, jiggers and buddles and was installed in purpose-built mills powered by water. The remains of one of Green's processing mills survive at Nantygarw, although they are difficult to interpret. The new Nantygarw Mining Company was registered in December 1893 and employed 50 men, which indicates a reasonably sized enterprise. Due to its remoteness the workforce would have been housed on site in barrack accommodation during the week, the remains of which still survive. Despite large returns the company went into liquidation in 1897 and although some activity continued until 1899, all work was then abandoned due to the construction of the Elan Valley Reservoirs (Hall 1993, 86–7). Transport must always have presented difficulties in this harsh and remote environment. Horses were used to carry the processed ore along the narrow mountain track eastwards to the Claerwen Valley and on to the railway at Rhayader, about 13 kilometres away.

The earliest workings seem to be represented by a collapsed level (12124, Fig 59) driven northwards close to the end of the original site access track (12132). A track leading from the level would have allowed ore to be carried to a row of ore-bins, of which perhaps two survive (12144–5). A possible trial level (12131), along the same vein, lies to the south of the stream.

Most of the visible features relate to a later phase of activity marked by the sinking of a shaft which exploited the same mineral vein as the level and the construction of the Green's processing mill. The stone-lined shaft (12116) has a timber frame surrounding the top and a sub-rectangular bob-pit (12117) on its eastern side. An area of collapse to the south makes it possible to see into the shaft head, where part of the original timber pump rod can still be seen. The remains of a stone-built building (12129) of unknown function are visible in the side of waste tips to the east of the shaft. A roughly circular levelled area about 3.8 metres in diameter about 25 metres north-east of the shaft may represent the remains of a whim circle (12127).

Power for pumping, and possibly winding, was provided by a substantial waterwheel set in a wheelpit (12141) (Fig 55) over a hundred metres to the east of

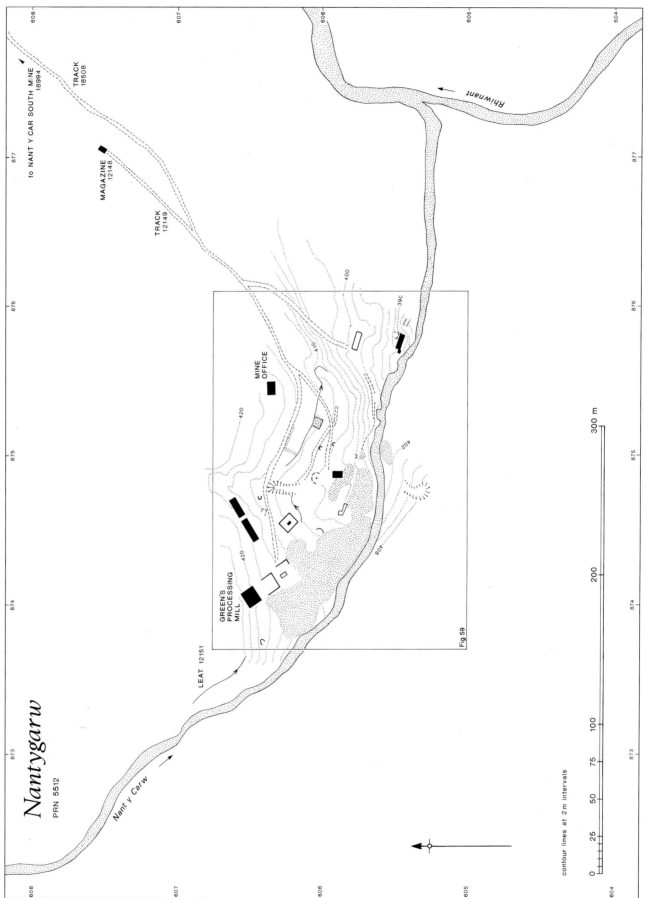

Nantygarw

PRN 5512

A plan of Nantygarw mine. See Figure 59 for detailed plan of the inset area.

Figure 55 Nantygarw mine: wheelpit (12141) viewed from the north-east with the Nant y Carw stream beyond. The wheel was most probably sited on the north side of the wheelpit, where fixing bolts survive alongside a small platform. (*CPAT 644–04*)

Figure 56 Nantygarw mine: remains of a Green's processing mill (12115) viewed from the north-west, looking towards the Nant y Carw stream. The upper building (12153) is filled with rubble with suggestions of an internal wall dividing the building lengthways. The lower building (12154), represented a stone-revetted platform, contains the remains of timber launders. The lowest part of the structure (12155) is now partly buried by spoil, but consists of a stone revetted platform, with the remains of a central machine base and a series of timber tanks and launders along the external wall face of the wall on the north-east side. (*CPAT 285–27*)

Figure 57 Nantygarw mine: remains of the chimney and hearth set centrally within the smithy (12118), viewed from the east.
The chimney survives to its full height of 4.2 metres. The remains of the Green's processing is visible on the slope above.
(*CPAT 285–33*)
Figure 58 Nantygarw mine: explosives' magazine (12148), viewed from the west, looking down the Rhiwnant Valley. (*CPAT 644–19*)

the shaft, the flat-rods presumably being carried on stanchions for which some fixing bolts are still visible along the north side of the stream. The wheelpit measures 10.5 by 3.25 metres across and survives to a height of 3.7 metres. The wheel appears to have been located on the north side of the wheelpit where some fixing bolts survive alongside a small platform. There is no surviving evidence for a leat supplying the wheel and it would seem likely that water was drawn directly from the stream about 55 metres to the west (where there is a small waterfall) and laundered to the wheelpit. Several fixing bolts and a timber post along the north side of the stream may be associated with the launder. The tail-race probably flowed directly over the entrance to a drainage adit (12142) cut beneath the wheelpit and remains open for some considerable distance. The workings of the wheelpit are no longer clear, though a balance-box (12152) survives at the south-east corner. It is likely that some structural evidence relating to the transfer of power to the flat-rods has been lost due to collapse along the south side. Three narrow rectangular slots (now infilled) within the main structure of the wheelpit show the position of a flywheel and gearing mechanism.

The site of the Green's processing mill installed in the 1890s lies on higher ground about 70 metres north-west of the shaft (Fig 56). The mill was almost certainly water-powered, but there is no surviving evidence of a wheelpit. A leat was constructed in 1893 to carry water from the natural upland lake at Llyn Carw, 2 kilometres to the west (Bick 1991, 22), which may correspond with the short length of leat (12151, Fig 54) that is visible to the north-west of the mill. The processing mill consisted of three contiguous structures, each housing machinery for successive stages of ore processing. The upper building (12153) measures 11.35 by 9.7 metres across externally and has walls surviving to a height of 4.3 metres. This substantial structure probably housed the crusher rolls, and though obscured by rubble there are suggestions of an internal wall which divided the building lengthways. The central structure (12154) consists of a stone-revetted platform with evidence of timber launders. The lowest part of the mill is now partly buried by spoil, but consists of a stone-revetted platform (12155), with the remains of a machine base in the middle and a series of timber tanks and launders along the outer wall-face to the north-east. To the south of the mill are large tips of jig and fine waste. It is clear that other processing activities were undertaken on the site, some, if not all of which may have been contemporary with the main mill. The remains of a small circular buddle (12126), 6.5 metres in diameter, can be identified partly buried by waste between the mill and the shaft. A jig platform (12122) lies next to the track to the east of the mill, and a second platform (12130), probably also for jigging can be seen to the east of the main shaft. A leat (12147), 1.6 metres wide, to the east of the level, may originally have led from the processing mill. The leat leads to the edge of a steep scarp where fixing bolts possibly mark the position of a launder which perhaps carried slimes from the mill to a settling pit (12139) further east. A small reservoir (12146) alongside the leat may represent another settling pit.

An interesting range of ancillary buildings is represented at the site, a number of which were probably of timber-framed construction set on stone platforms. The smithy (12118, Fig 57) consists of a rectangular platform, with the chimney and hearth set centrally within it, the chimney still surviving to its full height of over 4 metres. The mine office and possible manager's house lies at the east end of the site. The building, which measures 8.6 by 5.25 metres across, is divided into two rooms and consists of a stone footings with a concrete floor. Two other buildings to the east of the mill, similarly represented by stone footings with thin concrete floors, probably represent workers' barrack accommodation. The western building measures 16.5 by 4.1 metres across and is divided into three rooms. The eastern building measures 13.5 by 4.85 metres across and has a single internal division with the larger eastern room containing a rectangular slot suggesting the position of machinery. An intermittent rock-cut ledge running along the north side of the track east of the buildings suggests the line of an iron pipe, although the function is unknown. Buildings of similar shape, size and design were to be erected within a matter of a few years at the model village built a few miles away, at the foot of the Caban-côch dam, to house the influx of workers employed on the construction of the Elan Valley Reservoirs (Judge 1997, Pl 25). A grassy area to south of the track seems to represent a small garden (12150) tended by the workforce.

The explosives' magazine was safely positioned several hundred metres to the north-east of the mine office, approached by its own track. The stone-built structure, about 5 by 3.3 metres across, had brick quoins and door openings. A cross is picked out in lumps of white quartz in the stonework to the right of the door (12148, Figs 54, 58).

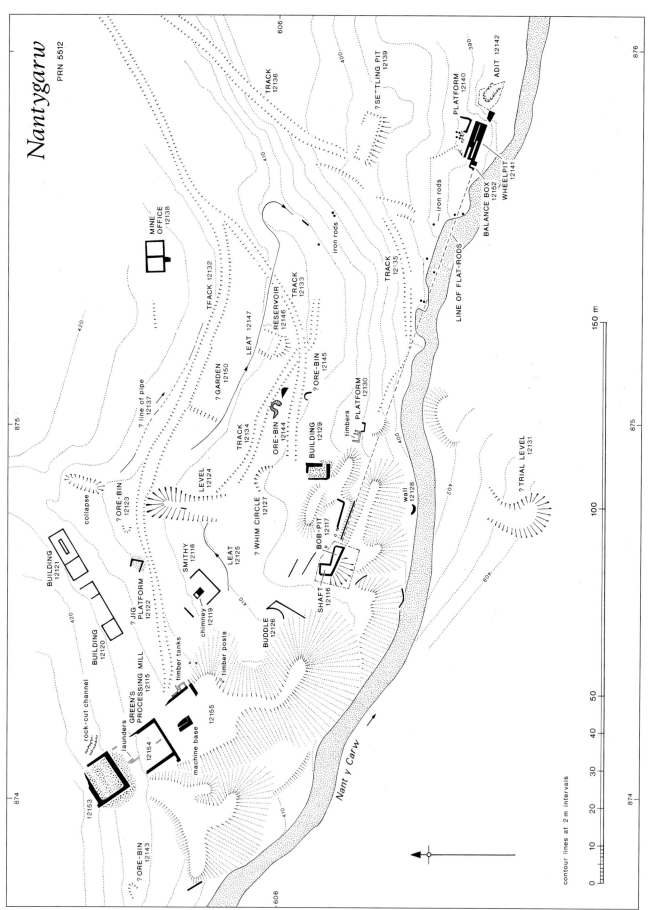

Figure 59 Nantygarw mine: detailed plan of the inset area shown in Figure 54.

Nantiago, Llangurig, Powys (Figs 10–11, 60–9)

Nantiago mine site lies at the head of a narrow stream valley on the eastern slopes of Plynlimon (SN82608630) (Fig 60), 10 kilometres north-west of Llangurig, forming a tributary of the river Wye. The solid geology is of Ordovician Upper Van mudstones and grits containing an ENE–WSW vein. A N–S cross vein has calcite with galena and sphalerite. The mine produced lead, silver and zinc ores.

The workings extend for over half a kilometre along the Nant Iago stream, between a height of 400–500 metres above sea level, covering an area of about 6 hectares on the edge of the extensive moorland of the Cambrian Mountains (Fig 61). A trackway to the north leads towards the equally remote mine at Nant yr Eira, described elsewhere in this volume. A trackway to the south joins the main Aberystwyth and Llangurig road after about 4 kilometres, a road which had been improved as a turnpike road by 1829. The reasonably extensive workings at Nantiago date from the mid-19th century to the early 20th century. New investment from the turn of the century led to the construction of a much larger dressing plant below the earlier dressing floor. It is these changes in processing technology which gave rise to the extensive spoil tips which form a dominant landscape feature within the valley and which provide a principal point of interest.

Nantiago was the subject of several mining ventures from the 1840s until the early 20th century. Originally known as Plynlimon Mine, it was inspected in 1846 by Matthew Francis for the lessee Robert Parry. His report noted a 12-foot waterwheel that he considered hopelessly inadequate for driving crushing and dressing machinery, and recommended further investment in two new waterwheels (Bick 1990, Part 4, 57). This venture was short-lived, however, and these improvements were never undertaken. The mine was working again by 1853, though only for a short period, to be revived once more in 1860 when a new waterwheel was purchased from the failing mine at Esgairlle, just along the main road towards Aberystwyth, but by 1865 the mine was up for sale (Bick 1990, Part 4, 58).

Production continued between 1873–88 under the direction of William Lefeaux, during which time a new 60-foot waterwheel was installed to pump the mine. The mine then again lay dormant until the formation of the Nantiago Mining Company in 1900. At this time John Mills and Company of Llanidloes Foundry erected a new 56-foot pumping wheel and a three-storey dressing mill powered by two Pelton-wheels and including a stone breaker, rolls, trommels and six four-compartment jigs (Bick 1990, Part 4, 58). In 1913 the site was sold to the Llanidloes Mining and Machinery Company, and although mining continued throughout the First World War, the mine finally closed shortly thereafter. Many of the structures, including the upper waterwheel, remained standing until at least 1932, as shown in a photograph of that date (Bick 1990, Part 4, 59). Barrack accommodation was provided for the miners staying at the mine during the working week. One worker is said to have cycled to the mine from near Shrewsbury each Monday morning (Bick 1990, Part 4, 58) – a distance of perhaps 50 miles!

Throughout the mine's history the principal workings consisted of a main engine shaft (18578, Fig 67) and a deep adit level (18566, Fig 68), the latter located in the northern side of a quarry (18567). The engine shaft was eventually sunk to 30 fathoms below the adit level and is still open, with part of the pump rod system remaining *in situ* (Fig 62). To the north of the shaft are the collapsed remains of a stone-built winding wheelpit (18579), together with the foundations of the winding house (18706). Various pieces of ironwork lie scattered around the shaft, including the winding wheel for the wooden A-frame, and a winding drum complete with cable (Fig 63). The overshot waterwheel was fed from a reservoir (18580) via a wooden launder. Stone quarries (18581, 18630) to the east of the shaft probably provided stone for construction work.

About 120 metres to the south-east is a second wheelpit (18575) which probably represents the new 60-foot wheel that was installed by William Lefeaux. The rock-cut wheelpit, measuring about 18 by 2.95 metres across, is surrounded by a surviving timber framework and has a rock-cut balance-box pit (18629) at its south-east corner. The wheel provided power for pumping via a system of flat-rods supported on a series of pier bases (18702–4) between the wheelpit and the shaft. It is evident that the wheelpit was rock-cut at least partly on economic grounds. The *Mining Journal* of 1860 records its construction, stating that 'nearly half of the wheelpit is cut out of solid rock which will save the expense in masonry work'. Since the wheelpit was cut below ground, however, a tunnel (18709) had to be cut for the tailrace. This led to a small reservoir (18631) from which water was sluiced either eastwards to the reservoir above the early dressing floors, or at a

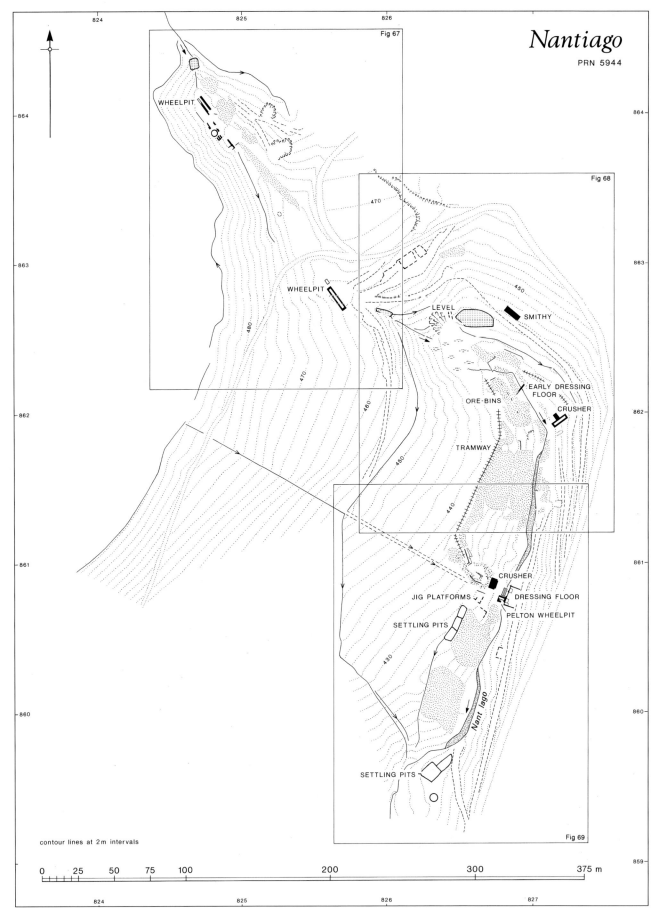

Figure 60 General plan of Nantiago mine. See Figures 67–69 for detailed plans of the inset areas.

Figure 61 Aerial view of Nantiago mine, from the east. The upper workings lie at the head of the valley to the right.
(Crown Copyright: RCAHMW 925075–44)

later date into the leat supplying the Pelton-wheels (see below).

The water supply for powering the winding wheel may initially have been drawn from the Nant Iago stream, but when this proved insufficient it was supplemented by water drawn from a point close to the source of the River Wye. This necessitated the construction of a substantial stone-revetted dam, 11 metres high, 12 metres wide and 100 metres long, about 2 kilometres to the west (SN812086650). The *Mining Journal* for 1860 records the completion of a leat (18576, Fig 67) which was said to have provided power for pumping, winding and crushing, and must therefore have fed both waterwheels.

Initially, ore appears to have been brought out of the mine from the main level and then transported via a tramway (18708, Fig 68) to a bank of poorly preserved ore-bins (18565). The early dressing floor (18565) lay in front of the ore-bins and seems to have been partly platformed on timber supports above the

stream, as suggested by several stone supporting walls and associated timbers which still survive on either side of the valley. The only structure which can now be identified on the dressing floor is a small, partly rock-cut wheelpit (18632), about 11 by 3.3 metres across, which abuts a crusher house (18632) serviced by the tramway. Water for the wheel was supplied by a leat drawn from a substantial stone-revetted reservoir (18564), fed by the Nant Iago stream. Just south of the wheelpit is a possible collapsed level (18560) which may have been used to transport ore to the early dressing floor.

As noted above, the formation of the Nantiago Mining Company in 1900 led to a substantial capital investment. A new 56-foot pumping wheel was erected by John Mills and Company, replacing the earlier 60-foot wheel, and at a later date a Crossley gas engine was installed to assist with pumping (Bick 1990, Part 4, 58). A new dressing floor was constructed further down the valley (18556, Fig 69). This, like the earlier

Figure 62 Nantiago mine: engine shaft (18578) from the north-west, with the remains of the iron winding wheel and wooden pumping rod at the top of the open shaft. The concrete structure visible to the right is the base for the pumping mechanism. (*CPAT 329–29*)

Figure 63 Nantiago mine: discarded manual winch lying alongside the engine shaft. (*CPAT144–04*)

Figure 64 Nantiago mine: remains of later dressing floor (18556) and processing mill including the crusher (18557) on the west bank of the Nant Iago stream, viewed from the east. (*CPAT 331–36*)

Figure 65 Nantiago mine: the later dressing floor, supported on timber planking above the Nant Iago stream. (*CPAT 144–35*)

Figure 66 Nantiago mine: the surviving Pelton-wheel. (18635) (*CPAT 329–03*)

dressing floor, was platformed across the stream, which appears to have been canalised to the west of the earlier ore-bins. The timber planking still survives, together with concrete bases and some of the machinery and support rods, including a collapsed trommel (Fig 65).

The main structure on the dressing floor was the processing mill. This was originally a three-storey structure including the crusher (18557) on the west bank of the stream, with a rock-cut stairway on the northern side leading to the upper floors. Constructed in stone and concrete, much of its detail still remains, including parts of timber flooring and support rods (see Fig 64). A new tramway (18569) was constructed to transport ore directly to the crusher.

Adjoining the south wall of the crusher are several jig platforms (18558), including the remains of some of the wooden jiggers. Two very substantial spoil tips of jig waste lie to the south-west. Immediately above the northern spoil tip is a run of three small settling pits (18554), with a leat (18700) flowing from the lower pit to direct slimes into the stream. Wooden launders (18698) appear to have carried slurry down-hill from the dressing floor for a distance of over a hundred metres to two settling pits (18553). The purpose of a platform (18555) along the line of the launder is unknown. Next to the settling pits is a second shaft, now capped with concrete (18552).

The processing mill and dressing floor machinery was powered by two Pelton-wheels, one of which still survives *in situ*, supported by a timber frame above a stone and concrete wheelpit (Fig 66). The Pelton-wheels were driven by water under the pressure of gravity, a considerable force being provided by directing the water down a steep gradient in two iron pipes. One of the pipes (18636, Fig 69) was fed by a leat (18572) drawn from the small reservoir (18631, Figs 67–8) below the tailrace outflow from the pumping wheelpit. A wooden tank and sluice (18699)

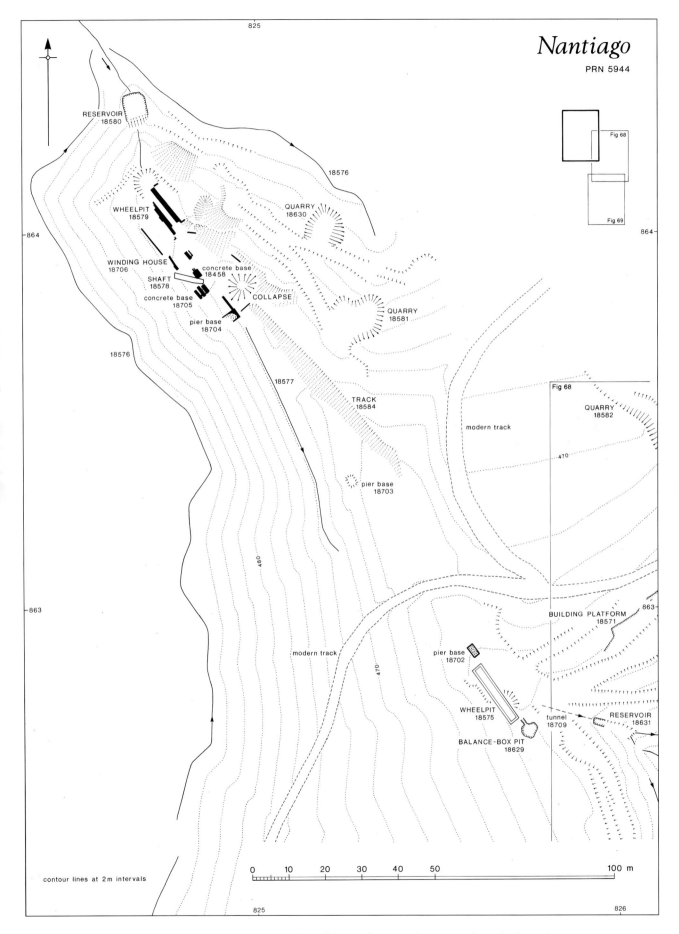

Figure 67 Nantiago mine: detailed plan of the northernmost inset area shown in Figure 60.

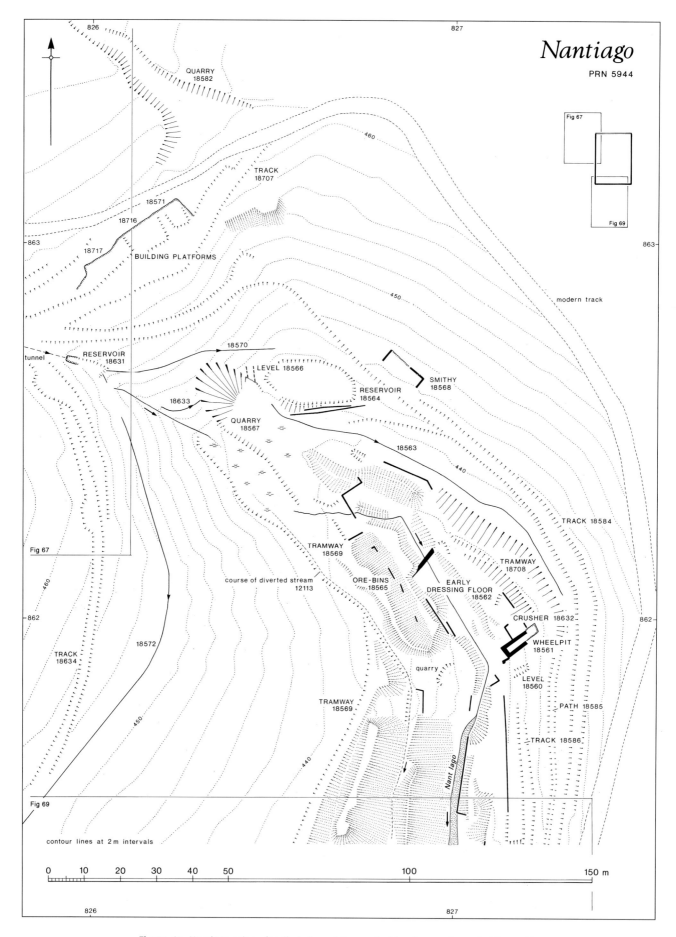

Figure 68 Nantiago mine: detailed plan of the central inset area shown in Figure 60.

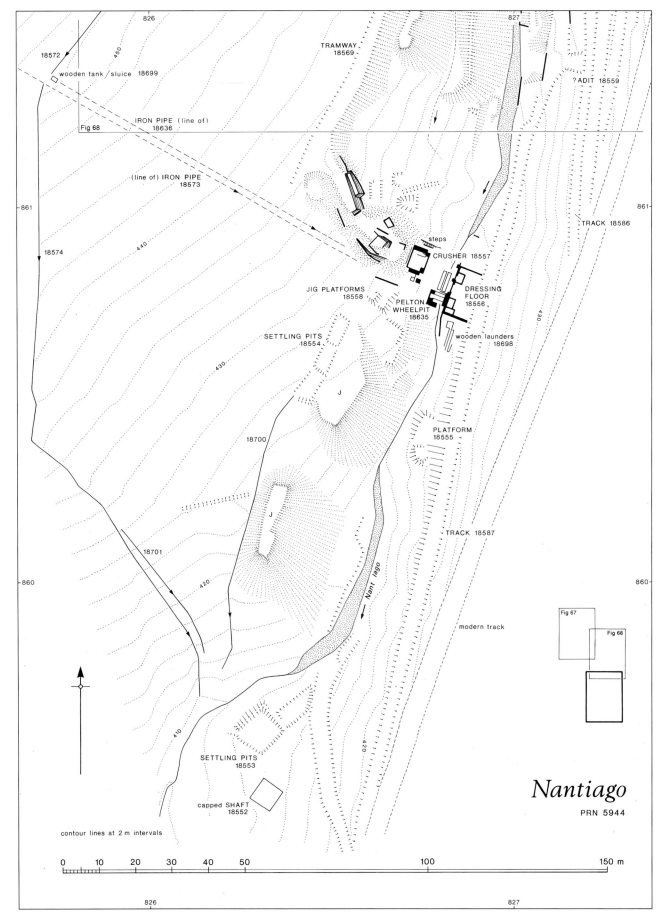

Figure 69 Nantiago mine: detailed plan of the southernmost inset area shown in Figure 60.

still survive at the end of the leat, where water was directed either into one of the iron pipes, or diverted to flow into the stream. A track along the western side of the leat (18634) appears to have provided access to the sluice. When pressure was low, an additional source of water was provided by the main leat via a second iron pipe (18573), although this would divert water away from the pumping and winding wheelpits.

None of the ancillary mine buildings survive in a good condition, but it is possible to identify the foundations of the smithy (18568, Fig 68) and three adjacent building platforms (18571, 18716–7) to the north of the early dressing floor. An undated mine plan in the Denbighshire Record Office (DD/WY/5300) suggests that the platforms correspond with a blacksmith-cum-carpenter's shop together with cottages or barracks. A horse shed and a pump house are also shown to the east, of which there is no visible trace.

The original mine access track (18587) evidently followed the eastern side of the valley, leading north of the early dressing floors, past the smithy and then on to the pumping wheelpit and to the shaft. This joined a second track (18707) which ran past the building platforms and headed on over the mountain to the Nant yr Eira mine, about a kilometre to the north.

Pen Dylife, Llanbrynmair and Trefeglwys, Powys (Figs 2, 9, 70–6, 134)

The Pen Dylife mine workings are sited along an exposed upland ridge, 16 kilometres north-west of the market town of Llanidloes (SN85509350) (Fig 70) and within 5 kilometres of the source of the River Severn. The solid geology, comprising Silurian rocks of the Frongoch formation, contains three main veins known as Esgairgaled, Llechwedd Ddu and Dylife lodes (Bick 1985, 3), the last of which also appears to known as the Dyfngwm lode (Jones 1922, Pl 21). Mineralisation includes galena, chalcopyrite and sphalerite which yielded lead, silver, zinc and copper ores.

The mining remains extend for about a kilometre along the ridge and cover an area of about 30 hectares, at a height of between about 400–50 metres above sea level. Just to the north is the valley of the Afon Twymyn stream, occupied by the remains at of the large 19th-century mine at Dylife. To the south, Pen Dylife overlooks the steep-sided Clywedog Valley containing the remains of the Dyfngwm mine. The Pen Dylife and Dyfngwm workings lie to either side of a substantial bank (18614, Fig 70) which probably marked the boundary between the two setts. Much earlier activity along the crest of the ridge is represented by the Roman fortlet of Penycrocbren, whose earthwork banks and single entrance on the northern side are clearly visible from the air (Fig 71). To the west of the fortlet is a low mound which marks the site of a gibbet, depicted on a map of 1774 (Bick 1985, 19), where gibbetting irons and a skull have been discovered. The northern boundary of the survey area is defined by the old track between Llanidloes and Machynlleth, perhaps representing a drovers' road (Moore-Colyer 2002, 48). Apart from mining, upland grazing has been the predominant land use for much of the site's history. The mining landscape at Pen Dylife falls within the Clywedog Valley landscape of special historic interest in Wales (Cadw 2001), which also includes the mining remains at Bryntail and Van, together with the Gwestyn and Penyclun mines described in detail elsewhere in this volume.

The well-preserved mining remains at Pen Dylife provide an a clear demonstration of the improvements that took place in ore extraction techniques from early times up to the end of the 19th century. The workings are dominated by a line of small pits and larger shafts seeking out the vein along the ridge, merging at the west with the large opencast workings of Dyfngwm mine (see Fig 71). Earlier mining activity appears to be represented by the smaller shafts as well as by a series of leats and small reservoirs that suggest that hushing was employed as a means of early prospecting and extraction. As elsewhere, the scale of mining operations increased dramatically from the mid-19th century, accompanied by the sinking of a new shaft and the construction an engine house. An unusual feature of Pen Dylife is the absence of the large spoil tips which generally characterise 19th-century workings. This was partly due to the fact that the ore mined at Pen Dylife was processed either at Dylife, or later at Dyfngwm, the two being connected underground from 1865.

The workings at Pen Dylife follow the Dylife vein along the ridge, with workings on the other two veins situated to the north, close to the present village. Before the early 19th century the workings were solely on the Dylife vein, which was exploited both from Pen Dylife and from near the later Llechwedd Ddu shaft, although as the century progressed large-scale workings

Figure 70 General plan of Pen Dylife mine. See Figures 73–6 for detailed plans of the inset areas.

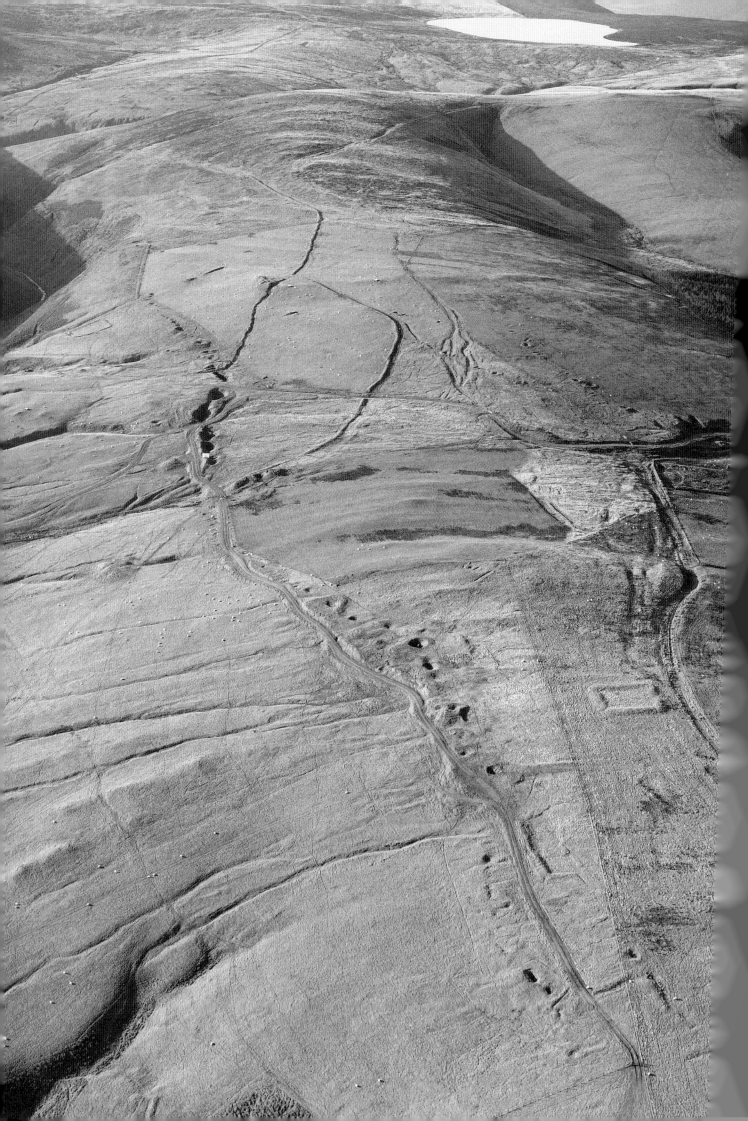

developed at both Llechwedd Ddu and Esgairgaled (Bick 1985, 3). Intensive mining activity gave rise to the small but once thriving village of Dylife, with its own church, chapels, and a public house. The church has sadly now gone, but rows of miners' cottages survive (see Fig 14), as does the Star Inn.

The origins of mining activity are uncertain, though the adjacent Roman fortlet of Penycrocbren hint at mining activity during this period (Jones 1961; Putnam 1962). The earliest documentary evidence of mining is in about 1640, when Thomas Bushell of Cardiganshire took a lease. By 1812 workings were under way on all three veins, and in 1818 the lease was taken over by Hugh Williams, later joined by John Pughe. During the 1840s work commenced on the Dylife adit cross-cut, which intersected the Dylife load from the Llechwedd Ddu adit. By 1849, however, a report by Francis Matthews stated that the Dylife vein had not been worked for some years (Bick 1985, 5–6). In 1858 the mining interests at Dylife were bought by Cobden, Bright and Company of Manchester, which invested heavily in the various workings at Dylife, Cobden having married Williams's daughter in 1840. One of the new company's principal aims was to expand the exploitation of the Dylife vein, which involved the sinking of Boundary Shaft (Bick 1985, 12–14). A 60-inch Cornish pumping engine with two 10-ton boilers was installed, though not without some difficulty: the engine house was the highest to be installed in Wales, a feat requiring fifty horses to haul equipment to the site. The subsequent cost of transporting coal to fire the boilers proved a great burden. In 1861, a 50-foot by 6-foot waterwheel was erected in the valley below for drawing at the Old Engine Shaft and at Boundary Shaft. The latter was achieved by running a pulley line over the mountain. The shaft was eventually sunk to 167 fathoms, making it the deepest in mid Wales, and included an underground balance-bob, a rarity in Wales. Working finally ceased in January 1880 (Bick 1985, 24–6). By 1863 a total of 250 men were employed underground at Dylife, 38 of whom were working on the Dylife vein. At this time the population of the village is reported to have been around a thousand, with three or four inns, a church, several chapels and a school. In 1865 the Dylife adit was connected to the deep adit at Dyfngwm, making

a through passage beneath the mountain (Bick 1990, Part 4, 18). By 1873, however, with failing prospects, the mine was sold to the Dylife Lead Mining Company, who concentrated work on the Dylife vein, sinking Boundary Shaft to 132 fathoms below the adit. In 1876 the company re-formed as the Great Dylife Lead Mining Company until it collapsed in 1884. Work resumed between 1886–91 under the name Blaen Twmyn, following which the only activity was an attempt by Hirnant Mines in the 1920s to rework the tips near the village and to reopen the Dylife adit at Dyfngwm, which subsequently collapsed (Bick 1985, 14–16).

The line of the Dylife vein is clearly traced by a run of shafts and trials which extend along the ridge, the majority of which are presumed to be of 17th- or 18th-century date. A further area of trials is located north of the boundary bank, overlying a series of early trackways (18595, Fig 70) running along the ridge. One of the principal interests of Pen Dylife is in the evidence for hushing along the south side of the ridge revealed by recent survey work which appears to belong to the earlier workings (Fig 72). It appears that water from the open moorland was collected against the boundary bank (18614) to the north-west and gathered at the point where the bank changes direction on the edge of the survey area, just to the north-west of a later small enclosure or animal pen (18624, Fig 73). The water was then released through a gap in the bank and directed eastwards down the slope of the hill along the hushing channel (18623, Fig 63), a slight bank across the channel just past the mid point possibly indicating the existence of a small reservoir (18662) to control the flow of water. The eastern end of the channel is disturbed by later workings and collapse but at the point where it turns to the south it is joined by a leat (18665, Fig 73) emanating from a possible reservoir (18659) which may have provided additional water. The channel heads southwards down the contour, leading to a further hushing channel (18625, Fig 74) which dramatically increases in width and depth as it approaches the edge of the Clywedog Valley near the site of a possible trial level (18656). Two other hushing channels (18647, 18669, Fig 74) can be identified further to the west, together with a possible hushing reservoir (18657). The hushing chan-

Figure 71 (*left*)
Aerial view of Pen Dylife mine from the east. The old mountain track or drovers' road (18654) between Llanidloes and Machynlleth and the Penycrocbren Roman fortlet are visible towards the lower right. The workings are represented by a series of shafts and trials following the vein along the ridge. The main hushing channel is visible running away into the middle distance. (*Crown Copyright: RCAHMW 925091–42*)

Figure 72 Pen Dylife mine: collapsed workings to the left and hushing channel (18623) and shafts towards the lower right, viewed from the north, with hushing channel bottom right. (*Crown Copyright: RCAHMW 945031–44*)

nels lead to the extensive opencast workings associated with the Dyfngwm mine, and suggests that, as at Craig-y-Mwyn, described elsewhere in this volume, hushing was employed as a means of prospecting and possibly also extraction (see Fig 72).

Further east, between the modern access track and Boundary Shaft, three low banks (18609–11, Fig 75) appear to dam natural undulations in the ground. It is possible that these are the remains of further collection reservoirs associated with early hushing, although there is no trace of associated channels or leats. At the eastern end of the site, however, there is further possible evidence of hushing, represented by a sub-rectangular reservoir (18596, Fig 76), 37 by 12 metres across, with leats feeding into it from the north and

east. To the south, beyond the modern track, are several dry channels (18651) which have evidently been cut by water. However, the form of these is such that they are not conclusive proof of hushing, and they might have formed naturally. A second reservoir (18603), 40 metres to the north, appears to have fed a leat (18600) which may have helped to supply the Boundary Shaft boiler house (18606).

The deeper shafts represent 19th-century workings – the Boundary Shaft (18605, Fig 75) belonging to Dylife mine, and the two whim shafts (18615, 18617, Fig 73) and a connecting level to the west belonging to Dyfngwm mine. The boundary bank (18614, Fig 75), after which Boundary Shaft is named, probably marked the division between the two mines above

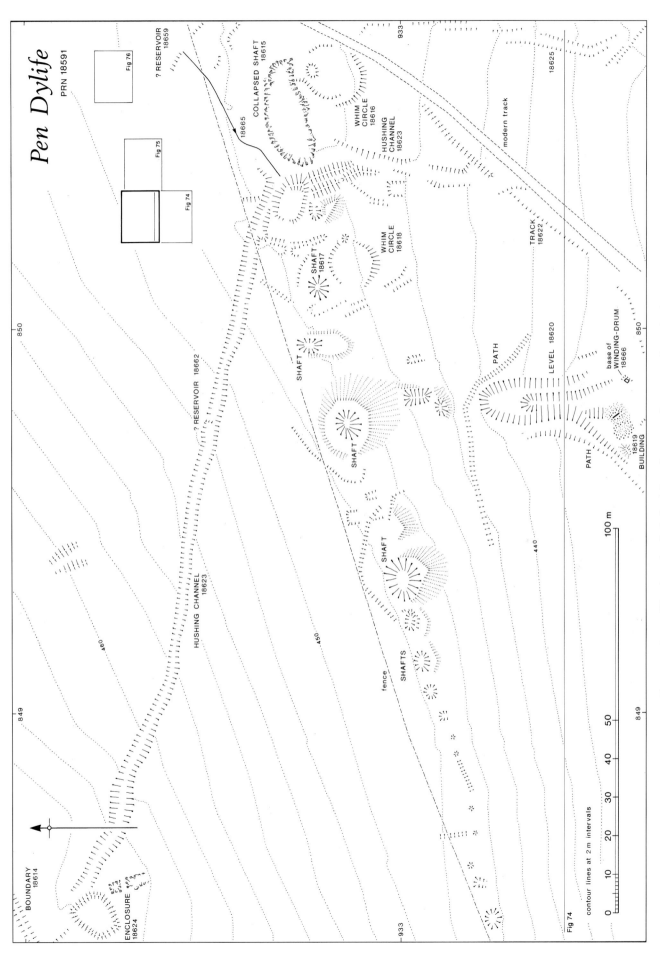

Figure 73 Pen Dylife mine: detailed plan of north-western inset area shown in Figure 70.

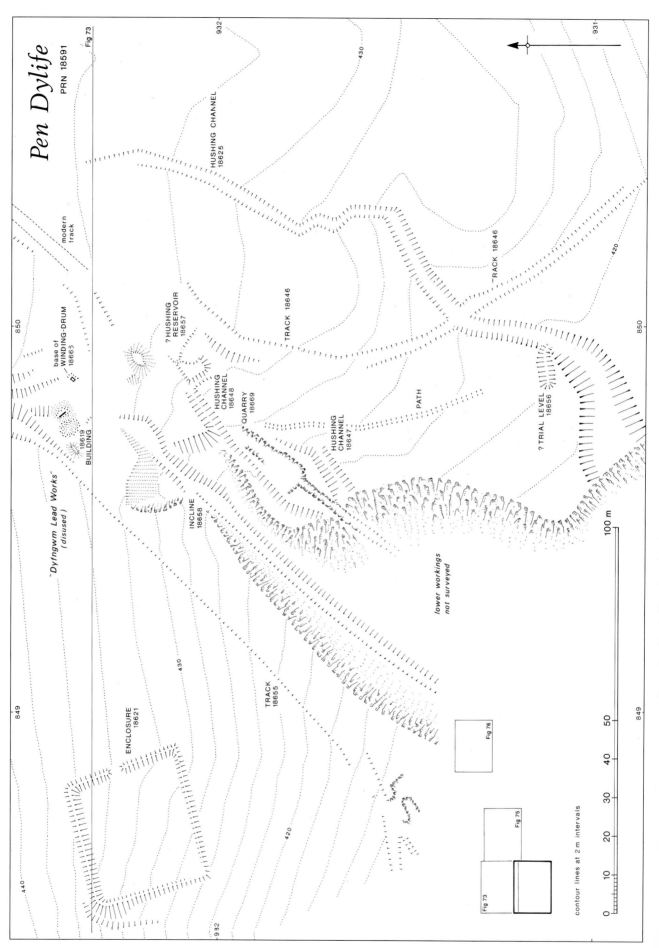

Pen Dylife

PRN 18591

Fig 73

HUSHING CHANNEL 18625

modern track

?HUSHING RESERVOIR 18657

TRACK 18646

TRACK 18646

base of WINDING-DRUM 18663

850

HUSHING CHANNEL 18648

QUARRY 18669

HUSHING CHANNEL 18647

PATH

?TRIAL LEVEL 18656

18619 BUILDING

"Dyfngwm Lead Works" (disused)

INCLINE 18658

lower workings not surveyed

430

TRACK 18655

ENCLOSURE 18621

849

440

932

420

Fig 76

Fig 75

Fig 73

contour lines at 2 m intervals

0   10   20   30   40   50   100 m

931

430

420

850

849

Pen Dylife mine; detailed plan of south-western inset area shown in Figure 70.

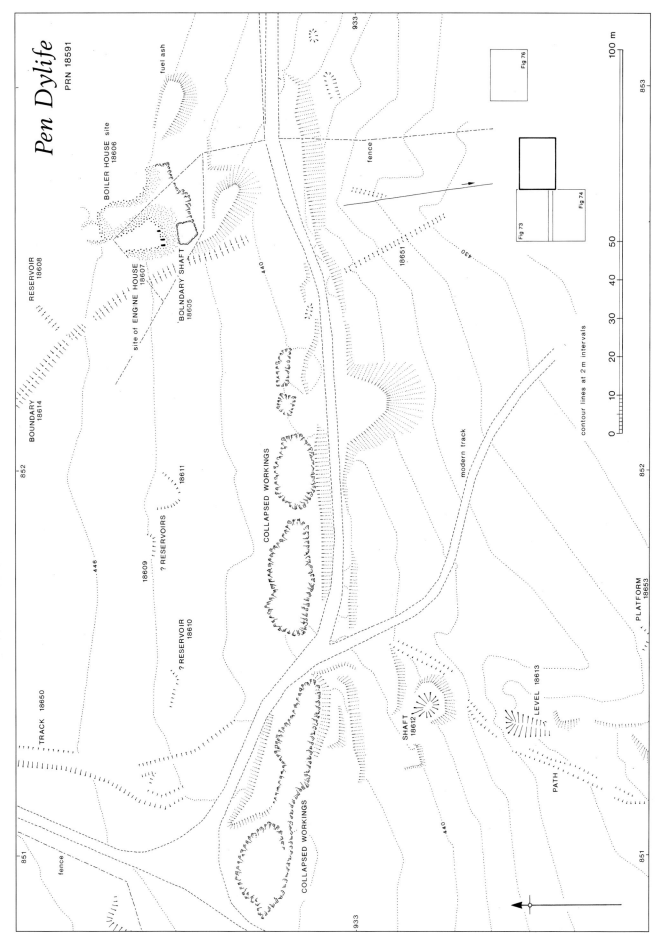

Figure 75 Pen Dylife mine: detailed plan of central inset area shown in Figure 70.

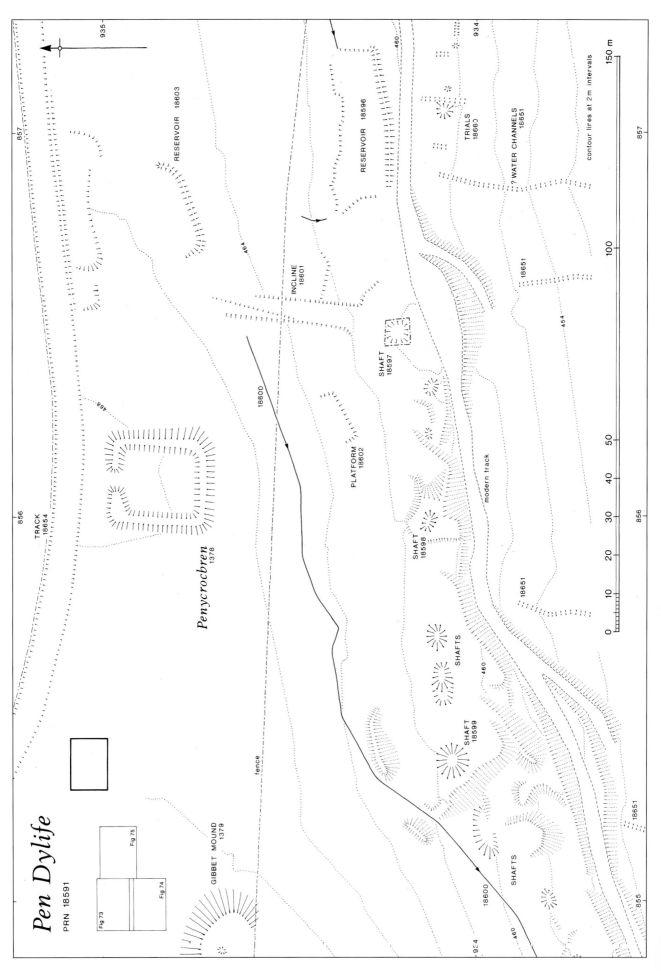

Detailed plan of north-eastern inset area shown in Figure 70.

ground. The Boundary Shaft workings were originally accessed by a shaft about 250 to the west (Jones 1922, 156), which is probably to be identified as one or other of the two whim shafts. Later, a deep adit was driven from the valley below, eventually connecting with the Dylife adit. The later workings also probably include three of the more substantial shafts towards the eastern end of the site (18597–9, Fig 76) amongst the presumed earlier workings. The easternmost shaft appears to have a short incline (18601) leading northwards towards the old mountain track, suggesting that ore may have been carried to lower-lying ground to the north or east via that route.

The Boundary Shaft, resulting from the investment by Cobden and Bright from 1858, is fenced and remains open to a considerable depth. North of the shaft are the collapsed remains of the engine house (18607) with the site of the boiler house (18606) to the east. A slight bank just to the north (18608), at right-angles to the boundary bank, marks the site of the reservoir which provided water for the boilers. The 60-inch engine was employed to pump the shaft. Winding was provided by the pulley which ran across the mountain for over a kilometre from the waterwheel at Dylife, passing beneath the old mountain track, where a gully can still be seen (18710, Fig 70).

As noted above, the workings of Dyfngwm mine at

Pen Dylife are assumed to lie to the west of the boundary bank and consist of several shafts, levels and collapsed workings (Figs 73–5). The main area of the mine lay beyond the survey area in the Clywedog Valley below, where there are significant remains of processing of ores. The two larger shafts on the hill (18615, 18617, Fig 73) both have adjoining whim circles (18616, 18618). The main level (18620) that was driven in from the south, apparently to meet one of the larger shafts, has now collapsed. At the entrance a spread of rubble marks the site of a building (18619) shown on the 1st edition Ordnance Survey map of 1887, whose purpose is unknown. The level was connected to the main mine site and dressing floors in the Clywedog Valley by an incline (18658) running through the opencast. The base of the winding drum survives at the head of the incline. To the west of the level lie the earthwork banks of a large square enclosure (18621, Fig 74) with an entrance along its eastern side. As at a number of other mine sites in mid Wales, the enclosure may have been used to impound horses employed at the mine. A second collapsed level lies further to the east (18613, Fig 75), driven in from the head of a shallow valley and aligned to a shaft (18612) to the north. Extensive spoil-tips south of the level include jig waste. A slight terraced area (18653) to the east may indicate the site of the jiggers.

Penyclun, Llanidloes, Powys (Figs 77–80)

Penyclun lies to the west of the Van mines, close to the Llyn Clywedog reservoir (SN93098730) (Fig 77). The solid geology is formed by the Ordovician Van formation. A single vein with an ENE strike contains lead and zinc ores, with barytes and witherite gangue. Penyclun mine produced lead ore.

The compact mining remains of Penyclun lie within an enclosed lowland landscape on an east-facing slope, below the ramparts of Penyclun hillfort, at a height of about 200 metres. The area has a rich mining history. Bryntail mine lies 1.7 kilometres to the west and Van mines 1.2 kilometres to the east. These, together with Penyclun and the mining landscapes at Gwestyn and Pen Dylife, described in detail elsewhere in this volume, form part of the Clywedog Valley landscape of special historic interest in Wales (Cadw 2001). Much of the mining landscape at Penyclun has recently been lost to land reclamation, but the site is of particular interest for the rare survival of a small Cornish engine house and stack. Its setting, which

includes the main shaft, connecting adit and other structures, covers an area of about 1.5 hectares.

Penyclun was for a while the most productive mine in Montgomeryshire. It seems that ore was first discovered by the resident farmer around 1845, being kept secret for some time, until being divulged by his son while under the influence of drink (Bick 1990, Part 4, 40). Several letters relate to the management of Penyclun by William Lefeaux. A report by David Jones in March 1853 refers to Lefeaux's wish to include the farm buildings in the lease, for conversion to labourers' cottages, and notes the recent completion of a smelting house. A letter of 1860 from James Paull to John Taylor mentions a recent visit to Penyclun, where the sinking of the new east shaft had begun, with a wheelpit being cut to erect a 60-foot wheel for pumping, crushing and dressing. By 1863, under the direction of Jehu Hitchins, the new shaft had been sunk to 77 fathoms (Bick 1990, Part 4, 40). This venture proved to be unsuccessful, however, and in

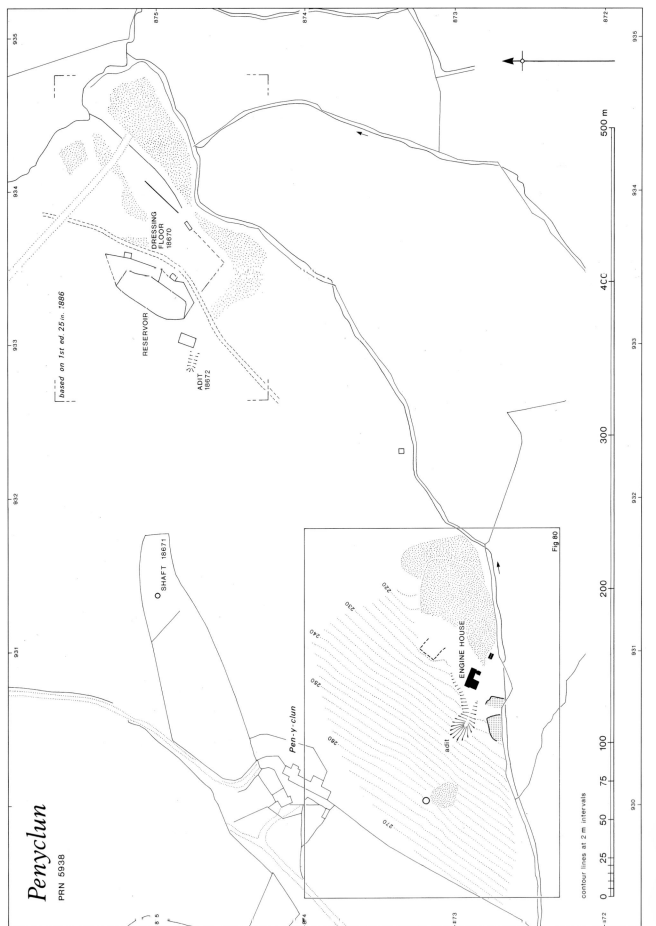

Penyclun

PRN 5938

based on 1st ed. 25in. 1886

DRESSING
FLOOR
18670

RESERVOIR

ADIT
18672

SHAFT 18671

Pen-y-clun

ENGINE HOUSE

adit

Fig 80

contour lines at 2 m intervals

0 25 50 75 100 200 300 400 500 m

(Penyclun mine. See Figure 80 for detailed plan of the inset area.

Figure 78 (*above*)
Penyclun mine: engine house
(18338) and chimney (18340), from
the north-east.
(*CPAT 276–21*)

Figure 79
Penyclun mine: engine house
(18338) viewed from the south-
east. This small Cornish rotative
engine house measures only 5.5 by
4 metres across, still stands to its
full height of about 8 metres. The
roof has long since fallen in and the
structure is now unfortunately in a
relatively poor state.
(*CPAT 276–27*)

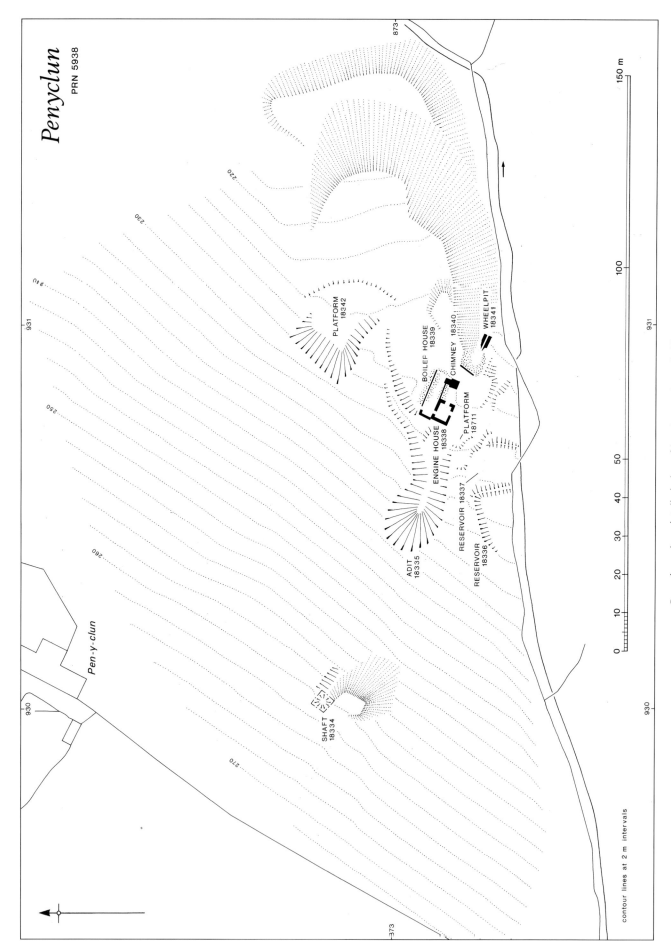

Penyclun

PRN 5938

SHAFT
18334

Pen-y-clun

ADIT
18335

PLATFORM
18342

BOILEF HOUSE
18339

ENGINE HOUSE
18338

CHIMNEY 18340

RESERVOIR 18337

RESERVOIR
18336

PLATFORM
18711

WHEELPIT
18341

contour lines at 2 m intervals

A superior detailed plan of inset area shown in Figure 77.

1866 the property was for sale. In 1868 the lease was acquired by Mr Howell, who installed a new water-wheel in 1873 (Bick 1990, Part 4, 40). A 30-year lease of 1890, between Sir Herbert Lloyd, Watkin Williams Wynne and John Paull of Greenfield, Llanidloes, refers to the extraction of copper, zinc blende, calamine and black jack. The last reference to Penyclun is an agreement of 1933 between Sir Herbert Lloyd, Watkin Williams Wynne and Isaac Breeze Jones of Llanidloes to work the waste tips for barytes.

The surviving remains are largely associated with the earlier workings by Lefeaux and Hitchins, and include a small Cornish engine house (18340, Figs 78–9). The engine house was aligned on the drainage adit (18335) and shaft (18334) to the west and was probably used for both pumping and winding. There is no clear evidence of how power was transferred to the shaft, but this is likely to have been by means of a flat-rod system supported on stanchions. The engine house is a two-storey structure built of stone with brick dressings. The building is about 5.5 by 4 metres across and survives to a height of about 8 metres. Only the footings of the 13 by 4 metre boiler house against the north wall of the engine house survive. Its chimney still stands to its full height but now leans somewhat

precariously. A large platform to the north was possibly the site of the mine office (18342).

The engine house appears to date from Hitchins's unsuccessful venture, since the sale details of 1866 list 'two valuable steam engines' (Bick 1990, Part 4, 40). An earlier source of power, possibly to be associated with Lefeaux, was provided by a small waterwheel, also aligned to the adit and shaft, whose wheelpit (18341) survives to the south-east of the engine house. The earthwork remains of two reservoirs just to the west may have provided water for the wheel, or for the later boilers, or possibly for both.

The ore processing areas in the lower part of the mine, several hundred metres to the north-east, have recently been cleared as part of a land reclamation scheme. Some clue as to what has been lost is given on the 1st edition of the Ordnance Survey map of 1886 (Fig 77, top right) which shows a reservoir, dressing floor and adit. The latter was probably a drainage adit connected with a shaft 150 metres to the west (18671) which is said by Bick to have been worked by Howell in the later 19th century. Little surface trace of these features is now evident, though it is probable that evidence is still preserved beneath the levelled tips of processing waste.

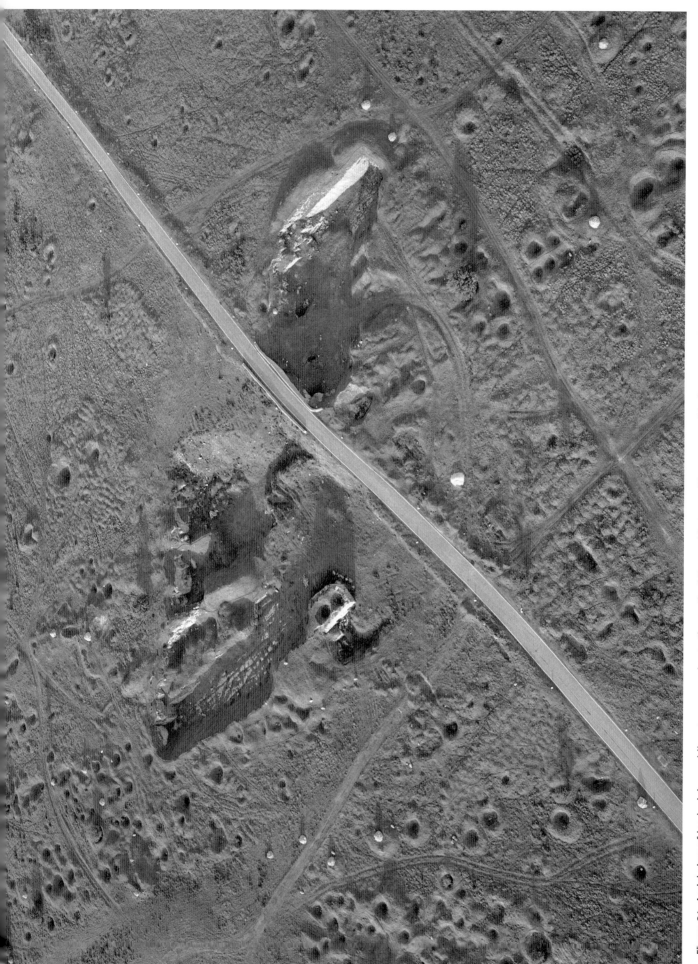

Figure 81 Aerial view of lead mining and limestone quarrying to the north of the road between Rhes-y-cae and Halkyn. Many of the shafts in this area have little development waste and were either fairly shallow or have been backfilled. Some have concrete beehive cappings. The quarries are associated with the pair of limekilns at the centre of the photograph.

3 Interpreting the mining landscapes of north-east Wales

by Pat Frost and Nigel Jones

Halkyn Mountain, Holywell, Flintshire (Figs 6, 81–90)

Halkyn Mountain lies 2 kilometres south of the town of Holywell and 5 kilometres west of Flint (Fig 4). The mining landscape covers an area of more than 500 hectares on the low upland plateau between the Clwydian Range and the Dee Estuary, at a height of between 200–90 metres above sea level. The hills form part of the belt of Carboniferous limestone which runs inland for 30 kilometres to the south of Prestatyn (see Fig 4). Mineralisation includes galena, sphalerite and chalcopyrite. The area was once one of the most important zinc and lead orefields in Wales, with silver as a valuable by-product.

The main mining area on Halkyn Mountain falls between the small mining settlements of Halkyn, Rhes-y-cae, Brynford and Pentre Halkyn (Fig 82), much of which was once common land. Though somewhat fragmented by land improvement and more recent stone quarrying it remains one of the most extensive and dramatic mining landscapes in Wales and is recognised as a landscape of outstanding historic interest in Wales (Cadw 1998; Britnell *et al* 2000). In addition to the almost continuous mineral workings shown in Figures 88–90, intermittent workings continued for about a further 3 kilometres north-west to Gorsedd and a kilometre south-east to Rhosesmor. Lines of shallow surface open-cuts, bell-pits and deeper stone-lined shafts graphically etch out the course of the rich mineral veins known by such names as the Long Rake, Old Rake, Chwarel Las, Pant-y-pydew, Pant-y-pwll-dwr veins and the Pant-y-ffrith and Caleb Bell cross-courses (Figs 83–4, 87). Other elements of this landscape include the palimpsest of tracks which criss-cross the area, leats and reservoirs which would have served the ore processing areas, occasional horse whim circles, and scattered miners' cottages and mine offices,

some converted to modern dwellings and others now in ruins.

The mining of lead ores on Halkyn Mountain had almost certainly begun by Roman times, though unequivocal evidence of workings of the period have yet to be identified. A Roman 'pig' or ingot of lead was found in 1950 during the construction of Carmel school, about 2 kilometres to the north-west of Brynford. The pig was inscribed with the letters C NIPI ASCANI, standing for the name of a private lead producer, C Nipius Ascanius, and is undoubtedly composed of lead that had been mined and smelted on Halkyn Mountain. Similar pigs have been found near the Roman legionary fortress at Chester about 20 kilometres to the east, two of which are inscribed with the letters DECEANGL, the name of the native tribe that inhabited north-east Wales at the time of the Roman conquest. The remains of Roman domestic buildings and a bath house at Pentre Farm, Flint seem likely to have been owned by a Roman official responsible for supervising this lead smelting industry, which probably exported lead along the Dee Estuary to Chester and beyond (O'Leary *et al* 1989). Copper vessels said to be of Roman origin were discovered in the mid-18th century during the sinking of a shaft on Long Rake (Davies 1949, 176–8), a vein which extends in an east–west direction across the common, cutting through Rhes-y-cae (Fig 90). Evidence of Roman lead smelting (presumably from ores brought down from Halkyn Mountain) was found on excavations in the Pentre Oakenholt area of Flint (Atkinson and Taylor 1924), on the shores of the Dee Estuary, about 5 kilometres to the east of Pentre Halkyn.

Mining is also known to have been carried out on

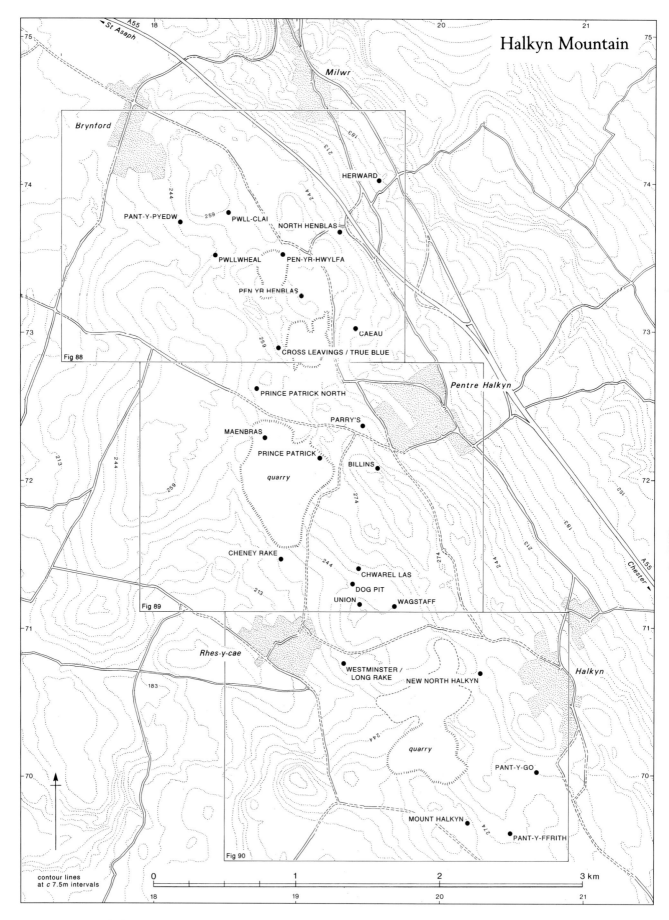

Figure 82 General plan of Halkyn Mountain, showing the location of the principal named 19th- and 20th-century mines. See Figures 88–90 for detailed plans of inset areas. Workings continue to the north-west of Brynford.

Figure 83 Aerial view of Halkyn Mountain showing the intensive area of mine shafts south-east of Pentre Halkyn (SJ 195715). The area lies to the east of Pant-y-pwll-dwr limestone quarry (see Fig 89), just visible in the top right-hand corner. The lines of shafts, of varying depths, follow rich east-west veins including those known as Billings and Chwarel Las, which were principally worked for lead. The linear workings in the right foreground are probably a north-south cross-cut. Working in this area probably began in the Roman period and continued up to the early 20th century. (*Crown Copyright: RCAHMW 935136–45*)

a significant scale during the Middle Ages, perhaps peaking in the later 13th century when lead was in much demand for roofing the newly constructed Edwardian castles at Flint and Rhuddlan as well as those further afield, in Caernarvonshire, Anglesey, and in mid Wales. Records survive from the 1350s of the codes of law and privileges of the free miners of Englefield, which encompassed the Holywell-Halkyn area. As noted in an earlier chapter, they were free men, who could pasture their stock on common land and sell their ore on the free market on condition that they paid their dues to the lord who owned the

mineral rights (Williams 1994, 62). Medieval workings, like the Roman workings before them, have yet to be positively identified in the field. It is likely that earlier workings have been obscured by the more intensive workings which commenced in the 17th century: mines of all periods being largely restricted to the narrow ore veins marked by lines of smaller bell-pits and trial pits and shafts, often no more than about 4–5 metres across.

In the 1630s the crown granted the rights to mine lead in the parish of Holywell, in the hundreds of Coleshill and Rhuddlan, to the Grosvenor Estate,

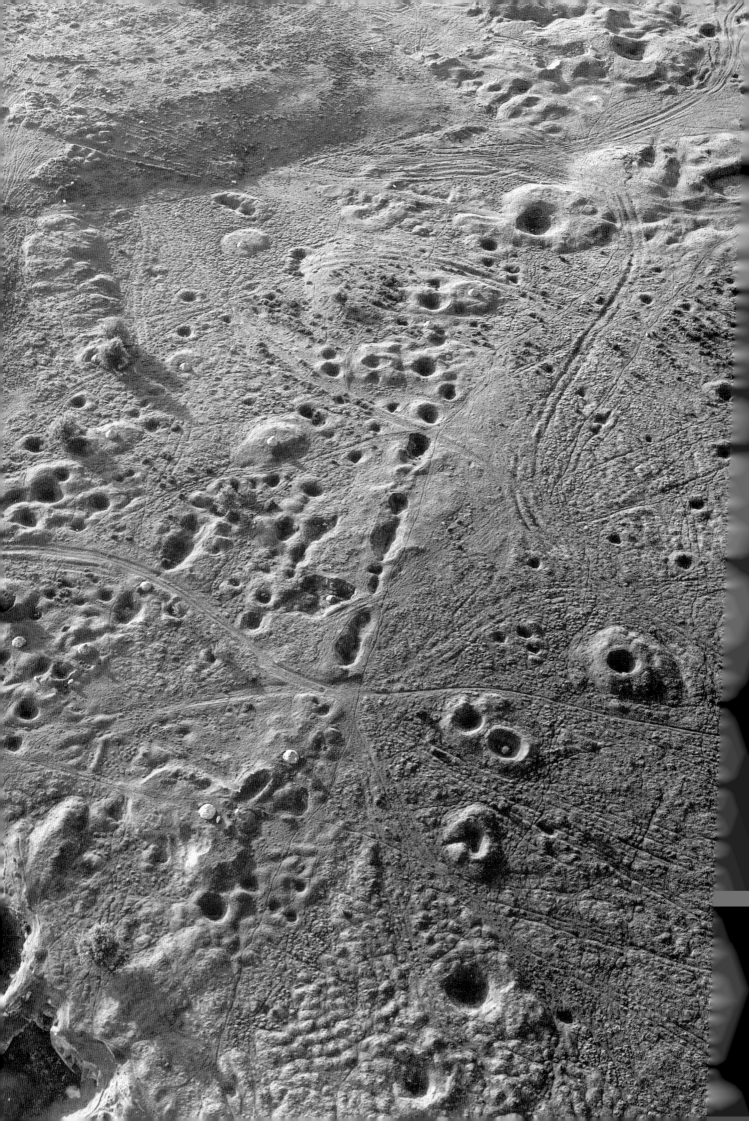

retaining for itself the rights in Halkyn and Northop. At this early date leases were let as annual bargains, measured in terms of a mere 30 yards. The lack of investment that this engendered early on was one of the causes of the lines of relatively shallow pits and shafts of which well over 4,000 have been recorded within this mining landscape. Though some of the shallower shafts and trials are still open, many have collapsed and are simply represented by depressions. The original depth of the shafts is indicated by the amount of spoil which appears as chains of smaller heaps, ring-like mounds around the mouth of the shaft, or as large consolidated mounds.

The London Lead Company, or the Quaker Company as it is more commonly known, was actively mining in Flintshire from about 1695. In 1698, the company was already involved in disputes with the Grosvenor estate over mining on Old Rake, Halkyn, one of the richest veins on the mountain. Rich ore was being wound up in baskets at Old Rake and Long Rake, where by 1701 the company had a building which included a smithy, count-house, storeroom for ore, lodgings for its agent, and a chimney for the convenience of the miners in winter. The Quaker Company inaugurated a more methodical approach to mining on the mountain: new and larger shafts were sunk and ore processed at the mine was being transported by cart to the company's new smelting-house at Gadlys, about 2 kilometres to the north-east of Pentre Halkyn, which was in production by 1704.

Until the invention of the steam engine the raising of ore had been by simple methods such as rope and bucket, windlasses and later by horse whims. Consequently, shafts remained fairly shallow, generally in the form of bell-pits not exceeding 10 metres in depth. The Quaker Company were responsible for introducing several technological innovations such as a windmill for pumping out water and winding ore at Pant-y-pwll-dwr Rake, followed by a later installation of an engine house for a Newcomen steam engine by 1729, one of the first of seven to be installed by the company on Halkyn. The Quaker interests on Halkyn included Maeslygan, Old Rake, Long Rake, Silver

Rake, and Moel-y-crio. Shafts up to about 60 yards (55 metres) in depth were sunk by the 1720s. Another innovation introduced by the company was the use of adits which served as drainage and access levels. Previously, a majority of mines would have been under water and unworkable during the winter months. These improvements enabled mining to take place all year round as well as the exploitation of deeper, richer veins. By the end of the 18th century most of the richest veins on Halkyn Mountain were already being worked, and further expansion necessitated deeper workings along these lodes.

Other factors which gave rise the increased scale of mining during the early 18th century and beyond were the abundance of coal in Flintshire and the development of its use as a replacement for charcoal in smelting lead and as fuel for the steam engines. The proximity of the Dee Estuary also made the task of shipping ore to manufacturing centres and smelteries elsewhere along the coast much easier. One of the drawbacks was the shortage of water power which had been such a boon in other mining areas and because of this a great dependence was placed on coal-fired steam engines as a source of power for most mines in the area during the 19th century.

The gradual expansion of the industry and the need for higher levels of capital investment led to the replacement of small mining ventures by large-scale mining companies during the course of the 19th century. By the late 19th century Flintshire as a whole became the most productive mining area in Wales and second in importance to the Pennines in Britain as a whole. Earlier workings had exhausted the more easily worked sources of ore. Deeper mining required more capital investment, particularly for drainage which became increasingly essential as workings sank further below the water-table. A number of smaller drainage adits were dug by individual companies, but two major drainage tunnels were cut through the mountain as part of a cooperative venture. The Halkyn Deep Level Tunnel was driven initially by the Grosvenor Estate in 1818, and taken over by the Halkyn District Mines Drainage Company in 1875. It drained the mines on

Figure 84 (*left*)
Aerial view of Halkyn Mountain showing continuous mineral workings in the area of the Wagstaff or Union vein, north-east of Rhes-y-cae (SJ196710). Some of the larger and possibly deeper shafts are surrounded by heaps of development waste. The smaller pits without heaps of development waste are likely to be shallower bell-pits which produced less waste, though some of the pits or shafts may have been partly filled in with development waste when the shaft next to it was sunk. Some of the deeper shafts were capped by Clwyd County Council in the 1970s for safety reasons. The beehive-shaped caps (sometimes known as 'Clwyd Caps') were built of concrete set on a steel frame.
(*Crown Copyright: RCAHMW 935136–47*)

the south-east side of the mountain, such as New North Halkyn and Mount Halkyn, before continuing south towards Hendre and Llyn-y-pandy. In 1897 a group of companies formed the Holywell-Halkyn Mining and Tunnel Company and began to drive the Milwr Tunnel from the Dee Estuary at Bagillt. It cut across the centre of the orefield from north to south, and was eventually extended to the Mold mines in 1957. By these means, all the earlier mines which worked the mineral veins along the course of the tunnel could to be reworked to even greater depths, and over 300 metres deep in the case of some of the mines on Halkyn Mountain. Other improvements in mining technique during the 19th century included the invention of the rock drill, the use of compressed air underground, and the use of dynamite.

Documentary evidence is often slight, and it is only in rare instances that detailed records and plans of the mining sites survive. Often, the only documentary reference to the hundred or so mines in the area, with names such as Dog Pit, Prince Patrick, Queen of the Mountain, or True Blue, is a note in the *Mining Journal* relating to production figures, changes in ownership, and occasionally the installation of new equipment, and returns for the production of lead recorded by the Mining Record Office from 1845. In some instances there are reports by the agents which can give a valuable insight into the workings at a particular date. Although company records survive for many of the mines, they are frequently incomplete and are difficult to relate to what is still visible on the ground. Mine plans and sections of the workings have sometimes survived, but they often only relate to underground workings, and contain little or no indication of what lay above ground. For many sites the earliest surviving surface plans are provided by the 1st edition of the Ordnance Survey, generally of the 1880s. The surface workings and structures were occasionally recorded in contemporary photographs, although sadly such records are very scarce. Despite the relatively recent date of many mines, the interpretation of the surviving field evidence is of critical importance

to our understanding of the mining and processing techniques that were employed at different periods.

There were peaks in production around 1850 and 1895 but the industry underwent a general decline at the end of the 19th century due to foreign competition. The Sea Level Tunnel was extended southwards in the second and third decades of the 20th century, enabling new veins to be exploited. The years following the end of the Second World War saw the amalgamation of a number of companies with both mining and quarrying interests, small-scale mining operations continuing until the 1970s.

Although many of the sites remain relatively well preserved in the unimproved core areas of this landscape, some sites have been lost to more recent limestone quarrying and landscaping for agricultural and residential use, particularly around the periphery. Mine sites immediately north of Brynford have been landscaped for use by Holywell golf course, and the construction of the A55 trunk road cut through many of the mine sites further north, particularly in the area of Smithy Gate (SJ177754). In the area around Pen-y-ball Top (SJ175755) only part of the early mining remains have survived as a result of reclamation for agricultural use. In places only the larger shafts and surrounding spoil tips survive, together with the earthwork remains of tramways belonging to the Grange and Coetia Butler quarries. Numerous shafts were capped in concrete for reasons of safety as part of a programme undertaken by the former Clwyd County Council in the 1970s. Derelict land reclamation schemes involving shaft capping, infilling and disposal of large-scale waste, have levelled much of the late 20th-century workings, particularly in the area to the south-west of Halkyn village, which included workings of Halkyn District United Mines on the Pant-y-go vein. Further schemes resulted in the loss of the Prince Patrick mine to the Pant-y-pwll-dwr quarry and some of the workings on the Pant-y-pydew vein to the Pen yr Henblas chert quarry.

Few mine buildings or other above-ground structures have survived, as a result of natural decay as well

Figure 85 (*right*)

Aerial view of Halkyn Mountain showing two well-preserved late 19th century or early 20th century horse whims or horse gins (SJ20257016) belonging to the former New North Halkyn mine, north of Mount Villas. The sites lie near the eastern edge of Pant quarry (see Fig 90) which is just visible in the top right-hand corner. A winding drum on a post at the centre of the whim was turned by one or two horses and would have raised and lowered a cage for extracting the ore. The cage was supported by A-frames set above the shaft on the left-hand side of the whim. The ore extracted from these shafts was probably processed at the mill built next to Lewis's Shaft. Horse whims, introduced into north-east Wales in about the mid-17th century, made it much easier to sink shafts to greater depths.

(*Crown Copyright: RCAHMW 935137–50*)

Figure 86 Aerial view of Halkyn Mountain showing late 19th-century mining and limestone quarrying (near SJ195710) to the north of the road between Rhes-y-cae and Halkyn (see Fig 90). The sites lie in the area of the Wagstaff and Union mines, which were first worked by the Quaker Company from 1696 and continued in production until the First World War. Many of the shafts in this area have little development waste and were therefore probably either fairly shallow or have been backfilled. A pair of limekilns and a number of shafts capped with modern concrete beehive-shaped caps are visible in the lower right-hand corner of the photograph. (*Crown Copyright: RCAHMW 935136–42*)

as a deliberate policy of clearing away derelict buildings. Parts of one or two original stone engine houses survive, as at Glan Nant, near Holway, last used as a pigsty, and possibly at Halkyn, together with a former chimney base. Traces of a possible stone-faced winding wheelpit also survive at Holway. Former mine offices or manager's houses now converted to dwellings survive at Parry's mine, west of Pentre Halkyn, and Clwt Militia mine, north of Calcoed. Several original smithies survive, as at the former Glan Nant, Carmel, Ty Newydd and Mona mines, now converted to other uses. Other surface structures shown on earlier maps of which there is now no visible trace include winding gear, powder magazines, and sawpits, though a small number of horse whims are still identifiable, including two to the west of Halkyn, belonging to the former

New North Halkyn mine (Figs 85, 90). Numerous reservoirs, leats, and tramways are also shown on earlier maps, some of which can still be clearly identified in amongst the mine shafts. Limestone boundary stones up to about a metre high have survived here and there, which marked out different mining concessions, the positioning of boundary markers having been frequent subject of dispute between the Grosvenor Estate and the crown agents in the second half of the 19th century. Much of the ore processing appears to have been carried out away from the mountain, but areas of dressing floor waste and sunken areas probably representing buddles survive at Holway.

Other significant industrial activity within the landscape of Halkyn Mountain has included quarrying for chert, 'marble', hydraulic lime, limestone for building

Figure 87 Aerial view of Halkyn Mountain showing lines of shafts running along the rich Pwll-clai and Pant-y-pydew veins, Holywell Common. The settlement of Pwll-clai (SJ186738), seen from the north-east, lies at the centre, on the far side of the road between Brynford and Pentre Halkyn (see Fig 88). Fewer workings are visible in the fields to the lower right-hand corner, suggesting that this area has been reclaimed. A curving ditch just below the road was formerly a leat which served water-powered machinery at the Pwll-clai dressing floors. (*Crown Copyright: RCAHMW 935135–56*)

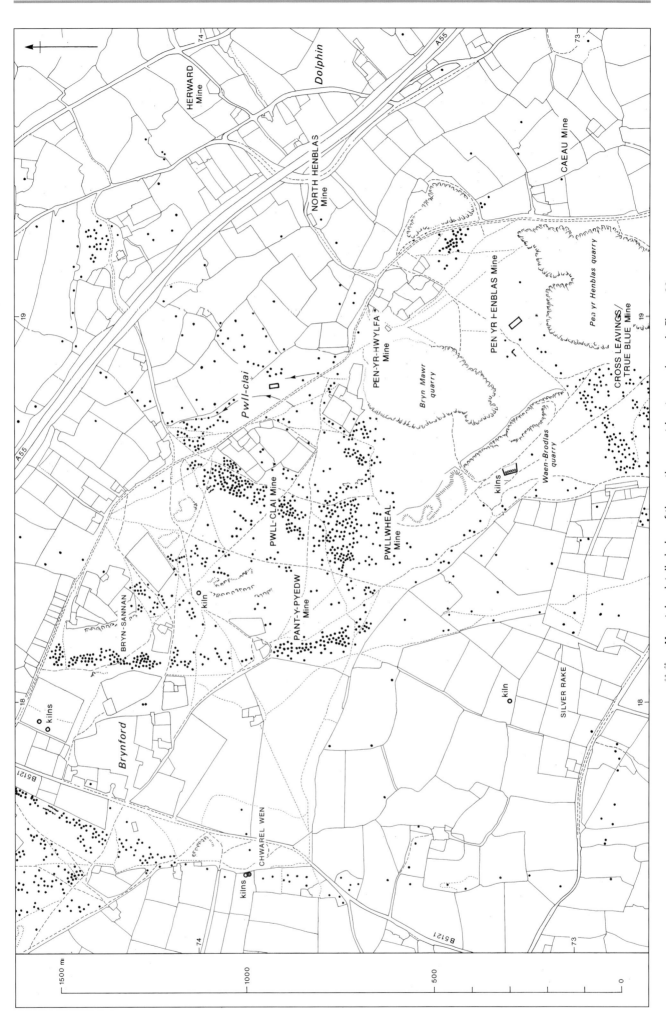

Mountain detailed plan of the northernmost inset area shown in Figure 82.

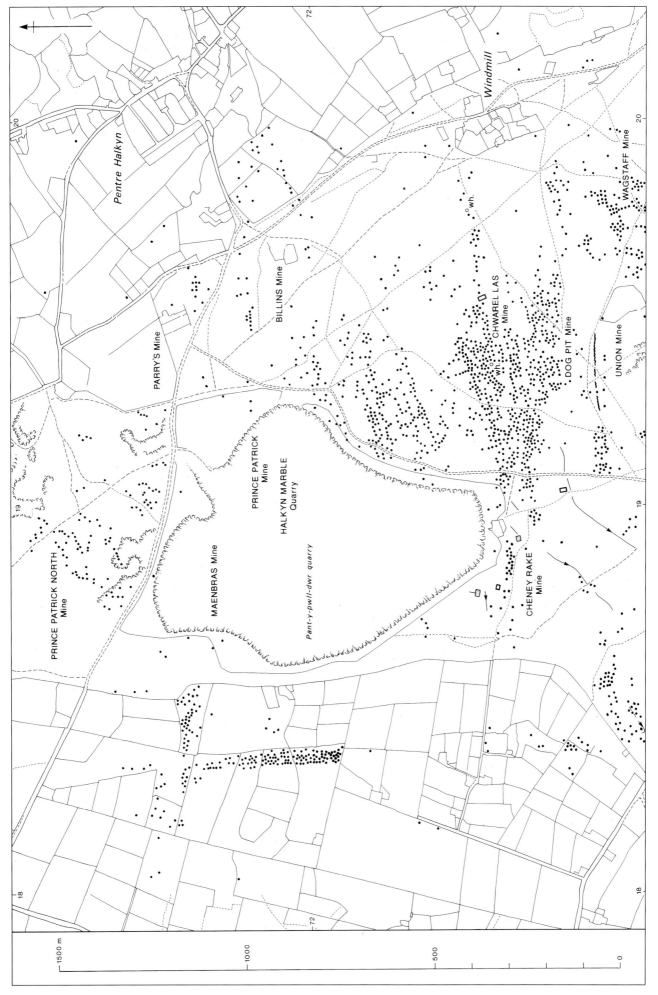

Figure 89 Halkyn Mountain: detailed plan of the central inset area shown in Figure 82.

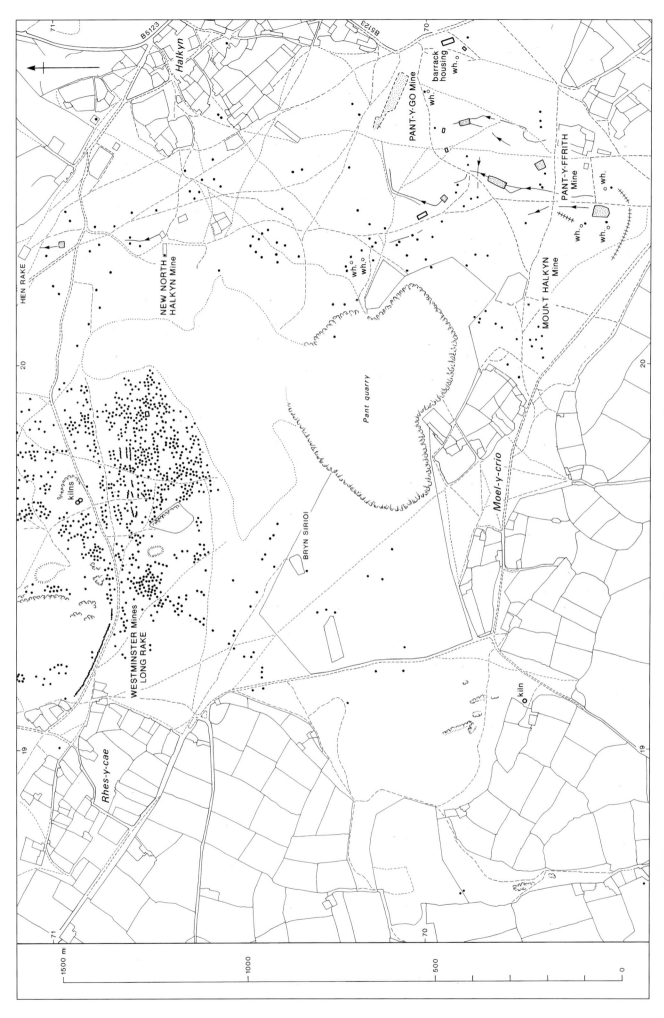

A detailed survey of the southernmost inset area shown in Figure 82

B5123

Halkyn

PANT-Y-GO Mine

barrack housing

wh. o

wh. o

wh. o

PANT-Y-FFRITH Mine

wh.

wh. o

wh. o

wh. o

wh. o

HEN RAKE

NEW NORTH HALKYN Mine

MOUNT HALKYN Mine

20

20

Pant quarry

kilns

BRYN SIRIOI

Moel-y-crio

WESTMINSTER Mines LONG RAKE

19

19

Rhes-y-cae

o kiln

1500 m

1000

500

0

and agricultural lime: each of which has also left an indelible mark on the landscape – often intermixed with the lead mining remains. Chert for grinding and for the production of stoneware and porcelain for the Minton and Wedgwood factories in the Potteries was being quarried between the 1770s and the early 20th century at Pant-y-pwll-dwr, Pen-yr-henblas, Pen-yr-garreg, Pen-yr-hwylfa, Bryn Mawr and on the north side of Moel y Gaer. 'Halkyn Marble' was quarried at Pant-y-pwll-dwr from the 1830s and exported to the surrounding region. Hydraulic lime that would set below water was also produced at the Grange, Holway and at Pant-y-pydew between the 1830s and 1890s, being in demand for the construction of the new docks being built in Liverpool, Birkenhead and Belfast. Limestone for building, gravestones and gateposts, and lime-burning was quarried at a number of centres, notably again at Pany-y-pwll-dwr and between Halkyn and Rhes-y-cae (Fig 86). Many former limekilns are known from early maps of plans though some of these, as at Pen-y-parc, Bryn Rodyn, and Billins no longer survive. Other limekilns survive only as foundations or low mounds, though a bank of five well-preserved kilns survive at Pant-y-pydew and a bank of two between Rhes-y-cae and Halkyn (see Fig 81). Deposits of glacial clay and sand were also being quarried, particularly towards the southern end of the area. Clay suitable for the production of porcelain was being dug from quarries at Foelddu, between Halkyn and Rhes-y-cae, between the 1820s and 1890s. Clay pits and a brick kiln were set up at Waen-y-trochwaed, west of Rhes-y-cae, in the late 19th century. A glacial esker was extensively quarried for sand at Moel-y-crio in the first few decades of the 20th century. Stone quarrying continues to the present day, with several of the larger quarries, now several hundred feet deep, and impacting upon the surrounding landscape.

Belgrave, Llanarmon-yn-Iâl, Denbighshire (Figs 91–4)

Belgrave mine (SJ20205885) (Fig 91) lies on the same belt of Carboniferous limestone as Halkyn Mountain, just under 20 kilometres to the south. It occupies a slightly higher plateau, between 400 and 450 metres above sea level, a kilometre north of the village of Eryrys and 6 kilometres south-west of Mold. This relatively compact mine, covering an area of about 5 hectares, exploited the Belgrave vein which runs south–east from the Alyn Valley for about a kilometre across the limestone ridge towards Nercwys Mountain, which yielded lead and silver ores.

The general area, known as Pot Hole Mountain, is one of undulating upland pasture. Belgrave is sited towards the western edge of the plateau, along an old trackway which leads down to the Alyn Valley to the west. The main workings are 19th-century and represented by shafts and trials along the vein (Figs 91–2), but there are a number of smaller shafts and trials which may belong to an earlier period. In addition to the workings the mining landscape contains the remains of a substantial Cornish engine house, together with the foundations for another (Fig 93). The outline of the mine office, cottages and a possible smithy are also evident, as are the earthworks of two reservoirs, a whim circle and several ancillary buildings.

The below-ground workings at Belgrave were fairly extensive and judging by royalties paid to the Grosvenor Estate were probably amongst the richest of the mines in the Llanarmon District during the first half of the 19th century (Smith 1921, 16). The vein was worked from a deep adit level at a depth of 96 fathoms in the Alyn Valley, with three main levels cutting in eastward at Bryn-yr-orsedd, about a kilometre to the north-west, and at least ten shafts strung out along the limestone ridge. The deepest shafts were sunk on the eastern side of the ridge, within the survey area shown in Figure 94. There is evidence for a dressing floor at Bryn-yr-orsedd but the extensive heaps of jigging waste at Belgrave clearly show that some ore processing was carried out near the shafts (Fig 94).

Much of the mine's history is poorly documented, although the main period of production seems to have been in the earlier part of the 19th century. In 1845 the mine was leased by Westminster Estates to Ebenezer Fernie of Tavistock, and then to William Williams in 1847. No returns are recorded for the years between 1857–81, and the mine is recorded by the Ordnance Survey as being inactive in 1874. However, returns were made by the Belgrave Mines Company in 1881–82, when fourteen people were employed underground and three on the surface (Burt et al 1992, 2, 26). A letter of 1924 in the Grosvenor Estate papers refers to mines secured from the estate by the Llanarmon District Mining Company in 1892,

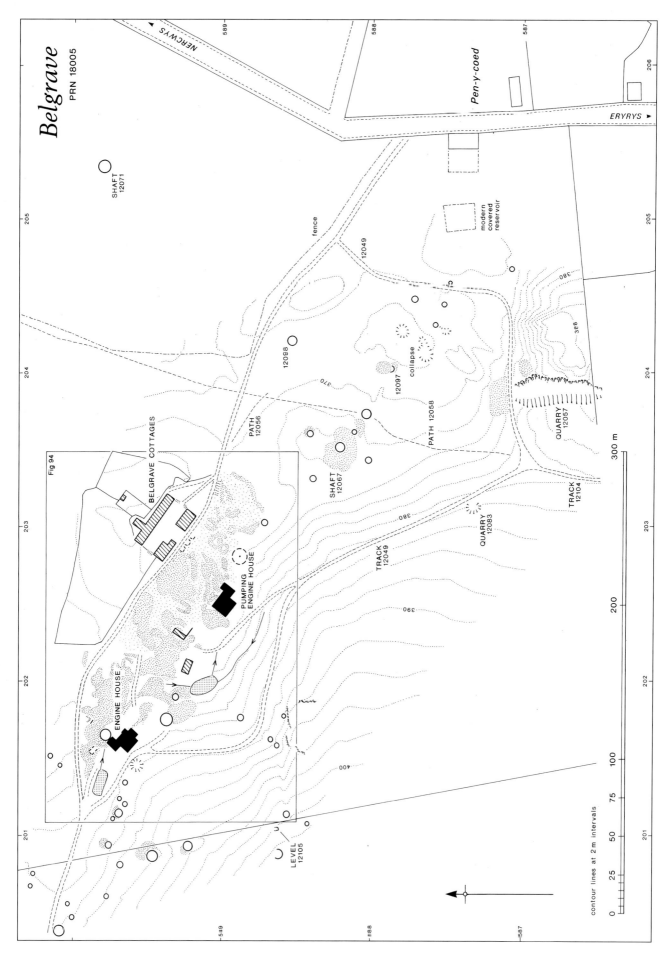

Belgrave PRN 18005

SHAFT 12071

NERCWYS

Pen-y-coed

ERYRYS ►

modern covered reservoir

fence

12049

collapse

12098

12097

PATH 12056

PATH 12058

QUARRY 12057

SHAFT 12067

TRACK 12104

QUARRY 12083

TRACK 12049

BELGRAVE COTTAGES

Fig 94

PUMPING ENGINE HOUSE

ENGINE HOUSE

LEVEL 12105

contour lines at 2 m intervals

0   25   50   75   100   200   300 m

See Figure 94 for detailed plan of the inset area.

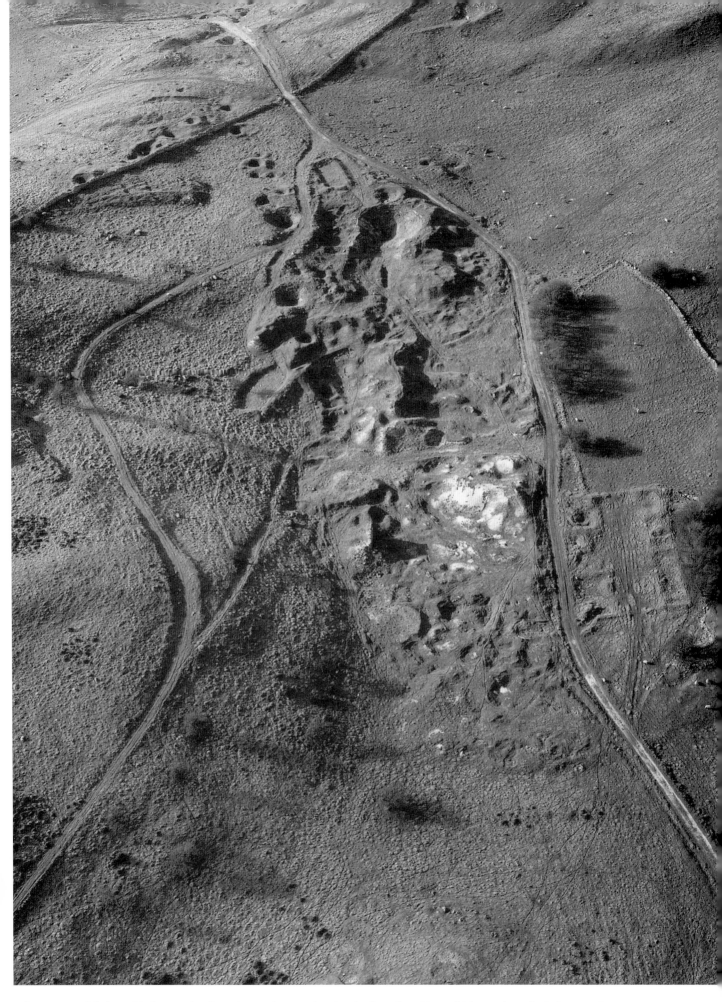

Figure 92 Aerial view of Belgrave mine from the south-east, showing the line of workings which run along the Belgrave vein across the hill to Bryn-yr-orsedd. (*CPAT 90-MB-302*)

Figure 93 Belgrave mine: remains of the wall of the pumping engine house (12060) towards the south-east side of the mine. A steam engine once housed in the building drove a beam-pumping engine at the main shaft via a system of flat-rods, pumping water from underground to fill reservoirs for feeding the boiler of a winding engine house and possibly for water-power for driving machinery on the dressing floor. The underground workings appear to have been drained by gravity-fed adits which ran into River Alun towards the west. (*CPAT 381–22*)

with a view to constructing a drainage scheme; the letter includes Belgrave in a list of mines already water-logged and closed down.

In 1928 take-notes were granted by the Grosvenor Estate to the Robert Group Quarries, initially for two years: these permitted the removal of waste, limestone and spar from the site, and the concession was subsequently extended to 1936. The resulting reworking of the spoil tips has largely removed any evidence of processing at the site. Two or three shafts were capped in the 1970s. The old engine shaft was recorded as being circular and stone-lined and there was said to be a date-stone of 1804.

The main shaft (12036, Fig 94), which was sunk to about 300 metres, has now collapsed, resulting in the loss of part of the adjacent structures. The Ordnance Survey 1st and 2nd edition maps of 1874 and 1900 depict a complex of buildings surrounding the shaft and show some development of these structures between the two surveys. An undated mine section shows the engine shaft, with a head frame, Cornish engine house and a boiler house with a separate chimney on the east side of the shaft, and a horse whim on the west. It is still possible to identify the stone foundations of the winding engine house (12037), a structure about 10 by 7 metres across. A

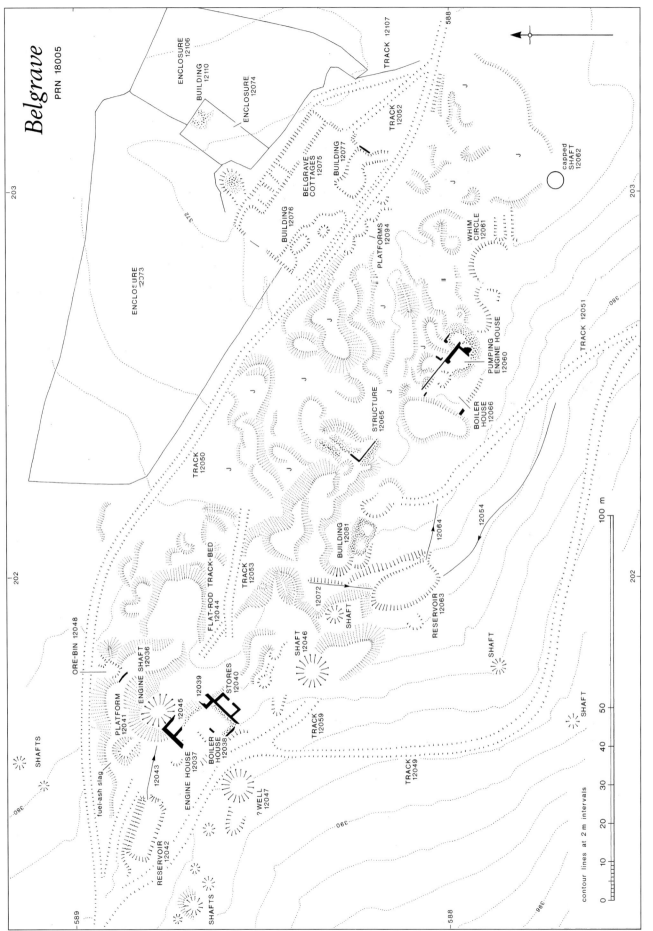

Figure 94 Belgrave mine: detailed plan of the inset area shown in Figure 91, towards the north-west corner of the mine.

stone structure extending towards the shaft from the north side of the engine house (12045) may be the loading for a flywheel or the condenser pit. The foundations of the boiler house (12038), about 10 by 8 metres across, are visible to the east side of the engine house, together with possibly the rectangular plinth of the chimney at the north-east corner and a further building (12040), possibly stores, against its eastern wall. The well-preserved earthworks of a reservoir which would have provided water for the boilers lie to the north-west (12042). The source of water for the reservoir is unknown, but may have been the well shown on the Ordnance Survey 2nd edition map of 1900 which seems to correspond with the area of collapse (12047) about 20 metres to the south of the reservoir. A platform abutting the north-west side of the shaft may be the site of a horse whim (12041). The spoil tip around the platform is composed of fuel ash from the boilers. An ore-bin (12048) built into the spoil tip can be seen on the northern side of the shaft.

A second stone-built Cornish engine house (12060), about 100 metres to the south-east, was used to pump the main shaft (see Fig 93), its northern wall still surviving to a height of up to 4 metres. The pumping arrangement was sited on the north side and power was transferred via flat-rods, the track-bed for which (12040) is still visible close to the shaft. The boiler house (12066) adjoined the southern side of the engine house, with the plinth for the chimney possibly at the north-west corner. The earthworks of a reservoir which provided water for the boilers lie about 30 metres to the west (12063). It appears to have been fed by two leats, one from the south-east and one from the north which may have been culverted beneath spoil tips and linked to the upper reservoir (12042) associated with the winding engine house. A stone quarry on the southern boundary of the mine (12057, see Fig 91) probably supplied materials for the construction of the engine houses and other ancillary buildings.

To the east of the pumping engine house is a whim circle (12061) about 10 metres in diameter. The undated mine section mentioned above shows a shaft immediately to the east of the engine house but there is no evidence of this, and it is possible that both the whim and the engine house were used for winding the capped shaft (12062) which lies further to the south-east.

Large spreads of waste cover much of the area surrounding the two engine houses. The reworking of the spoil tips during the 1920s and 1930s, together with more recent agricultural disturbance, appear to have largely removed any evidence for structures associated with ore processing. The waste indicates jigging, but there is no evidence that buddles were used for ore separation.

Other structures associated with the mine are poorly preserved. The grassed-over remains of a three-roomed building, possibly the mine office (12081), lie to the north of the lower reservoir. The main ancillary buildings, surviving as earthworks and foundations, form a complex to the north of the main access track, enclosed by a boundary wall. Additional enclosure walls to the north may represent gardens. The buildings included a row of miners' cottages (12075) formerly known as Belgrave Cottages, about 36 by 5 metres across, with an outbuilding near the north-west corner. Two buildings (12075–6), each about 13 by 8 metres across, lay along the track, on opposite corners of the enclosure. The form of the foundations and the collapsed rubble of a possible chimney suggest that the eastern building may have been a smithy. The buildings are shown on the Ordnance Survey 1st edition map of 1874, and appear to have been substantially unaltered since that date. The cottages were still occupied in 1907, after the closure of the mine, and were the subject of extended legal dispute concerning ownership, as indicated by documents in the Grosvenor Estate papers.

Eisteddfod, Minera, Wrexham (Figs 95–114, 136)

The Eisteddfod mining landscape (SJ250525) occupies an extensive area of over 20 hectares of moorland at the northern end of Esclusham Mountain, at a height of about 350 metres. The various mines within this landscape occupy the Carboniferous limestone plateau close to the village of Gwynfryn, 2 kilometres west of Minera. The limestone, which outcrops in various places, is crossed by several major mineral veins aligned north-west to south-east (Fig 95). Mineralisation is mainly galena, with some silver and sphalerite ores. The landscape forms the western end of a continuous series of mineral workings extending for between two and four kilometres to the east and south-east, including the well-known mines at Minera, in the

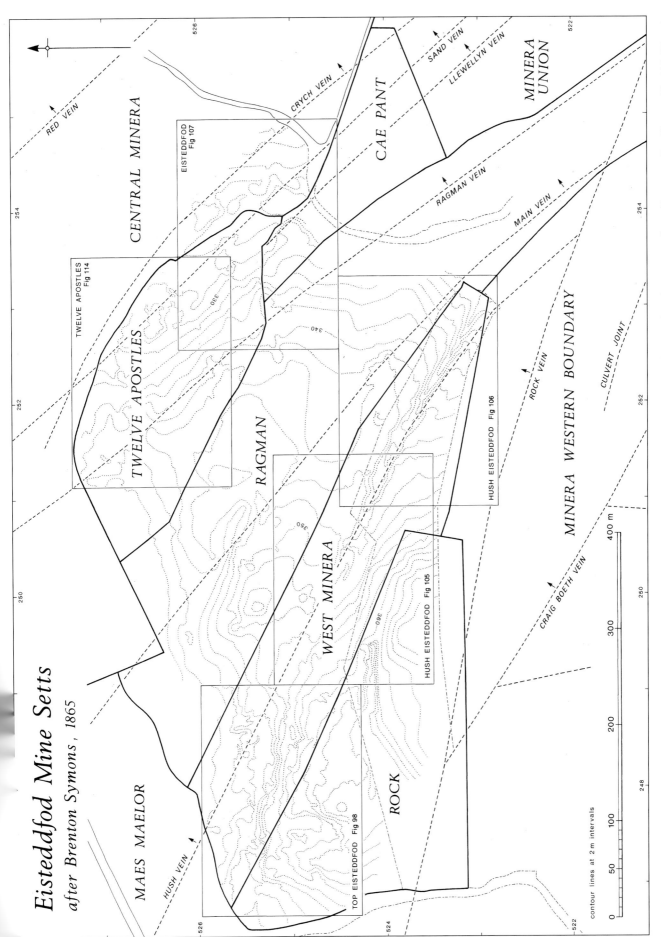

Figure 95 The names of mines and mineral veins in the Eisteddfod area shown on Brenton Symonds's map of 1865, illustrated at the same scale as Figure 97. See Figures 98, 105–07 and 114 for detailed plans of the inset areas

Figure 96 Aerial view of Top Eisteddfod and the Hush seen from the south, with part of the northern edge of the Minera limestone quarry in the lower left-hand corner. (*CPAT 90-MB-287*)

more heavily populated, lower-lying areas between Bwlchgwyn and New Brighton.

The landscape, named after the place-name adopted by one of the principal 19th-century mines towards the south-east of the area, contains what is perhaps the last remaining area of intensive lead mining in north-east Wales to remain relatively undisturbed by later development. Although the expansion of the Minera limestone quarry has led to the loss of the southern part of the area, the remainder is a well-preserved relict landscape bearing the scars of centuries of mineral extraction from at least the medieval period to the end of the 19th century, when the introduction of new technology permitted deeper and larger-scale operations to be undertaken below ground.

The workings described here span a period of nearly 500 years, from at least the 14th century up to the late 19th century. Since there is only a loose correspondence with the named mining setts which are known to have existed in the mid-19th century the landscape has been subdivided into a number of areas for descriptive purposes – Top Eisteddfod, Hush Eisteddfod, Ragman, Eisteddfod mine, and Twelve Apostles, shown at a smaller scale in Figure 95 and in greater detail in Figures 98, 105, 106, 107 and 114. The workings in the Ragman sett are for the most part only shown at the smaller scale although some of the elements which fall within it also appear on some of the larger-scale drawings. Each of these areas has its own distinctive character but they are all interlinked by trackways and leats which thread their way between the workings. The landscape of Top Eisteddfod is composed of a complex series of closely spaced shafts and several shallow limestone quarries (see Figs 96 and 100). To the south-east the workings merge with those of Hush Eisteddfod which is dominated by a conspicuous linear open-cut known as the Hush (see Fig 101). The only substantial surviving structures lie at the eastern end of the landscape within the Eisteddfod mine sett. Here, the remains of the engine house lie adjacent to a large shaft from which the spoil tip fans out in typical 'finger' spoil heaps (see Fig 108). There are several other shafts, some with whim circles, together with the dressing area, which includes a number of small structures, including an ore-bin. The tumbled remains of a row of cottages provide the only evidence for workers' accommodation within the general landscape, although surviving dwellings around the fringes, and also in Gwynfryn, presumably originated as miners' housing. Twelve Apostles (see Fig 114) is the only sett with clearly defined boundaries, represented by a substantial earthwork bank. Within this area the workings are concentrated along two veins running north-west to south-east, with the main workings along the Sand vein, comprising several large shafts and spoil tips, as well as the ruins of a number of small buildings and structures, some associated with a small dressing area. The workings of the adjacent Ragman sett to the west (Fig 97) are on a smaller scale and the main interest here lies in what may be an early dressing floor, together with a large, silted reservoir which was fed by a leat drawing water from the Aber Sychnant stream 3.5 kilometres to the south, close to Pool Park mine (see Fig 125).

It has been widely assumed that the earliest mining activity in the Minera district is to be found within the Eisteddfod mining landscape. Working is thought to have begun during the Roman period, though as yet there is no archaeological evidence to support this. The earliest documentary references date to the 14th century and provide evidence of a flourishing lead mining industry at Minera, probably undertaken on a seasonal basis by families which combined mining and farming as their means of livelihood (Pratt 1976; Williams 1994). By the later 17th century the miners were free from hearth tax and were granted a plot of land sufficient to build a house and curtilage, together with sufficient wood for repairs to their houses and their pits. Some of the mineral veins at Eisteddfod lay close to the surface, and although evidence for medieval workings has probably been largely been obscured by later mining it seem likely that these early workings were open-cuts, worked down from an

exposed outcrop. The area known as Eisteddfod Hush may have been one of the earliest workings, where the Hush vein may have been worked from the surface, resulting in the deep linear scar which forms a prominant feature in the present landscape. The intensive surface workings around Top Eisteddfod also suggests early mining activity.

There is little evidence concerning the state of mining industry during the earlier post-medieval period, but it seems likely that it was confined to relatively shallow workings until at least the late 18th century. Detailed records of mining activity generally only survive from the mid-19th century onwards, and even some of these are ambiguous. It is consequently difficult to interpret due to complex changes of ownership and leasing and the scarcity of plans showing the mining setts being worked by individual mining companies at any one time.

The clearest picture is provided by two maps, the first drawn by Isaac Shone in 1863 and the second in 1865 by Brenton Symonds, which show the names and boundaries of the mining setts being worked in the 1860s (see Fig 95). Symonds's map is of particular help since it also shows some of the shafts, as well as identifying the main veins. It shows that in the 1860s the landscapes described in this volume were largely divided between five mining companies – Rock, West Minera, Ragman, Cae Pant and Twelve Apostles. In 1875, some of these companies were amalgamated with Central Minera, working the area to the north-east, to form the Consolidated Minera Lead Mining Company in 1875, under a 21-year lease from the Duke of Westminster. This venture only lasted until 1886, however, when mining in the area ceased.

It seems likely that the ores raised from Eisteddfod were transported to Deeside to one of several smelteries that developed there from the 1750s onwards. By the end of the 18th century, however, a local smeltery had been established at Brymbo, 4 kilometres to the east, by John Wilkinson who had taken over the Minera mine in 1783 (Lewis 1967, 138–40).

Limestone quarrying for building stone and for the production of lime was also being actively undertaken in the area from the 17th century onwards, although the earliest specific reference to quarrying in the area covered by this survey is contained in a lease granted to in 1819 James Kyrke and John Burton for quarrying limestone and building kilns on Eisteddfod (Ellis 1995, 29–31). The quarries were operating between the 1830s and the 1850s as the Steddfod Lime Company, managed by Kyrke. The precise location of

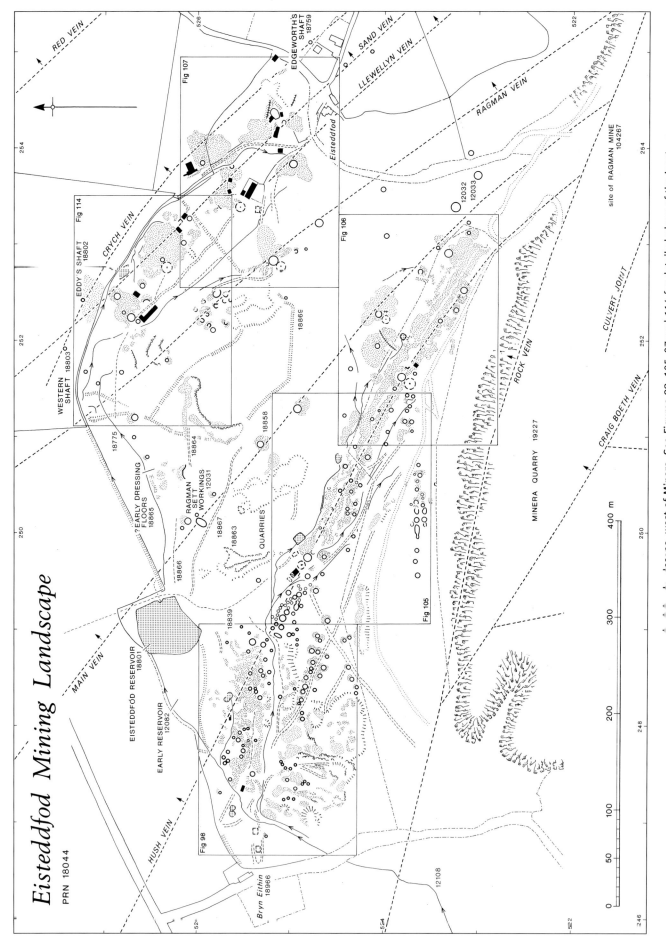

Eisteddfod Mining Landscape

PRN 18044

RED VEIN

Fig 107

EDGEWORTH'S SHAFT 18759

SAND VEIN

LLEWELLYN VEIN

RAGMAN VEIN

Eisteddfod

Fig 114

CRYCH VEIN

EDDY'S SHAFT 18802

Fig 106

site of RAGMAN MINE 104267

12032
12033

WESTERN SHAFT 18803

18866

18775

18858

EARLY DRESSING FLOORS 18865

18864

RAGMAN SETT WORKINGS 12031

ROCK VEIN

CULVERT JOINT

CRAIG BOETH VEIN

18867

18863

QUARRIES

18866

MINERA QUARRY 19227

MAIN VEIN

18839

EISTEDDFÖD RESERVOIR 18801

Fig 105

EARLY RESERVOIR 12082

HUSH VEIN

Fig 98

12108

Bryn Eithin 18966

400 m

300

250

200

100

50

0

... west of Minera. See Figures 98, 105–07 and 114 for detailed plans of the inset areas

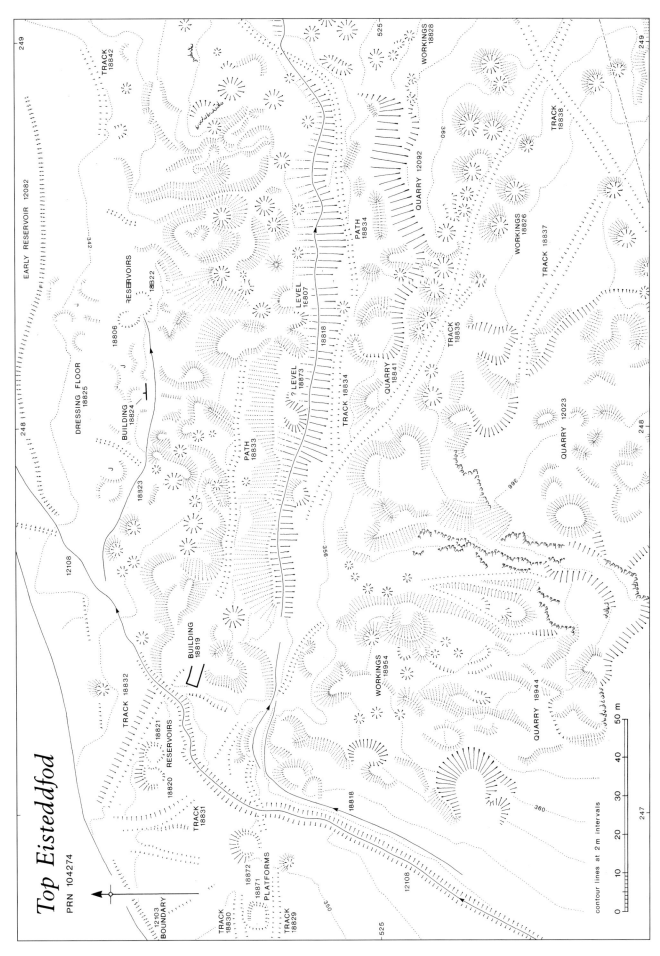

Figure 98 Eisteddfod mines: detailed plan of the workings at Top Eisteddfod, towards the western side of the Eisteddfod mining landscape (see location in Fig 97)

the company's quarries is unknown but it was possibly within the area of the later Minera limestone quarry, to the south, seen in Figure 96.

The earliest stone quarries are probably represented by the numerous shallow workings of the rock outcrops scattered throughout the survey area; these can be difficult to distinguish from shallow lead workings and are difficult to date from field evidence alone. One of few reliable clues is provided by the presence of drill marks, visible in the larger quarry at Top Eisteddfod (18944), which have to postdate the invention of the rock drill in the 1870s.

Top Eisteddfod (Figs 98, 101)

The area shown as Top Eisteddfod in Figure 98 falls within the mining setts of Rock and West Minera shown on Isaac Shone's map of 1863 and Symonds's map of 1865 (see Fig 95), the boundary between the two lying approximately along the line of a track running from south-east to north-west (18835).

No records relating to Rock mine appear to have survived and no mining returns were entered. The recent survey shows that the area has had a long history of mining, and includes a dense concentration of small trials and shallow workings. Some of these predate the large stone quarry (18944, Fig 98) which together with an area of earlier quarrying to the south-east (12023) occupied much of the area, and may date to the medieval period. Most of the workings produced relatively little development waste, indicating that they were fairly shallow, and this, together with the absence of other evidence of large-scale workings characteristic of the mid-19th century onwards, suggests that the remains are of relatively early date. It is possible that the area was leased under the name of the Rock sett when Symonds's map was drawn up but that no workings were actually undertaken during this period.

There are several areas of small-scale quarrying scattered across the area, some of which may represent early opencast workings in places where mineral veins were exposed at the surface. An open level (18807, Fig 98) is to be seen cutting southwards into the hillside towards the centre of the complex, next to a possible collapsed level (18873).

There is evidence of a dressing floor (18825) on the flat ground at the northern end of the area, where several low mounds of jig waste and the foundations of a building (18824) indicate a processing site. Two small reservoirs next to it (18806, 18822), fed by a leat from the west, seem likely to have been associated with ore dressing. A further pair of reservoirs (18820–1), whose purpose is less certain, can be seen at the western end of the site.

Hush Eisteddfod (Figs 99–106)

Much of the area in the north-east corner of Figure 98, and the areas shown in Figures 105 and 106 fell within the West Minera mine sett shown on the maps of Shone and Symonds as a linear strip running north-west to south-east, bounded by Rock and Minera Western Boundary to the south and Ragman to the north. Its eastern boundary appears to have coincided with a present boundary at the east end of the linear quarry known as the Hush, which also defined the limit of the survey. Mining returns for lead were entered for the years 1881 and 1882, but prior to this returns for both lead and silver were entered for the Hush Eisteddfod Lead Mining Company, during the period 1876–77. The mine was amalgamated with the Consolidated Minera Lead Mining Company in 1884, before ceasing to operate in 1886 (Burt *et al* 1992, 149).

One of the most interesting and significant feature of this landscape is the long channel known as the Hush, about 15–20 metres wide and about 350 metres long (see Figs 105–06). The channel has been cut into the surface along the line of the Hush vein and the most dominant landscape feature visible from the air (Figs 99 and 104). Its name is clearly derived from the term 'hushing', a technique employing the use of water power to flush away the overburden in order to expose underlying mineral veins. Small-scale hushing may possibly have been employed at an early stage of prospecting or exploitation, but the workings visible today are clearly the result of successive and extensive opencast workings which were cut down into the limestone along the line of the vein. On the floor of the Hush is a series of linear spoil tips which have resulted from the successive periods of working along the exposed limestone, which has been gradually cut back

Figure 99 (*right*)
Aerial view of Top Eisteddfod and the western end of Hush Eisteddfod, from the south-east, showing part of the workings illustrated in Figures 98 and 105.
(*CPAT 90-MB-291*)

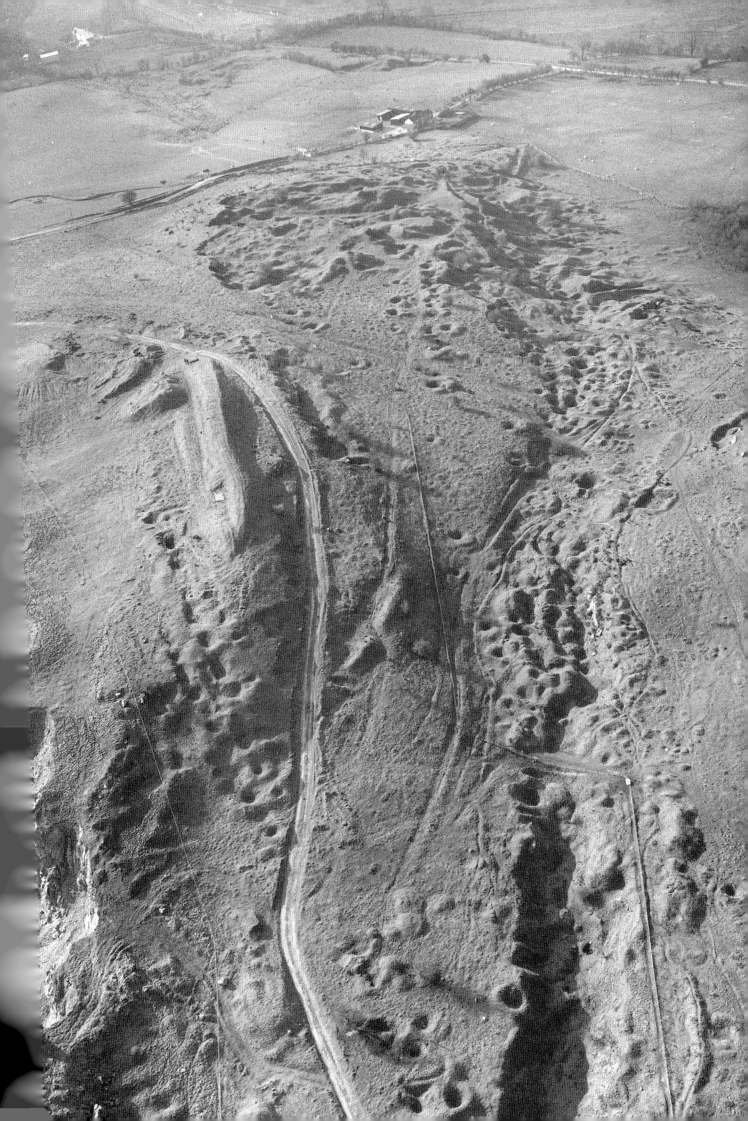

Figure 100 Eisteddfod mines: mounds of spoil and probable dressing waste along the north side of the Eisteddfod Hush. The waste is thought to derive largely from shallow surface workings of the medieval and early post-medieval periods. (*CPAT 351–31*)

Figure 101 Eisteddfod mines: part of the quarried limestone face on the northern side of the Eisteddfod Hush towards its western end. The level or adit next to the figure (18808, see Fig 105) was probably dug to meet a mineral vein. (*CPAT 357–01*)

Figure 102 Eisteddfod mines: ore-bin (18813, see Fig 105) near the engine house at the western end of the Hush, forming part of the later and deeper workings along the Hush vein, in this instance probably during the mid to late 19th century. Ore extracted from a shaft (18816), by the shrub in the background, would have been dropped into the top of the bin after being lifted from below ground and temporarily stored there before processing. The ore would then have been raked through an arch the front of the bin and sorted in the area in the foreground. The absence of mounds of processing waste in the area suggests that the sorted ore was then taken elsewhere for further processing. (*CPAT 348–07*)

Figure 103 Eisteddfod mines: reservoir (18817, shown on plan in Fig 105) on the northern edge of the Hush, towards its western end. It was probably used to store water for the boilers on the engine house (18811) about 20 metres to the west. It was fed by a leat (running diagonally across the foreground) dug along the north side of the Hush to draw water from the Aber Sychnant stream. (*CPAT 348–13*)

Figure 104 Aerial view showing a shaft and whim circle (18946, 18810, see Fig 106) on the north side of the Hush, visible towards the centre foreground. The area in which the shaft lies is shown on Brenton Symonds's map of 1865 as falling within the Ragman mine sett, and probably represents mid to late 19th-century workings. The boundary with the West Minera mine, which included the Hush, lay just beyond. (*CPAT 90-MB-290*)

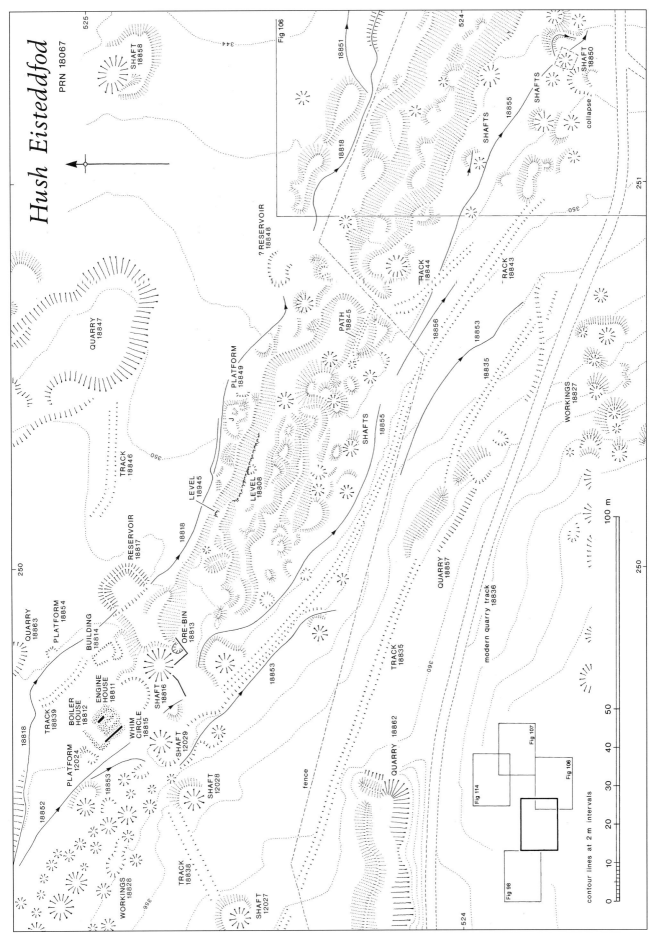

Figure 105 Eisteddfod mines: detailed plan of the western end of Hush Eisteddfod, in the southern part of the Eisteddfoc mining landscape (for location see Fig 97).

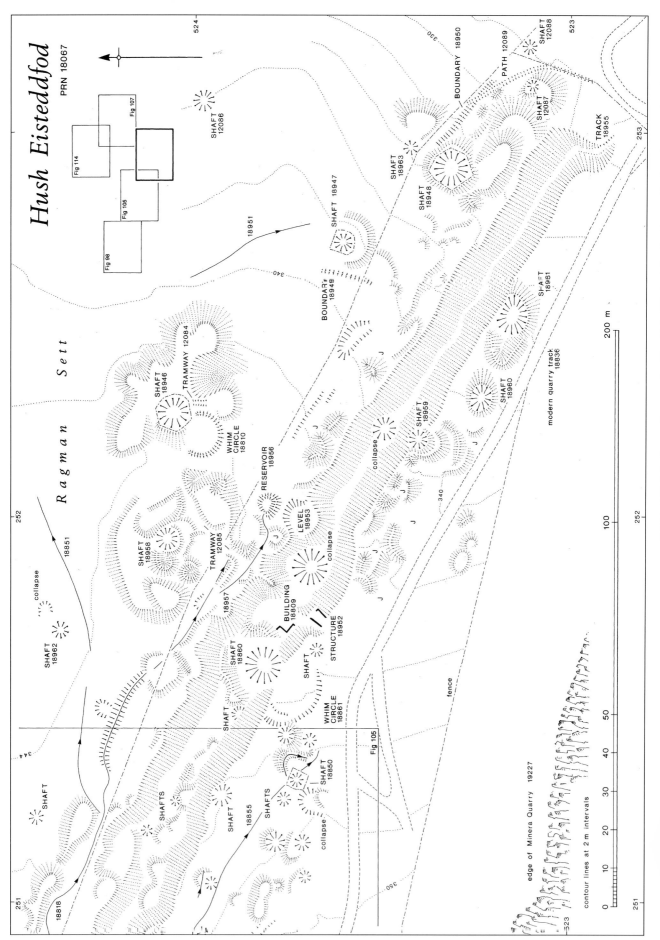

Hush Eisteddfod

PRN 18067

Fig 114
Fig 107
Fig 105
Fig 98

Ragman Sett

contour lines at 2 m intervals

edge of Minera Quarry 19227

...located in the southern part of the Eisteddfod mining landscape (for location see Fig 97).

to widen the open-cut (Fig 100). A blocked level is visible at the base of the quarried limestone face towards the northern end (Fig 101), with a further collapsed level just to the west, about halfway up the slope.

There are numerous shafts and trials both along the edges of the Hush and within it. These mostly appear to have been fairly shallow, but there are several later and much larger shafts which are likely to represent the workings of the Hush Eisteddfod and West Minera companies during the later 19th century. The Hush itself is not closely dated but may have been created by a series of successive workings along a particularly lucrative vein from the medieval period up to the early 19th century.

The maps of the 1860s by Shone and Symonds suggest that the boundary between West Minera and the Ragman sett to the north lay beyond but roughly parallel with the northern side of the Hush. A large whim shaft (18946) which lies about 50 metres to the north of the Hush (see Fig 106 and the aerial photograph in Fig 104) is shown by Symonds's map as falling within the Ragman sett, whilst the large shaft about 100 metres to the south-east (18948), fell within the West Minera sett. A low boundary bank alongside this latter shaft (18950) may originally have marked the boundary between the two setts.

One of the major 19th-century shafts in this area lies at the western end of the Hush (18816, Fig 105) and is associated with a well-preserved stone-built ore-bin on the south-east side (Fig 102) and a building platform to the north (18814). Cages in the shaft were evidently initially raised and lowered by a horse whim (18815). This was superseded by a winding steam engine housed in an engine house (18811, about 7 by 5 metres across), with an adjoining boiler house (18812, about 8 by 4 metres across) whose foundations are still visible just to the north-west. A substantial reservoir to the east (Fig 103) probably stored water for the boilers. The reservoir was fed by a leat which drew water from a source to the west of Eisteddfod, and flowed eastwards through Top Eisteddfod. A leat leading from the reservoir carried water along the northern edge of the Hush, at one point running along a raised embankment, with one or two small reservoirs and other subsidiary leats along its course. Adjacent tips of jig waste and several platforms suggest that the water was also used for jigging. The courses of other three leats can be traced along the southern side of the Hush which were earlier than the main leat associated with the engine house.

Although the ultimate destination of the leats is uncertain, it seems likely that they supplied water for dressing ore at the main Ragman Mine site to the south-east, now lost to the modern quarry.

A second substantial shaft lies on the floor of the Hush about half way along its length (18860, Fig 106). The shaft was associated with a whim circle (18861) and the foundations of two stone structures – a building on the floor of the Hush (18809) and another structure (18952) built on its southern side. The latter appears to have been quite substantial and may represent the means by which the ore produced by the shaft was hauled up to the southern edge of the Hush.

Ragman (Figs 95, 97, 104, 106)

Symonds's map of 1865 (see Fig 95) places the Ragman mine sett towards the centre of the Eisteddfod landscape – bounded by West Minera (Top Eisteddfod and Hush Eisteddfod) to the south and the Twelve Apostles to the north – working parts of the Ragman and the Main veins. Most of the workings belonging to this set are only shown in this volume on the smaller-scale drawing in Figure 97, though a number of the structures belonging to it appear on some of the larger-scale drawings.

The Ragman Mining Company operated from 1862–70, but only entered returns for the period 1865–67 (Burt *et al* 1992, 146). The 1st edition Ordnance Survey map of 1872 shows at least two engine houses and several other buildings towards the south-east end of the sett, in an area since lost to the Minera limestone quarry. The surviving remains include one of the larger shafts on the north side of the Hush, associated with a horse whim circle (18946, 18810, see Figs 104 and 106).

The large reservoir at the north-west end of the set (18801, Fig 97), now largely silted up, was fed by a leat which drew water from the Aber Sychnant stream, 3.5 kilometres to the south. It is first shown on the Ordnance Survey 1st edition map of 1872, and has a well-preserved sluice which fed a further substantial leat following the northern boundary of Twelve Apostles and flowed through the main Eisteddfod area before continuing south-east towards the Ragman dressing-floor area. Evidence for an earlier and larger reservoir (12082) is represented by a low earthwork bank, which would have formed the southern edge of the reservoir (see Fig 97 and the top of Fig 98). This reservoir is shown on an undated mine plan and on a plan of Bwlch Gwyn mine of 1858, where it is called

Steddfod Pool. It is just possible to trace a leat (18866) flowing eastwards into the Twelve Apostles sett, which may be associated with this earlier reservoir.

Eisteddfod mine (Figs 107–11)

The north-east corner of Eisteddfod shown in Figures 107 and 114 was worked by a succession of short-lived companies during the 19th century and it is consequently difficult to piece together its history. The earliest map of the area, dated 1858, shows it to be part of the land leased by the Bwlch Gwyn mine, which made returns for lead and silver between 1850 and 1858 (Burt et al 1992, 11). A second company known as Eisteddfod made returns for lead and silver in 1859 and appears to have continued at least until 1865 (Burt et al 1992, 132–3). The maps of Shone (1863) and Symonds (1865) suggest that by that time the area was split between Twelve Apostles and Central Minera. The latter made returns for 1859–67 and continued in operation until 1870 (Burt et al 1992, 147). Two undated mine plans for this area were deposited under the name of Minera Union, although they may relate to workings by early companies, suggesting that ultimately the whole area came under the control of Minera Union. A further complication is the presence of the Steddfod Company between 1855 and 1861, which has been attributed the same location as Eisteddfod (Burt et al 1992, 132–3, 155).

The two undated mine plans mentioned above suggest that the earliest workings were associated with three shafts which can still be identified on the ground. One is shown within a walled shaft enclosure (18737, see Figs 107 and 111) which also appears on the Symonds map of 1865, although the shaft itself has now been filled in. The enclosure is surrounded by substantial tips of development waste and in one place the wall revets a spoil tip standing to a height of 1.6 metres. The south-west side of the enclosure has been roughly rebuilt, possibly as an animal pound. The foundations of two buildings (18738–9) butt against the sides of the enclosure and on the northern side is a raised embankment which has the appearance of a tramway. An ore-bin (18740) is built into the spoil heap to the south-west of the enclosure, in line with traces of a tramway (18755) which is shown running towards Edgeworth's Shaft, about 90m to the east, on one of the undated mine plans (see Fig 97 for the location of this shaft).

The foundations of a number of other structures are visible in the area to the west of the shaft enclosure, including a possibly open-fronted two-roomed

building (18741) built into the spoil tip, and three other building platforms (18742, 18764–5) slightly further to the west. The presence of the building platforms near the ore-bin suggest that the area between may have been used as a dressing floor (18789), but there are no obvious tips of processing waste to confirm this interpretation.

A second shaft is shown on the undated mine plan as a whim shaft surrounded by extensive spoil tips, and referred to by Symonds as Engine Shaft, lying on the Crych vein in the field to the north-west (18736). The horse whim is no longer visible on the ground and was evidently replaced by the winding engine house (18735) whose remains can be seen to the north-west of the shaft. Dressed masonry, still standing to over 1.6 metres in places, defines the engine bed and flywheel pit and there is a wheelpit for a winding drum on the north-east, aligned upon the shaft (Figs 109 and 110). The boiler house lay on the south-west side but survives only as a platform. The engine house, which possibly belonged to the Central Minera Company, is shown on the Ordnance Survey 1st edition map of 1872. It appears to have been out of use by 1899 when the 2nd edition map was published, and by then the existing building constructed against the wheelpit is shown. This is built of reused masonry and is now used as an animal shelter.

An arc of stone walling (18737) to the south of the Engine Shaft appears to represent a third shaft, surrounded by a wall (Fig 111). A fourth shaft, again infilled, was probably sited near the remains of a small stone building (18746) immediately to the north of the Eisteddfod Cottages, and associated with a well-preserved horse whim circle (18748) and a large spoil tip of development waste. Both of these shafts are shown by Symonds to fall within the Twelve Apostles sett, but are otherwise undated and cannot be securely attributed to the workings of any particular company.

Eisteddfod Cottages (18745) now lie in ruins, though substantial sections of stone walling still survive. There are traces of outbuildings against each end and a separate range, possibly latrines, at the north-west corner of a yard area enclosed by a stone wall. An enclosure to the south, between the cottages and a track, was probably a garden. The cottages probably represent miners' accommodation, and although their date of construction is unknown they appear on a plan of Bwlch Gwyn mine dated 1858.

The track (18761) which passes to the south of the cottages once formed the boundary between Twelve Apostles to the north and Ragman and Cae Pant or

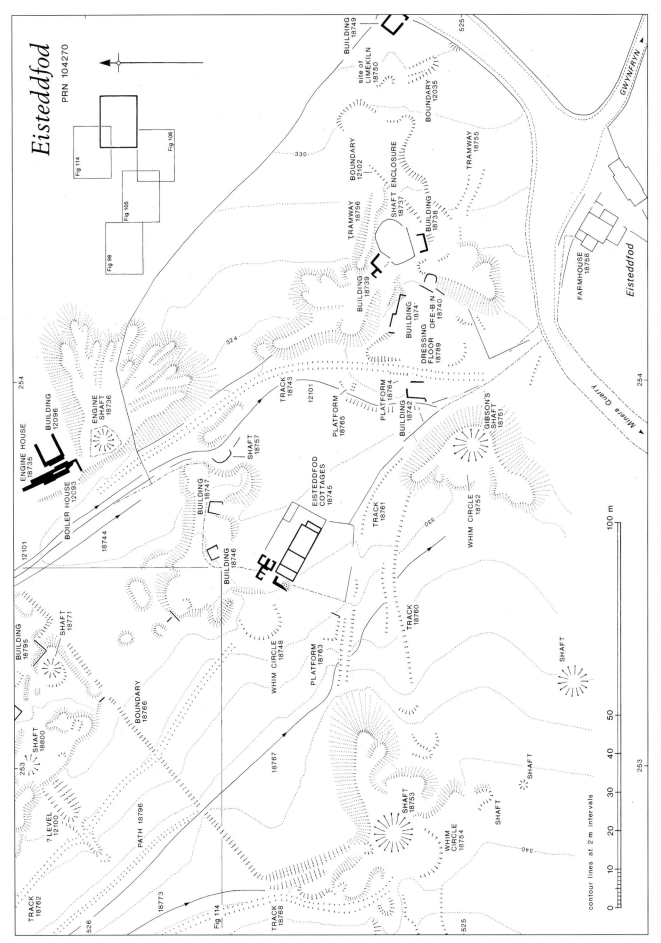

Figure 107 Eisteddfod mines: detailed plan of Eisteddfod, at the eastern end of the Eisteddfod mining landscape (for location see Fig 97).

Figure 108 Aerial view of the mining landscape west of Gwynfryn (see Fig 107), seen from the north-east, with the now derelict Eisteddfod farmhouse (18758) towards the top left-hand corner and waste heaps belonging to the Twelve Apostles dressing floor to the lower right. Gibson's Shaft (18751) lies near the track towards the left and the remains of the later 19th-century winding engine house (18735) belonging to Central Minera are visible in the foreground, next to the large heaps of development waste from the shaft. The curving leat visible towards the centre of the photograph took water from Aber Sychnant stream, possibly for supplying the boilers of the engine house and for driving water-powered machinery on the dressing floor to the left of Gibson's Shaft. (*CPAT 90-MB-289*)

Figure 109 Remains of the later 19th-century engine house at Central Minera (18735, see Fig 107), viewed from the south-east. The figure is standing on the engine bed for the original horizontal engine, to the left of the wheelpit. The original boiler house would have lain to the left, with a chimney beyond. The building to the right of the wheelpit has been adapted as an animal shelter. The engine would have raised and lowered cages carrying ore from the shaft (18736) in the foreground. (*CPAT 349–02*)

Figure 110
Wheelpit of of the later 19th-century engine house at Central Minera (18735, see Fig 107), viewed from the north-west. The stonework once supported the wheel which drove the winding-drum, raising and lowering cables in the shaft beyond.
(*CPAT 349–05*)

Figure 111
Stone-walled shaft enclosure (18737, see Fig 107) viewed from the west. The enclosure once surrounded one of the main shafts, now filled in, indicated by the surrounding heaps of development waste. The remains of an ore-bin and the main ore dressing floor lie in the foreground.
(*CPAT 348–25*)

Minera Union to the south. Two substantial whim shafts lie just to the south of the boundary. The one to the west (18753) appears to have lain on the edge of the Ragman sett in 1865, while the eastern one (18751), shown as Gibson's Shaft on one of the undated mine plans, fell within the Cae Pant sett according to Symonds. Further workings continue to the south of the two shafts, beyond the area surveyed, towards the entrance to Minera limestone quarry, on the eastern slopes of Eisteddfod. Cae Pant mine appears to have operated between 1865 and 1870, but only made returns for 1867–68 (Burt *et al* 1992, 128). Shone's map of 1863 does not show Cae Pant and includes this area under Minera Union. Although the *Mining Journal* of 1861 also refers to a 'Gibson's Mine' in the area it is possible that this is a mis-spelling of the name of Charles Gibbons, the owner of both Minera Union and Minera Boundary mines in the period between 1875 and 1889.

Twelve Apostles (Figs 112–14)

The Twelve Apostles mine sett, shown in Figure 114, can be more clearly defined on the ground than any of the other mineral workings at Eisteddfod, its boundary with the neighbouring Ragman sett to the south and the succession of companies working the area to the east being marked by a substantial boundary bank (18766). The area was worked for lead and silver by the South Minera Company between 1863–65, and by the Twelve Apostles Company between 1866–70, the latter taking its name from a group of twelve mine adventurers. It was finally worked by John Langford and Company in 1883–84 (Burt *et al* 1992, 156). Evidence from the plans of Shone in 1863 and Symonds in 1865 suggests that by the end the sett extended east of the boundary bank, as far as the leat (12101) flowing through Eisteddfod, to include Eisteddfod Cottages (see Fig 107).

There is a complex of possible early workings

Figure 112 The remains of a building (18788, see Fig 114) which may have included the mine office at Twelve Apostles.
(*CPAT 349–20*)

Figure 113 Shallow workings or open-cuts (18790, see Fig 114) in an area of possible early exploitation on the south-west side of the Twelve Apostles mine area. (*CPAT 349–26*)

towards the south-east corner of the sett, including open-cuts, shallow trials and spoil tips and a number of horseshoe-shaped earthworks which resemble ore-bins (18790, Fig 113). This suggests that the area was first worked for ore before the beginning of the 19th century, and possibly well before that date.

The main 19th-century workings at Twelve Apostles appear to have centred on two shafts – a large whim shaft, named by Symonds as Apostles' Shaft (18769), to the south of an area of grassed spoil tips, and a second shaft (18797) about 80 metres to the north-east, close to a range of buildings. An undated mine plan depicts both shafts, and also indicates a ladder pit (12019) which would have provided access as well as a trial (18799) midway between the two shafts. Workings visible on the ground include a number of other substantial shafts, earlier trials, and a possible collapsed level (12100) close to the eastern boundary of the sett.

There are traces of three sets of buildings at Twelve Apostles, probably representing administrative and processing activities. A range of buildings towards the centre of the sett (18788), consisting of four or five rooms whose dry-stone walls still stand to a height of about 1.3 metres, probably included the mine office (Fig 112). A three-roomed, open-ended building (18789), lies against a substantial spoil tip to the north-east. Two buildings towards the south-east corner of the sett, both shown on the 1st edition Ordnance Survey map of 1872 and on an undated mine plan, were possibly associated with ore processing. One appears to have been an L-shaped building (18793) partly cut into a spoil tip and partly set a slight platform. Little of the structure of the second building survives (18795), built against the boundary bank and a shaft mound.

The grassed-over spoil tips in this area consist mainly of jig tailings, suggesting a prolonged period of ore processing. No jig platforms are visible, however, and the only structures associated with the ore dressing area are the two buildings described above. Several

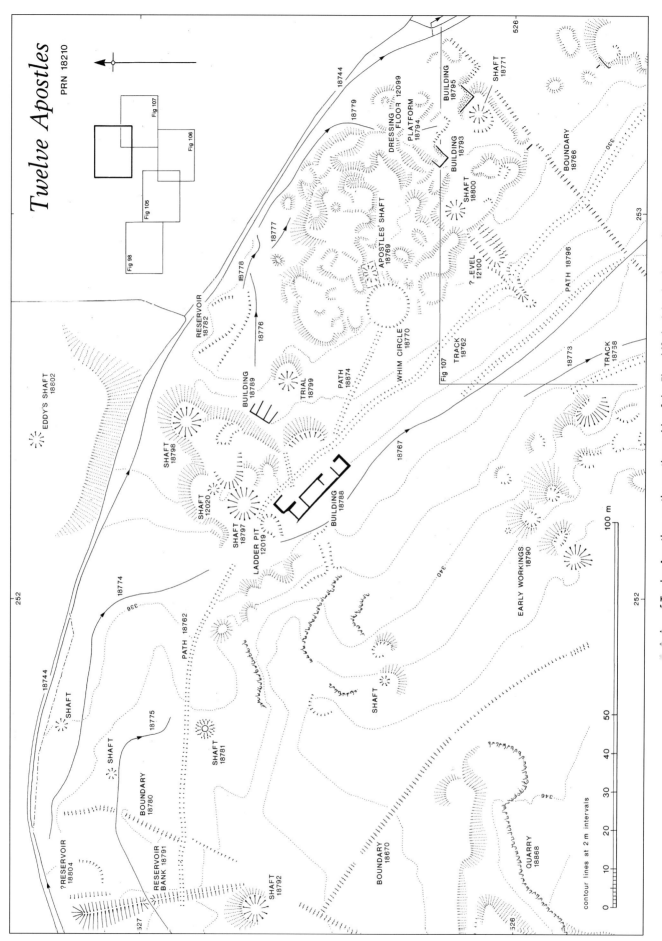

Twelve Apostles

PRN 18210

Twelve Apostles, on the northern side of the Eisteddfod mining landscape (for location see Fig 97).

short sections of leat and a silted-up reservoir (18782) can be traced along the northern edge of the tips. These presumably supplied water for ore processing and appear to have been associated with a substantial reservoir bank beyond the western boundary of the sett (18791). The bank, which may itself overlie an earlier reservoir (18804), seems to be most clearly associated with a leat (18774) which flowed past the mine office buildings and possibly served the main Ragman dressing floors. The bank was cut by a second leat (18775) which appears to have originated at the large reservoir (18801) at the northern end of the Ragman sett (see Fig 97).

Lower Park, Minera, Wrexham (Figs 115–21)

Lower Park (SJ25155138) (Fig 115) lies on the eastern edge of Esclusham Mountain, about 2 kilometres to the west of the mining village of Minera and a kilometre or so to the south of the Eisteddfod mines. Both lead and silver ores were obtained from numerous shafts within the mine sett, which exploited the main Park vein and two subsidiary veins to the south within the Carboniferous limestone (Smith 1921, 112).

The mine sett covers an area of about 10 hectares now lying within an area of improved pasture (see Figs 116 and 119) at about 370 metres above sea level. It overlooks the narrow valley of the Aber Sychnant stream to the west and the extensive disused workings of Minera quarry to the north, and forms part of an extensive though dispersed mining landscape extending to three or four kilometres southwards across the hills to the Pool Park, Cefn y Gist and Eglwyseg metal mines.

Lower Park mine is of particular interest in being one of the few early 19th-century mines in north-east Wales that saw little subsequent working or clearance. It therefore still retains many of its original features, including dressing floors, ore-bins and beehive capped shafts, which though perhaps unremarkable in themselves have rarely survived elsewhere within the region. The mine overlies an earlier agricultural landscape of late medieval and early post-medieval date consisting of field boundaries and tracks, and has been superimposed by a reorganised landscape of large stone-walled enclosures associated with the later 19th-century Park Farm (see Fig 116).

The history of Lower Park mine is inextricably linked with that of Pool Park which lies about a kilometre to the south. The earliest workings in the two setts were at Lower Park (Earp 1958, 67) near Park Farm (see Fig 115). Production figures given in the *Mining Journal* suggest that the most profitable years were between 1821 and 1824. Records in the Grosvenor Estate papers show that the land at that time was leased to John Burton and Robert Morgan, who by 1821 had sunk a shaft to depth of 100 yards. The following year, a 21-year lease was granted to James Kyrke, John Burton and others. The lease original includes a plan showing two shafts at Lower Park. The relatively shallow depth of limestone above the underlying Ordovician shales suggests that the mineral veins would have been almost completely worked out by the time the mine closed in 1863 (Earp 1958, 67). It was subsequently owned by Park Mines from 1863–65 and by the Lower Park Company between 1866–71 (Burt *et al* 1992, 152). The underground workings were connected to those of Park mine, and the main whim shaft at Lower Park may well have remained in use.

The earliest workings at Lower Park appear to be represented by a run of shallow trial pits (18900) towards the south-west corner of the sett (see Fig 115), close to a substantial boundary bank (18901) which may have marked the boundary of the mining sett. Similar trials are also to be seen in an area of outcropping limestone pavement to the north-west (18918), just to the east of Park Farm.

Many substantial shafts are to be seen within the mine sett, some of which are associated with whim circles. A number of the shafts have stone collars, a type which is otherwise unknown in the region. Several of the shafts have beehive-shaped dry-stone cappings, built after they had been abandoned. Another interesting feature of six of the shafts is the existence of ore-bins built into the tip of development waste surrounding the shafts. The bins are generally poorly preserved, although several still show evidence of their stone construction (Fig 117).

The largest shaft in the area of the sett (18890, see Fig 121) lies at the south-east corner of a stone-walled enclosure (18941) (Fig 118) which surrounds the dressing floors and ancillary buildings. The shaft, associated with a well-preserved whim circle on the south side and large spoil tips of development waste to the west (Fig 119), seems likely to have continued in use

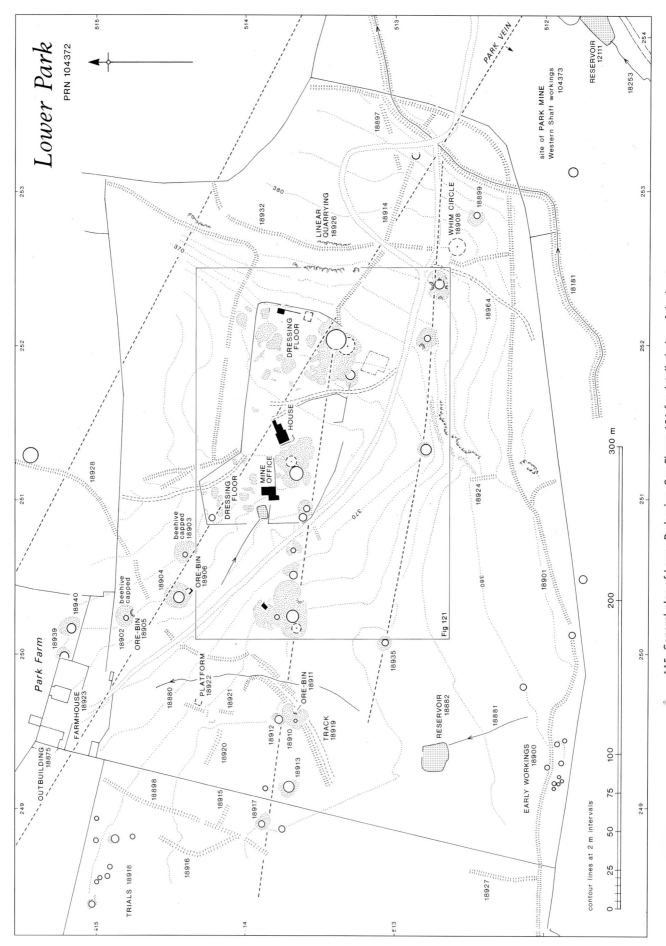

Lower Park

PRN 104372

site of PARK MINE
Western Shaft workings
104373

RESERVOIR
12111

PARK VEIN

WHIM CIRCLE
18908

LINEAR
QUARRYING
18926

DRESSING
FLOOR

HOUSE

DRESSING
FLOOR

MINE
OFFICE

beehive
capped
18903

ORE-BIN
18906

beehive
capped
18902

ORE-BIN
18905

Park Farm

FARMHOUSE
18923

OUTBUILDING
18875

TRIALS 18918

PLATFORM
18922

ORE-BIN
18911

TRACK
18919

RESERVOIR
18882

EARLY WORKINGS
18900

Fig 121

contour lines at 2 m intervals

300 m

115 General plan of Lower Park mine. See Figure 121 for detailed plan of the inset area.

Figure 116 Aerial view of Lower Park mine, seen from the north-east with the farmhouse of Park Farm towards the lower right-hand corner. The main shaft, mine office and dressing floor in the walled enclosure just below the track to the right, with other shafts strung out along the Park vein. Part of a relict field system is visible beyond the farmhouse, towards the right-hand side. One of the notable features of the mine is a number of 19th-century beehive-capped shafts (to the left of the track in the foreground). A mining lease granted to Adam Eyton, a lead smelter from Llanerch-y-mor and Edward Williams of Wrexham by the duke of Westminster in December 1882 stipulated that they should build a 'substantial stone wall around pits … when the pit goes out of use' and then 'fill up with earth and waste and cover with arch of stone'. The main period of working was between the 1820s and 1860s, before Hill Shaft and New Shaft were sunk further east along the vein on Esclusham in the 1860s and 1870s.
(*Crown Copyright: RCAHMW 935150–48*)

Figure 117 Lower Park mine: collapsed walling of one of the ore-bins (18886) on the side of a shaft (18895) towards the south-east corner of the workings, seen from the north-west (see location in Fig 121). The shaft mound is unusual in having three ore-bins on different sides. (*CPAT 357–10*)

Figure 118 Lower Park mine: foundations of a line of buildings (18883, see Fig 121) next to the dressing floor on the east side of the mine's central area, seen from the west. The buildings probably represent stores or shelters associated with the dressing floor. The remains of the wall of the enclosure (18941) surrounding the core area of the mine are visible just beyond the foundations of the buildings. (*CPAT 357–12*)

Figure 119 Lower Park mine viewed from the south-east, looking towards Llandegla. The large shaft (18890) and whim circle (18891) are visible in the middle distance with the mine agent's house (1005006) beyond, and Park Farm in the background.
(*CPAT 381–16*)

Figure 120 Lower Park mine: agent's house and garden of about the 1850s, with the remains of outbuildings to the left, seen from the north-west. An iron ladder, once used in the mine, leans against the outside wall of the house. (*CPAT 357–15*)

in conjunction with Park mine after the general closure of Lower Park in 1863.

Ore processing was evidently confined to two distinct areas within the walled enclosure. An area to the east (18878) consists of spreads and low tips of jig waste; there are no jigging platforms or other structures visible within this area but it seems likely that the row of collapsed stone buildings (18883) towards the eastern side of the enclosure represents shelters or workshops associated with ore processing (see Fig 118). An earthwork platform further to the south (18892) appears to have the remains of an ore-bin built into its southern side, and may therefore have been more directly associated with the extraction of ore from the shaft. The western dressing area (18877) also has fairly extensive spreads and low tips of jig waste, but in this instance there are several areas of finer spoil, possibly representing buddle waste. A roughly circular platform has the appearance of a buddle (12022) and there may be others less distinctly visible within the area of the

dressing floor just to the north. Circular buddles are thought to have been introduced into north-east Wales from Cornwall by the 1840s (Palmer and Neaverson 1989, 25), suggesting that the dressing floor dates to the mid-19th century at the earliest.

The use of buddles at the western dressing floor is probably confirmed by the presence of a substantial earthwork reservoir (105007) at the south-west corner of the dressing floor, fed by a system of reservoirs and leats which harnessed water from the moorland to the south of the sett. The reservoir alongside the dressing floor was fed by a leat (18879) from the north-west which probably originated in a second reservoir to the south of Park Farm farmhouse, now lost to agricultural activity. This in turn was probably fed by a leat from an upper reservoir (18882), created by an earthwork dam across a natural hollow towards the south-west corner of the sett (18882, see Fig 115) and fed by a leat from the south. The source of the leat which fed the upper reservoir is difficult to find on the open

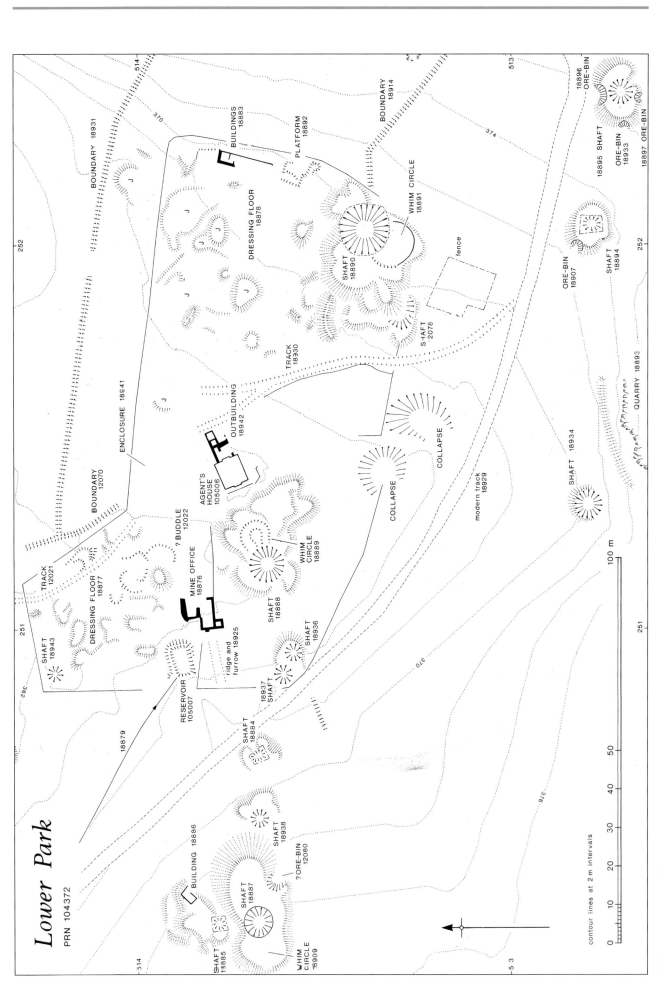

Lower Park mine: detailed plan of the inset area in Figure 115.

moorland, but it can possibly be traced contouring the hillside further to the south-west, just below a much more substantial leat (18181) which served the late 19th-century dressing floors at Minera. This larger leat, was over 4 kilometres in length. It drew water from the Aber Sychnant stream and ran past the Pool Park mine (see Fig 123) and through the south-east corner of the Lower Park sett.

The mine office and the agent's house lay within the walled enclosure, both being depicted on Symonds's map of 1865. The agent's house (105006, Fig 120) is now used as a barn. It is of stone construction with substantial dressed lintels above the windows and doorway on the south side, and has a number of outbuildings to the east, one of which includes a bread oven. An 'agent's house and garden' are also noted in a schedule of buildings submitted by Captain Sampson Mitchell for the Minera Mountain sett in 1899. The house was described as being 'in fairly good condition; roof over kitchen is leaking; lean-to back kitchen is bad and roof wants renewal'. The mine office (18876) now lies in ruins. It was about 6 by 3 metres across, with a chimney at the western end, a small annex to the south and a possible lean-to against the north wall. Park Farm, which lies in the north-west corner of the sett is also now in a derelict condition, though a barn still remains in use.

Pool Park, Minera, Wrexham (Figs 122–8)

The workings of Pool Park mine (SJ24905070) lie on the undulating, heather-covered moorland of Esclusham Mountain about 2.5 kilometres west of Minera, close to a narrow road which wends its way across the hills between Llangollen and Minera (Fig 122). About a kilometre to the north lies the Lower Park mine sett, described above. The mine lay in the angle between the steep-sided valley of the Aber Sychnant stream to the west and the equally steep-sided valley of one of its tributaries to the north, dissecting the Carboniferous limestone plateau, at a height of about 400 metres above sea level. The Pool Park and South Minera mineral veins, producing lead, silver and zinc ores, intersect close to the mine sett, their course traced by the run of shafts visible on the surface (Smith 1921, 113). Natural sink-holes in the limestone occur within the mine sett and within the surrounding moorland. An underground system of caves and fissures may have provided natural drainage for the early workings, though in the second half of the 19th century an adit was cut to drain the South Minera vein from a point several kilometres to the south-east.

The Pool Park mine sett included workings on both main veins, and extended from the valley of the Aber Sychnant stream on the west, through an area of more intense workings around the main site shown in Figure 122, to Pool Park Boundary Shaft (SJ25155050) and Mary Ann Shaft (SJ25405040) which lie within 250 metres to the south-east. The mining landscape covers an area of over 10 hectares, much of which remains devoid of vegetation and stands out starkly from the surrounding moorland (Fig 123). With the notable exception of the demolished engine house the area has been little affected by later activity, and remains fossilised in time (Fig 124). Two runs of shafts follow the main veins, but the main area of activity is focused upon a large shaft associated with extensive spoil tips, the remains of the engine house and a substantial embankment for a tramway linking the site to a second area of workings. Other significant landscape features include two leat systems which drew water from the Aber Sychnant stream to supply the Minera mines, one of which also supplied the Pool Park and Lower Park mines (Fig 125).

Documentary evidence for the history of the workings is drawn almost exclusively from mining returns, Symonds's map of 1865, and from references in the Grosvenor Estate papers. The mining returns give figures for the production of lead and silver between 1860 and 1874, with the addition of zinc from 1867–74, the most productive years being in the 1860s. The mine was owned by John Burton and James Kyrke from 1861–71 and by Sampson Mitchell and Sons from 1872–75, after which it was taken over by the Park Company. The mine appears to have closed in 1874 but a further return for zinc was made in 1881 (Burt et al 1992, 154).

Earlier workings appear to be represented by a number of the smaller shafts dotted along the veins, which though undated, are perhaps of 18th- or early 19th-century date. One of the most significant early mining features is a possible prospective hushing channel along the side of the valley bordering the site to the north, fed by two silted-up reservoirs further uphill (12018, see Figs 127 and 122). Prospecting here was ultimately unsuccessful, however, since there is no

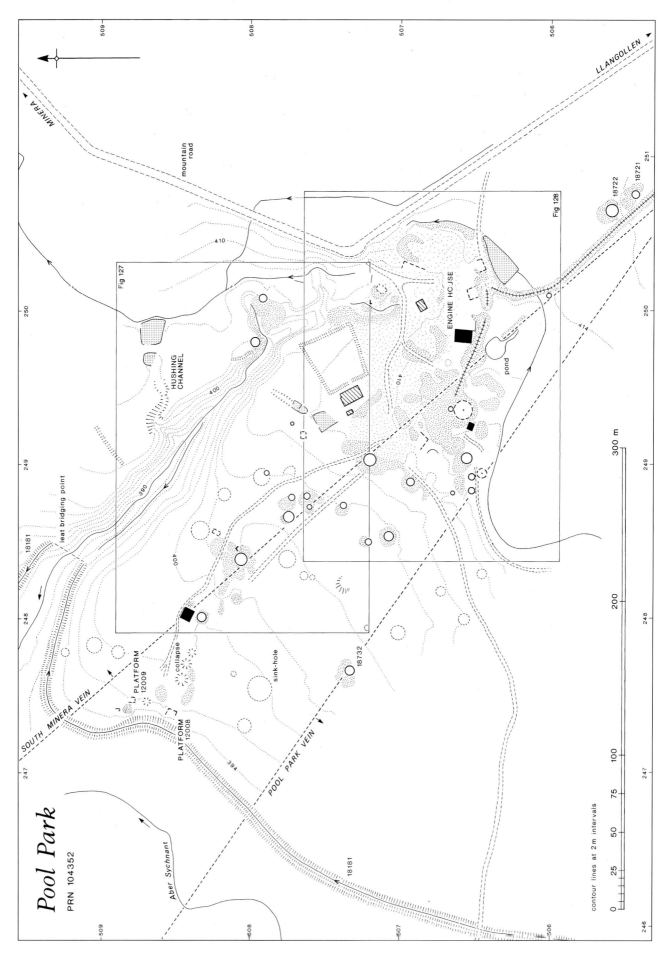

Pool Park

PRN 104352

Aber Sychnant

SOUTH MINERA VEIN

POOL PARK VEIN

PLATFORM 12009

PLATFORM 12008

collapse

sink-hole

leat bridging point

HUSHING CHANNEL

ENGINE HOUSE

pond

mountain road

Fig 127

Fig 128

MINERA

LLANGOLLEN

18181

18732

18722

18721

contour lines at 2 m intervals

0   25   50   75   100   200   300 m

See Figures 127 and 128 for detailed plans of the inset areas.

Figure 123 Aerial view of Pool Park mine, seen from the north-east. The mine shafts are strung out along the side of the stream in the foreground which feeds the Aber Sychnant stream, visible to the right. In the moorland beyond the mine is a scatter of natural sink-holes which join an underlying cave system in the limestone connected to the underground mine workings. The substantial leat running along the left-hand edge of the Aber Sychnant Valley is of late 19th-century date. It was formerly carried on a timber aqueduct over the stream in the foreground and fed two reservoirs (SJ263515) above the Minera mines, where the water was used to drive machinery on the dressing floor and to supply the engine house boilers. (*Crown Copyright: RCAHMW 935151–57*)

Figure 124 Pool Park mine: foundations of the engine house (18294, see Fig 128) towards the south-east corner of the mine, seen from the west. The structure once housed a steam engine, fired by coal brought up by cart over the mountain road from Brymbo. It is probably the engine house referred to in a report of 1896 by Captain Matthew Francis, which mentions a 15-inch winding engine with Cornish crusher rolls attached. The winding engine would have raised ore from the shaft (18292), about 50 metres to the west. (*CPAT 350–32*)

trace of workings in the immediate vicinity. Early ore processing is possibly to be seen towards the western end of the site, close to the Aber Sychnant Valley, where the presence of small tips of jig waste and two platforms (12008–9, see Fig 122) suggest the processing of ore from a number of early shafts.

By the 1860s mining was probably centred on the larger shafts – Engine Shaft (18292, Fig 128), now capped, within the main area of the workings, and Boundary Shaft and Mary Ann Shaft to the south-east of the survey area, all of which probably exploited the South Minera vein. Field evidence clearly shows that Engine Shaft was initially wound by a large horse whim (18293), about 13 metres in diameter, which has a small stone building (12002) against its western side. The horse whim was later replaced by a horizontal winding engine, housed in a stone-built engine house (18294) whose foundations can be seen about 50 metres further to the east (Fig 124). Like a number of

similar structures on Esclusham Mountain, the structure was demolished by the army during the 1960s. The surviving remains are difficult to interpret, but the dressed stone blocks of the engine bed and the flywheel pit aligned on the shaft, can still be identified. The position of the boilers is uncertain, but these were probably supplied by a large pond (18730) just beyond a tramway to the south of the engine house. Areas of collapse to either side of the tramway suggest that water was culverted beneath it. The foundations of a second building on the southern side of the engine house, about 6 metres across internally, seem likely to be those of a crusher house. Neither building appears on the 1st edition Ordnance Survey map of 1872, but both are shown on the 2nd edition of 1899. The two buildings are also mentioned in a report prepared by Captain Mathew Francis in 1896 for the Minera Mountain Mining Syndicate which stated that 'Pool Park Shaft is equipped with a 15-inch winding engine

Figure 125 Pool Park mine: substantial leat (18181, Fig 122) running along the edge of the Aber Sychnant Valley, looking towards Llandegla moor and Eglwyseg. The leat by-passed the west side of Pool Park, and supplied water to the large mines at Minera.
(CPAT 351–16)

Figure 126 Pool Park mine: remains of a two-roomed building (12001, see Fig 127), possibly an early mine office or stores, on the edge of the Aber Sychnant Valley towards the west side of the sett. (*CPAT 351–14*)

with Cornish crusher rolls attached and there is ample boiler power not only to wind, crush and dress, but to work a small compressor and engine which is available for carrying out the trial quickly with rock drills'. Francis also commented on the 'abundant and constant supply of water for all purposes, dressing on a large scale included'.

Two substantial raised tramways (18291, 18256) were constructed on embankments to transport ore from the Engine Shaft and Boundary Shaft to the dressing floors to the east and north-east of the engine house, where spreads of jig waste are visible (Fig 128). Only scant structural remains survive in this area, though it is possible to make out several platforms where jiggers were probably sited. Stonework with fixing bolts, visible to the north of the dressing floor, appears to represent a waterwheel (12014, Fig 128), fed by a leat system from the south, which is likely to have powered jiggers or possibly a buddle. A leat system feeding a structure here is shown on the Ordnance Survey map of 1872. Other structures possibly to be associated with ore processing include

two platforms which may represent washing sheds (12006, 12012), built against the raised tramway to the east of the engine house. These, together with a further building north-east of the engine house, which only survives as a heap of rubble (12013), are shown on an undated mine plan which predates the construction of the engine house. The spreads of jig waste at the mine are fairly extensive, and may represent successive phases of ore dressing. A roughly circular platform (18733) about 30 metres to the west of the engine shaft appears to be the site of an early buddle which was probably the source of the extensive spreads of buddle waste which surround the platform just to its north.

Two major leat systems fall within the mine sett. The more substantial one, sluiced from the Aber Sychnant some way upstream, bypassed the western side of the Pool Park mine and supplied the Minera mines, 2 kilometres to the north-east (18181, see Figs 122 and 125). The leat contours the valley side and was bridged across the tributary valley on the north side of Pool Park by means of a timber aqueduct which no longer

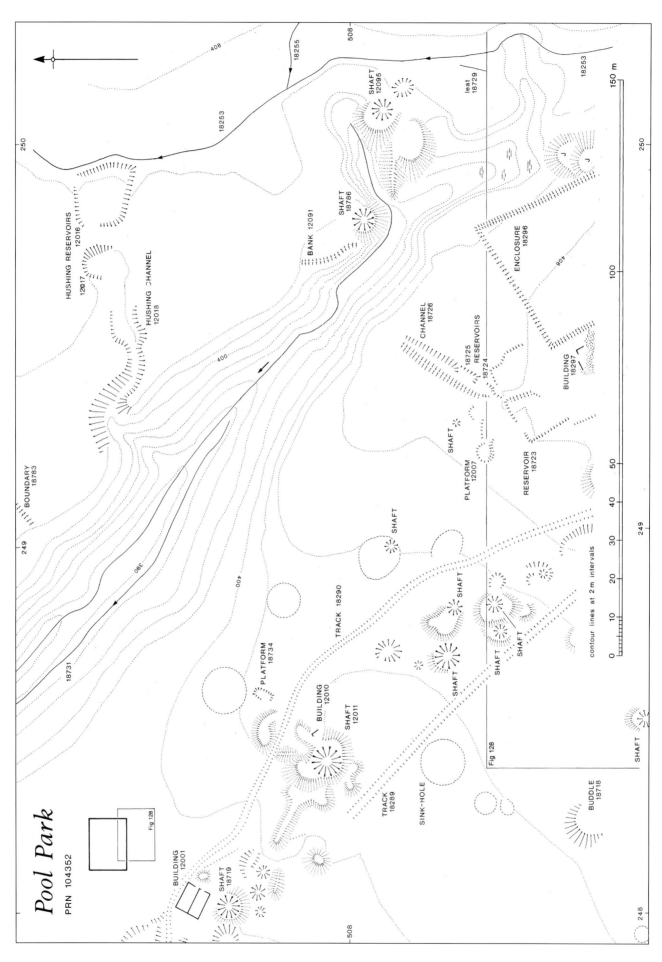

Pool Park

PRN 104352

Fig 128

BUILDING
12001

SHAFT
18719

BUILDING
12010

PLATFORM
18734

BUILDING
12011

SHAFT
12011

TRACK
18289

SINK-HOLE

TRACK 18290

SHAFT

SHAFT

SHAFT

SHAFT

SHAFT

BUDDLE
18718

508

Fig 128

contour lines at 2 m intervals

0 10 20 30 40 50 100 150 m

248

249

250

SHAFT

RESERVOIR
18723

PLATFORM
12007

SHAFT

ENCLOSURE
18296

BUILDING
18297

RESERVOIRS
18724

18725

CHANNEL
18726

J

J

leat
18729

18253

SHAFT
12095

BANK 12091

SHAFT
18786

SHAFT

18255

18253

408

508

408

400

400

380

380

18731

BOUNDARY
18783

HUSHING RESERVOIRS
12016

12017

HUSHING CHANNEL
12018

250

249

508

This plan of the northern inset area shown in Figure 122.

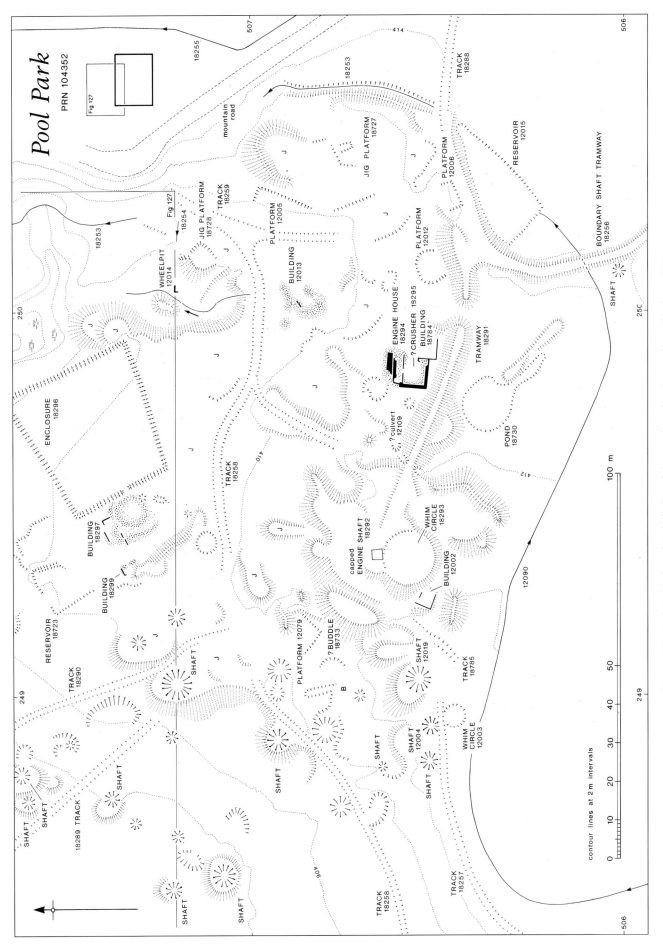

Figure 128   Pool Park mine: detailed plan of the southern inset area shown in Figure 122.

survives. It appears that the leat was augmented just before the bridging point by a subsidiary leat (18731) taken off the tributary. A second leat (12090, Fig 128), also sluiced from the Aber Sychnant upstream, was culverted under the tramway from Boundary Shaft to feed a large reservoir (12015) lying in the angle between the tramways to the south-east of the engine house. The reservoir evidently provided the main water supply for Pool Park and probably fed both the boilers of the engine house as well the small waterwheel on the northern side of the dressing floor mentioned above; it then continued northwards (18253) across the mountain in the direction of Park mine.

The foundations of several other buildings can be seen, the largest of which (18297) lies on the west side of a rectangular enclosure (18296) north of the engine

shaft, and also shown on the 1st edition Ordnance Survey map of 1872. The substantial heap of rubble which survives here indicates a structure of some size and significance, with a possible chimney against the north wall. Its function is uncertain, but it may be the remains of the smithy referred to in sale documents of 1899. The earthworks of a smaller building (18299) just to the west appear to be the mine office shown on Brenton Symonds's map of 1865. The rectangular enclosure was probably a pound for the horses used for transport and for winding the horse whims. Several hundred metres to the north-west are the remains of a further building of dry-stone construction (12001, Fig 126–7), divided into two rooms. This may originally have been used as offices or stores but is now used as a sheepfold.

Talargoch – Clive Shaft, Dyserth, Denbighshire (Figs 129–33)

Talargoch mine occupied fairly low-lying ground at the foot of the craggy upland of Graig Fawr, at the northern end of the Clwydian hills, looking out towards the coast of north Wales (Fig 129). The Clive Shaft and the immediately surrounding workings (SJ05628000) shown in the survey on Figure 130 is all that now remains of a once more extensive mining landscape. Workings once extended northwards for a kilometre or more to the village of Meliden and beyond, and included ore processing areas and other mine shafts which evolved during the 18th and 19th centuries. The engine house attached to Clive Shaft is the best-preserved example of a Cornish engine house in north Wales.

The underlying solid geology is of Carboniferous limestone, overlain with boulder clay and gravel. The Talargoch mine exploited three principal veins with lead, silver and zinc ores – Panton's vein to the north-west, the Talargoch vein in the centre, and the South Joint vein to the north-east. The Talargoch vein ran the length of the mine and was the most productive. At the southern end of the mine, around the Clive Shaft, a number of smaller veins ran at right-angles to the main veins and were exposed on the slopes of Graig Fawr, which were consequently the earliest veins to have been worked (Thorburn 1986, 9) (Fig 130).

Although mining is likely to have taken place in the general area from at least the Roman period, it was not until the 17th century that large-scale activity began in the area. Disputes over mineral rights were taking place in the middle of the 17th century between the

major landowning families in the area including the Grosvenors and the Mostyns. Draining the workings appears to have been a constant problem and it has been suggested that one of the first steam engines in Wales was erected on the bishop of St Asaph's land at Talargoch around 1716. In 1753, Paul Panton and Reverend Thomas Ince leased land for 21 years on the Earl of Plymouth's Estate between Talargoch and Dyserth, after which they constructed a leat, which took water from the Afon Ffyddion stream above Dyserth waterfalls (SJ057793), following the natural contours below Graig Fawr to Talargoch.

It is not known at what date mining commenced in the area of the Clive Shaft, but there appears to have been at least some working during the 18th century, if not earlier, and there was certainly a shaft here by 1803 (Thorburn 1986, 34–5). Earlier workings are probably represented by a number of shafts and possible shafts to the south and east of the later workings that have been identified as earthworks and as geophysical anomalies. The earthwork remains of a whim circle (64097) are evident to the south-east of the later engine house. The whim appears to have been used for winding at one of the adjacent shafts which have now been filled in, most probably in the period before the introduction of steam power.

By the late 1830s the mine workings had extended to the 150-yard level but continuing problems with drainage at the southern end of the mine prompted the mine agent, Ishmael Jones, to advise in 1842 that the only solution was to install a hydraulic engine. As

Figure 129 Aerial view of Talargoch, Clive Shaft, seen from the south-west showing the substantial stone-built engine house with the Drawing Shaft in front. The curving course of an early leat can be traced to the west of the road. (*CPAT 88–9–16*)

a consequence, the Clive Shaft was sunk between 1842–45 in the area known as Lletty Mwyn (Welsh 'mine lodging'), and equipped with an underground hydraulic engine.

By the 1850s Talargoch was one of the few profitable mines in the region. In 1857 the Talargoch Mining Company was founded and invested in the search for new sources of ore and in methods of increasing the depth of workings. The hydraulic engine at the Clive Shaft was replaced in 1862 by a 100-inch cylinder, housed in a new stone-built engine house, which remained in operation until the mine closed in 1884.

By the 1870s the mine output was dominated by zinc rather than lead and although production was high the cost of drainage forced the Talargoch Mining Company into liquidation in 1874. Attempts to float

a new company called the Old Talargoch Mining Company failed, and in 1875 the Talargoch Mining Company Ltd was formed. Although lead production continued to fall the output of zinc was still increasing. However, the costs of production were proving to be an increasing problem and in 1883 the company went into voluntary liquidation. The mine was auctioned in September 1883 and bought by Messrs Hughes and Lancaster of Acrefair, Wrexham, although their tenure was short-lived and underground working finally ceased in 1884.

By the 1880s the surface workings were concentrated in four main areas. At the northern end of the mine the Mostyn Shaft exploited the deepest workings using two rotary engines for winding and pumping. Walker's Shaft worked the Panton vein, drained by an 80-inch pumping engine, with other steam engines for

Figure 123. General plan of the mining complex at Talargoch, Clive Shaft

drawing and tools. The central area of Talargoch had been the focus of activity since the 17th century with several shafts, although latterly with only a pumping shaft using an 80-inch engine with a 9-foot stroke, together with a horizontal engine for winding. The area also housed the mine office, smithy, joiners' shop, fitters' shop, changing houses and stables. Finally, the Clive Shaft employed a 100-inch engine and a horizontal winding engine to drain the western workings. There were two dressing floors in operation, one at Coetia Llys at the northern end and the other at Maesyrerwddu to the north of the Clive Shaft.

The reworking of waste heaps continued ore production until 1905. By 1908 the mine was generally in ruins. Most of the Talargoch shafts were filled in and the buildings demolished in the 1950s, the only structure surviving being the engine house at Clive Shaft.

Initially, the Clive Shaft (64090) was equipped with a hydraulic engine which started operations in July 1845, with a 50-inch cylinder and a 10-foot stroke, constructed at John Taylor's foundry at Rhydymwyn (Thorburn 1986, 26). The engine was installed in a stone-lined underground engine house 50 yards below Lletty Mwyn. Water for the engine was supplied by a new leat, traces of which are still visible, which runs along the 300-foot (91-metre) contour to capture the east-flowing Afon Ffyddion stream, at a point about a kilometre and half to the south-east (SJ07027922). A small reservoir was constructed above and to the east of Lletty Mwyn, from which the water was carried downhill in 40-inch-diameter iron pipes.

The underground hydraulic engine was replaced in 1860 by a steam engine with a massive 100-inch cylinder and 10-foot stroke, housed in a new stone-built engine house (23382) which forms the dominant feature of the site today (Figs 129, 131–3). It was built by Thomas Roberts, a local man, and his sons. The former engine, built by the Haigh Foundry, Wigan, apparently worked 24 and 25 inch bucket lifts at around 3½ strokes per minute. The massive three-storey engine house is constructed of roughly dressed, local limestone with lime mortar and walls battered slightly inwards towards the top. The remains of a boiler house (64091) lie against the eastern side of the engine house, though little of this is now visible. A road led to the boiler house from the north and would

Figure 131 Talargoch, Clive Shaft: the engine house (23382) from the south-east with the earthwork remains of the winding engine base (64095) in the foreground. (*CPAT 1161–25*)

Figure 132
Talargoch, Clive Shaft: the engine house
(23382) from east with the remains of the
boiler house (64091) in the foreground.
(*CPAT 1161–0*)

Figure 133
Talargoch, Clive Shaft: the engine house
(23382) from the west with the Clive Shaft
and drainage culvert to the left.
(*CPAT 1161–07*)

have been used to supply the large quantities of coal consumed by the seven boilers which it is known to have housed. Evidence from the earthwork and geophysical surveys (ArchaeoPhysica 2002), as well as from the Ordnance Survey, suggest that a flue ran along the southern end of the boiler house, continuing about 30 metres south-east to the base of the chimney (64096), of which little now remains. The surviving stonework suggests a square plinth about 6.3 metres across with a circular chimney 2.8 metres in diameter internally at the base.

Water for the boilers was supplied via the aqueduct (64098), composed of 40-inch-diameter iron pipes, which had originally been constructed in the 1840s to supply the underground hydraulic engine. There is no indication of a structure leading downslope from the reservoir to the east of the survey area and consequently there is no visible evidence to suggest how the aqueduct was once carried across the line of a later railway. At the base of the steep slope the course of the aqueduct can be traced as a shallow gully, leading westwards to join a substantial embankment. Geophysical survey has suggested that this may be a masonry structure, rather than a simple rubble bank. At the western end the aqueduct turns north and then west towards the boiler house.

To the west of the engine house the remains of two structures are visible on top of the substantial spoil tip. A stone and brick-lined, arched, drainage culvert (64093) which lies close to the north-west corner of the engine house would have carried water raised to the surface by the pumping engine. Beyond this are the remains of the balance bob-pit (64092).

The Drawing Shaft (64094) lies to the south-west of the engine house, surrounded by a wire fence, and remains open to some depth. There is now no surface evidence for the headgear which would have stood over the shaft, although the remains of the engine base (64095) for a horizontal winding engine can still be identified to the south of the boiler house. Some masonry survives, together with fixing bolts for the 24-inch by 4 foot 6 inch horizontal steam engine which would have been powered using steam from the main boilers. The surviving remains, together with evidence from the Ordnance Survey, suggest that the engine bed was originally about 13 metres by 4 metres across, with the winding drum on the south-east side, aligned to the Drawing Shaft. The substantial spoil tip surrounding the shaft has several levelled platforms around its base, particularly on the west side, which may have been for small structures or shelters.

4 MANAGING MINING LANDSCAPES

by Mark Walters

This final section of the volume examines a number of management and conservation issues relating to former mining landscapes together with their potential value in a wide range of educational initiatives. Many of these questions are viewed from local perspective but will also be of relevance to former mining areas elsewhere in Britain and beyond.

The management and conservation of mining landscapes in mid and north-east Wales hold many challenges for the future. Belonging to the more recent past, they have often have been perceived as being intrinsically less important than more ancient archaeological remains. They have been seen as being hazardous and unsightly and a target for reclamation schemes which would return the land to more productive use. Mining landscapes often cover extensive tracts of remote and poorly accessible upland or marginal land. They are often in multiple ownership and in some instances subject to statutory and other designations which are unrelated to the boundaries of the mining site. The various components of the landscapes are also often surprisingly fragile, being subject to natural weathering, erosion, decay and collapse. All of these factors have tended to militate against the setting up of conservation initiatives.

Greater awareness of the meaning and significance of mining landscapes will undoubtedly play an important role in securing their long-term preservation. Rather than being seen as a blight, mining landscapes are increasingly seen as something which enriches our understanding of the past and which physically and visually touch upon the lives of former communities which owe their very existence to the mining industry. In many cases, mining represents a transient phase of landscape evolution, bracketed between what went before and what will follow, and a strong case can be made for managing at least the best of what has survived for the lessons it can teach us about a broad range of environmental issues. Many of the problems relating to the management and conservation of mining sites are not easily resolved, but a number of new opportunities are presented by the growing emphasis upon more sustainable forms of agriculture, together with various initiatives designed to improve public access to the countryside and provide visitor attractions. Statutory protection will have a role to play in some instances but does not provide a general panacea. In a Welsh context, the inclusion of a number of metal mining landscapes in the two published registers of *Landscapes of Historic Interest in Wales* (Cadw 1998; 2001) and the recent designation of Blaenafon as a World Heritage Site will undoubtely reap rewards in the long run.

Handling modern pressures on former mining landscapes

It is worthwhile looking briefly at some of the pressures that beset mining landscapes in the study area and to explore the question of how some of these conflicts might be resolved here as elsewhere in Britain.

Many of the mining landscapes of mid and northeast Wales are located on marginal land and consequently the pressure from large-scale redevelopment for housing or industry is often relatively slight.

Planning developments which have most often affected mining landscapes include the conversion of existing buildings and the construction of new isolated houses or agricultural buildings which, though relatively slight in landscape terms, can have a cumulative effect over the longer term. The visual impact of larger-scale developments such as renewable energy schemes has yet to arise but in cases of this kind the impact on the

Figure 134 Pen Dylife mine, Llanbrynmair, Powys: the foundations of the wheelpit for the 63-foot diameter Red or Martha Wheel constructed in the 1850s which used to pump and draw from the Llechwedd Ddu shaft. The wheelpit once held the largest diameter waterwheel employed on a metal mining site in Wales, but is almost unrecognizable beneath heaps of discarded rubbish. Regrettably, many mining sites in upland Wales are seen as a convenient dumping ground for old machinery and often attract fly-tipping.

(CPAT 153–26)

setting of mining landscapes might also need to be assessed. In north-east Wales the potential impact of industrial developments and small-scale housing developments upon mining landscapes is significantly higher in view of the higher population densities in that area. Here, a number of the former lead mining settlements have extended well beyond their original boundaries and in some instances have begun to impinge upon the mining landscapes which once lay in the countryside around them. As a consequence, close and active monitoring of planning applications by the principal heritage consultees is needed to ensure that appropriate schemes of mitigation are applied through the planning process. As far as the mining landscapes which fall within registered historic landscapes in Wales are concerned, there are now published guidelines for how the impact of proposed developments should be measured (Cadw 2003).

A number of agricultural activities continue to have a small-scale though nonetheless deleterious effect upon mining landscapes, particularly in the remote upland areas, including the creation of new farm tracks, small-scale quarrying, the levelling of buildings and other structures on the grounds of safety or in order to reuse materials, as well as the general dumping of rubbish (Fig 134). Activities of this kind are difficult to monitor, except in the case of scheduled monuments, and often the best that can be hoped for is to try and instill a sense stewardship amongst landowners, particularly where there is the opportunity to actively manage and conserve mining remains as part of an agri-environment scheme such as the all-Wales Tir Gofal scheme.

Large-scale afforestation schemes by the Forestry Commission had a considerable impact upon a number of mining landscapes in western Montgomeryshire,

Figure 135 Aerial view of Nant yr Eira mine, Llangurig, Powys, viewed from the north-west, showing areas of recently cleared forestry plantation which have revealed a two-roomed building which may be a barracks. Commercial coniferous woodlands planted since the 1940s unfortunately still mask large areas of former mining landscapes in western Montgomeryshire, Gwynedd and Ceredigion. (*Crown Copyright: RCAHMW 985036–68*)

Radnorshire and Breconshire in mid Wales after the end of the Second World War. In many instances damage was caused by preparatory ploughing and the creation of access tracks and forest rides during subsequent planting. Whilst the effects of root growth was largely confined to the surface layers, storm damage and the regeneration of saplings often led to the displacement of standing walls and structures. The harvesting and replanting of mature plantations might also result in the continued disturbance of structures and earthworks well beyond the initial damage. Improved liaison between archaeologists and foresters in recent years has fortunately resulted in a much greater awareness of the importance of mining landscapes and their conservation within actively managed woodland. In some instances trees have been cleared, revealing previously invisible mines and structures such as those at Nant yr Eira (Fig 135), Ceulan and Rhoswydol in mid Wales. Modern techniques and machinery employed to plant and harvest woodland are significantly less damaging than those used in the 1940s and 1950s and greater care is now taken to avoid obvious structures and earthworks. In addition, the provision of enhanced public access to woodland has led to a number of opportunities for the interpretation of mining sites along waymarked forestry trails.

Large-scale reclamation schemes undertaken by local authorities in the 1970s and 1980s with grant-aid from the Welsh Development Agency (WDA) used to be a major threat to former industrial sites in Wales.

Figure 136
Aerial view of Eisteddfod mines, Minera, Wrexham, looking south across Top Eisteddfod towards the now disused Minera limestone quarry, with Lower Park mine and Esclusham Mountain in the background. Quarrying as well as mining has left its mark on the landscape. Eisteddfod also contains several quarries which would have provided building stone and lime for use in agriculture.
(CPAT 90-MB-284)

Some of this work was essential for health and safety reasons, such as making shafts safe or removing contaminated waste-tips. Considerable destruction of mining remains took place without record at a number of sites in Wales, however, through a lack of our ability to manage the changes that were taking place. A number of mining landscapes were more or less completely destroyed, as for example at the Goginan, Cwmbrwyno and Ystrad Einion mines in Ceredigion. The shaft capping scheme carried out on the Flintshire orefield in the 1970s inadvertently led to the loss of valuable archaeological information when the areas around the shaft heads were cleared down to bedrock level in order that concrete caps might be fitted. This led to the destruction of buildings and structures around the head of the shaft, such as engine houses, boiler houses, ore-bins and angle or bob-pits, as well as evidence for earlier workings near the surface. There is fortunately now a growing awareness of the significance of these kinds of archaeological remains and consequently, during more recent reclamation work at the Van mine in mid Wales and at the Holway and Trelogan mines in north-east Wales, for example, prior evaluation and subsequent mitigation permitted the excavation and recording of significant elements of the mining complex while a number of individual structures were preserved by burial beneath waste material rather than being entirely destroyed. Where there are hazards that need to be averted, restricting access by means of fencing is now generally seen as a preferred option from the point of view of heritage conservation.

In the 1940s the Second World War and its aftermath led to a substantial increase in demand for natural resources. Many former mines and quarries were awarded interim development orders (IDOs) to allow them to be re-opened should the need arise. Many of these IDOs were renewed in the 1990s by their current owners via the minerals planning departments in local authorities. At that stage it proved difficult to apply conditions which required archaeological assessment, evaluation or preservation *in situ*, on the grounds that this might affect the economic viability of a mine or quarry or conflict with health and safety considerations. However, in the event of a mine or quarry re-opening, it would now need to conform to current environmental impact assessment requirements. This normally allows mitigatory measures to be applied, but the scope for achieving preservation *in situ* is often limited. None of the abandoned metal mines in Wales are currently economically viable but a number are affected or potentially affected by stone quarrying. In north-east Wales the important mining landscape at Eisteddfod was narrowly missed by extensions to the Minera limestone quarry (Fig 136) and is now protected, though parts of the Lower Park mine are still under threat. One limestone quarry is still active on Halkyn Mountain and extensions continue to destroy both surface and sub-surface mining evidence. While the surface features can be recorded and excavated through the use of planning conditions there has generally been little opportunity for recording the underground workings which are encountered here, due to health and safety issues.

Welsh mining landscapes displayed

Many of the mining landscapes of mid and north-east Wales described in this volume are on private land or are other otherwise inaccessible, but there are a number both here and elsewhere in Wales which can be visited (see Fig 140). Important sites which are open to the public outside the area include the Great Orme Bronze Age Mines Museum near Llandudno, the Mid Wales Lead Mining Museum at Llywernog, and the Dolaucothi Roman Gold Mines, north of Llandovery, together with the waymarked trails at the Hafna and Llanrwst mine complexes in the Gwydir Forest near Betws-y-coed, in north-west Wales. A brief outline is given to some of the mining sites within the study area where some provision is made for visitors.

The Nant yr Eira mine near Llangurig in mid Wales,

described in some detail earlier in this volume, is one of the most isolated and evocative metal mine sites in Wales. It lies within a few hundred metres of the summit of Plynlimon, the highest mountain in mid Wales, and is surrounded by dense coniferous forestry plantations. The waterfall and narrow Bronze Age open-cut workings hidden away at the northern end of the site are of particular interest. More obvious are the remains of later workings including ore-bins, crusher house wheelpit, smithy, barracks, jig platforms and buddles. Access is by means of a long metalled forestry track from the Hafren Forest picnic site (SN85658690) where a display panel gives a brief history of mining activity and details of other archaeological sites to be seen in the area and forms the

Figure 137 Aerial view of Bryntail mine, Llanidloes, Powys, showing the layout of the 1850s dressing floor below the Western Engine Shaft with the large Barytes Mill erected in about 1870. (*Crown Copyright: RCAHMW 98-CS–903*)

starting point for a 7-kilometre archaeological trail created by the Forestry Commission. The Elan Valley Trust at the Cwm Elan, Nant y Car and Dalrhiw mines is currently designing similar trails using existing public footpaths.

The Bryntail Lead Mine (SN91358680) (Fig 137), is spectacularly sited below the Clywedog dam, just to the west of the small market town of Llanidloes, and close to the Gwestyn and Penyclun mining landscapes described in this volume. The mine, first worked in the 18th century, was expanded between 1845 and 1867 and continued with barytes and witherite extraction and processing between 1874 and 1932. The site was renovated during the construction of the Clywedog dam in the mid 1970s and displays some typical structures associated with lead and barytes processing. A number of mining artefacts were found during the excavation of the dam foundations and these are displayed in cabinets in the Severn Trent Water control centre on the west side of the dam.

The Minera Mine Museum (SJ27475089), just to the west of Wrexham, lies to the east of the Eisteddfod, Lower Park and Pool Park mining landscapes described above. The Cornish pumping engine house and chimney (Fig 138), dating to 1857, had been a feature of the Meadow Shaft site for many years and were well known to the local community. Less well known were the spectacularly well-preserved remains of an entire dressing floor which lay beneath tons of waste material next to the shaft. These remains started to come to light during the first phase of reclamation in 1988 when the Welsh Development Agency agreed to fund a watching brief and exploratory excavation. An industrial archaeologist was employed full-time for the second phase and systematic excavation of the whole Meadow Shaft dressing floor area took place together

Figure 138
Minera Lead Mine Museum, Wrexham: the restored Meadow Shaft engine house dating to about 1857 with the base for a small winding and crushing engine in the foreground.
(*CPAT 241–4A*)

Figure 139
Two well-preserved and restored ore-bins at the Minera Lead Mine Museum, Wrexham, dating to about 1858. The rebuilt ore-house of about the 1860s in the background now houses the visitor centre.
(*CPAT 241–7A*)

with excavations at Taylor's Shaft to the north and on the halvans plant and New Minera Shaft sites to the east (Silvester 1993). These excavations took place between 1991 and 1994, subsequent to the main reclamation phase, and were funded by Wrexham Maelor Borough Council who had acquired the site. Mining at the Meadow Shaft began in the mid-18th century under a group of companies in Chester, honouring a charitable bequest to plough profits back to the city's poor. The shaft was subsequently widened and deepened in 1851 and a 42-inch engine installed for pumping. In 1858 a new dressing floor was built which worked up to the early 1890s and a buddle and ore-house were added in the 1860s. The dressing floor became rapidly obsolete due to the high rates of production of lead and zinc from the mine and was subsequently buried under tons of smelter and boiler

waste. After excavation the dressing floor structures were stabilised and some of the processing features reconstructed including the ore-bins (Fig 139), picking floor, jiggers, and buddle. The shaft collar was refurbished and the shaft capped. The engine house was completely restored and a hydraulically operating pumping beam and cylinder were installed with an attached balance-box. The ore-house was also rebuilt and is now used as the site office, museum and ticket and retail sales area. A way-marked path has been created around the site as well as a number of circular walks within the country park to the north and south of the Meadow Shaft site. These make use of old tramway and railway and enable other features of the lead mining and limestone quarrying industries around Minera to be seen (Fig 140).

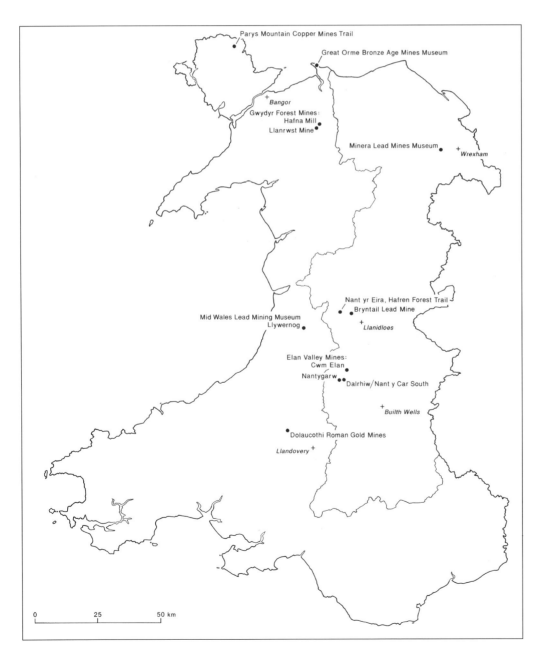

Figure 140
Metal mining sites in Wales where some provision is made for visitors.

Appendix 1:
Gazetteer of metal mines in mid Wales

The gazetteer lists the non-ferrous metal mines in mid Wales shown in the distribution map in Figure 3, covering the historic counties of Montgomeryshire, Radnorshire and Breconshire, corresponding with the present-day unitary authority of Powys. The gazetteer lists the following information: mine name, alternative mine names and community (the Welsh equivalent of civil parish); record numbers (PRNs) as listed in the regional Historic Environment Record (HER) maintained by the Clwyd-Powys Archaeological Trust (CPAT); the principal ores that were obtained; national grid reference. Further details of individual mines are contained in the report on the rapid survey undertaken by CPAT (Walters 1994) and in the regional HER. The following abbreviations are used to indicate the types of ores produced by the mines: Ag – silver; Au – gold; Ba – barytes; Ca – calcite; Co – cobalt; Cu – copper; Fe – iron; Mn – manganese; Ni – nickel; Pb – lead; Si – silica sand; Zn – zinc.

Mine	PRN	ores	grid reference
Aberdaunant, Llanidloes Without	8480	Pb	SN 90658655
Allt-y-Main, Meifod	8485	Pb Ba	SJ 16301440
Bacheiddon, Cadfarch	5077	Pb	SN 83709708
Brynfedwen, Llanbrynmair	8461	Pb	SN 85509701
Brynpostig, Llanidloes Without	8484	Pb	SN97128222
Bryntail, Llanidloes Without	1842	Pb Ba	SN91338685
Bwlch Creolen, Llanrhaeadr-ym-Mochnant	5927	Pb	SJ09752305
Calcot, Churchstoke	18980	Ba	SO29769721
Cefn Côch, Llanwrtyd Wells	5518	Pb Cu	SN84005355
Cefn-Pawl, Beguildy	1100	Pb	SO17107983
Ceulan, Llanbrynmair	8460	Pb	SN86209740
Cliffdale, Churchstoke	8853	Pb Ba	SO30209763
Clochnant, Penybontfawr	18981	Pb	SJ04412293
Craig Ddu, Penybontfawr	18982	Pb	SJ06152395
Craig Rhiwarth/North Llangynog, Llangynog	8430	Pb	SJ05552656
Craig-y-Mwyn, Llanrhaeadr-ym-Mochnant	8438	Pb	SJ07422852
Cwm Bach, Rhayader	18983	Pb	SN94406980
Cwm Elan, Rhayader	5945	Pb Zn	SN90006510
Cwm Fron/East Cwm Fron, Llangurig	18969	Pb	SN97108090
Cwm Orog, Llangynog	5925	Pb Zn Ba	SJ05202730
Cwmbychan, Glantwymyn	8448	Pb	SH85850110
Cwmbyr, Cadfarch	6160	Pb Zn	SN78639475
Cwmrhaiadr, Cadfarch	8451	Pb Zn	SN75559465
Cyfarthfa/Nant Ddu, Cadfarch	8497	Pb Cu	SN83409307
Dalrhiw, Llanwrthwl	5511	Cu Pb	SN88566079
Dyfngwm/Castle Rock, Llanbrynmair	5942	Pb Zn Cu	SN84909310
Dylife, Llanbrynmair	5648	Pb Zn Cu	SN85609390

Mine	PRN	ores	grid reference
East Van, Llanidloes Without	5937	Pb	SN94958850
Fedw/St Harmon, St Harmon	8436	Pb	SN97657930
Fron-Felin, Llanbrynmair	18984	Pb	SH87250071
Geufron, Llanidloes Without	8479	Cu	SN88588570
Glaslyn, Cadfarch	18985	Cu	SN81289425
Glyn, Llanidloes Without	18986	Pb Ba	SN92478724
Gorn, Llanidloes Without	5939	Pb	SN98008400
Gwaith y Mwyn, Nantmel	8487	Ag Pb	SN99906780
Gwestyn, Llanidloes Without	5943	Cu Pb	SN89408610
Hafodfeddgar, Llangurig	18987	Cu Pb Zn	SN87558585
Hyddgen, Cadfarch	6158	Pb	SN78209070
Llandrindod, Glascwm	18978	Pb	SO06605935
Llanerchyraur, Llanbrynmair	5941	Pb	SN86759820
Llangynog, Llangynog	8433	Pb	SJ05502555
Llanymynech Ogof, Carreghofa	30	Pb Cu	SJ26602222
Llanymynech, Carreghofa	18971	Pb Cu	SJ26602222
Maesnant, Llangurig	18988	Pb Cu	SN85368666
Marcheini Fach/Drosgol, St Harmon	18989	Pb	SN95657413
Melinygloch, Aberhafesb	18970	Pb	SO06649434
Middletown Hill, Trewern	18990	Pb Ba	SJ30931322
Moel Fadian, Cadfarch	18991	Cu	SN83019490
Nant Gyrnant, Llanwrtyd Wells	18992	Cu Pb	SN85804740
Nant y Blaidd, Llanrhaeadr-ym-Mochnant	18993	Pb	SJ09032833
Nant y Car North, Llanwrthwl	5513	Pb Cu	SN89086192
Nant y Car South, Llanwrthwl	18994	Cu Pb Zn	SN88676090
Nant yr Eira, Llangurig	725	Pb Cu	SN82708730
Nantiago, Llangurig	5944	Pb	SN82608632
Nantmelin, Llanidloes Without	18995	Cu Pb	SN86008772
Nanty/Pantmawr, Llangurig	3673	Pb	SN85258210
Nantybrain/Abergwesyn, Llanwrtyd	5517	Pb	SN83205045
Nantygarw, Llanwrthwl	5512	Pb	SN87436060
Nantyricket, Llangurig	8476	Cu	SN86558678
Newchapel/Cwm-Mawr, Llandinam	18996	Pb	SN98958335
Newtown	1042	Pb	SO09609100
Ogof Wyddan/Witches Cave/Machynlleth Park, Machynlleth	8458	Pb Cu	SH76050011
Pen Dylife, Llanbrynmair	18591	Pb Zn Cu	SN85509350
Penyclun, Llanidloes Without	5938	Pb	SN93098730
Pontneddfechan, Ystradfellte	20978	Pb Ag Si	SN90300970
Pwll-Glas/Trefeglwys, Trefeglwys	18997	Pb	SN97408929
Rhoswydol, Cadfarch	5940	Pb	SN83809730
Roundton, Churchstoke	7085	Pb Ba	SO29249466
Siglenlas, Llangurig	8478	Pb Cu	SN86588390
Talachddu, Felin-fach	5864	Pb Cu	SO08403425
Tyisaf/Cae Conroy, Llanbrynmair	18998	Pb	SN87709790
Tylwch, Llangurig	18999	Pb	SN96208068
Van, Llanidloes Without	5936	Pb	SN94258760
West Fedw, Llandrindod Wells	18972	Pb Zn Cu	SO11205823
West Wye Valley, Llangurig	8474	Pb Zn	SN82328465
Wye Valley, Llangurig	18979	Pb	SN82658510

Appendix 2:
Gazetteer of metal mines in north-east Wales

The gazetteer lists the non-ferrous metal mines in north-east Wales shown in the distribution map in Figure 4, covering the historic counties of Flintshire and Denbighshire. This corresponds with the former county of Clwyd and the present-day unitary authorities of Flintshire, Denbighshire, Wrexham, and the eastern part of Conwy. The gazetteer lists the following information: mine name, alternative mine names and community (the Welsh equivalent of civil parish); record numbers (PRNs) as listed in the regional Historic Environment Record (HER) maintained by

the Clwyd-Powys Archaeological Trust (CPAT); the principal ores that were obtained; national grid reference. Further details of individual mines are contained in the report on the rapid survey undertaken by CPAT (Frost 1994) and in the regional HER. The following abbreviations are used to indicate the types of ores produced by the mines: Ag – silver; Au – gold; Ba – barytes; Ca – calcite; Co – cobalt; Cu – copper; Fe – iron; Mn – manganese; Ni – nickel; Pb – lead; Si – silica sand; Zn – zinc.

Mine	PRN	ores	grid reference
Aberduna/Coed Cynric, Mold	18000	Pb Ag	SJ20506180
Alltgymbyd, Llandegla	18001	Pb	SJ20455473
Ashton, Holywell	18002	Pb Ag	SJ17807470
Axton, Llanasa	103308	Pb	SJ10508040
Bedol Aur, Holywell	18004	Pb	SJ18007500
Belgrave, Llanarmon-yn-Iâl	18005	Pb Ag	SJ20205880
Berthen Farm, Ysceifiog	18006	Pb	SJ17407180
Billins, Halkyn	18007	Pb Ag	SJ19607200
Blaen-y-Nant, Llanarmon-yn-Iâl	18008	Pb	SJ19905820
Bodelwyddan, St Asaph	18009	Pb Ag Zn	SH 99707490
Bodidris, Llandegla	18010	Pb	SJ20905390
Brindigrif, Whitford	18011	Pb	SJ12607940
Bron Eyarth, Efenechtyd	18012	Ba	SJ12305560
Bron Eyarth/Coed Marchon, Efenechtyd	18013	Pb	SJ11605560
Bron-heulog, Llanfairtalhaiarn	18014	Pb	SH93807150
Brynalyn/Pwllhelyg/Great New Westminster, Llanarmon	18018	Pb	SJ19305880
Bryncelyn, Mold	103154	Pb	SJ20346641
Bryncloddiau, Ysceifiog	103627	Pb	SJ15357380
Bryncoch/Pantymwyn East/Mold Mines, Rhydymwyn	18019	Pb Ag Cu	SJ20206480
Brynford Hall, Holywell	18020	Pb Ag	SJ18957475
Brynford/Valentine, Brynford	18021	Pb Ag	SJ17707440
Bryngwiog/Nantygo, Halkyn	103375	Pb	SJ19206910
Bryngwyn, Mold	18022	Pb	SJ21406180
Brynhyfryd, Gwernymynydd	18023	Pb	SJ19706400
Bryn-Nantllech, Llansannan	18016	Cu	SH94006850
Brynsion, Caerwys	18024	Pb	SJ13607190
Brynyffynnon, Mold	18025	Pb	SJ21606230

Mine	PRN	ores	grid reference
Brynyfryd, Mold	18026	Pb	SJ21406200
Brynyrhenblas, Holywell	18027	Pb	SJ18207440
Bryn-yr-odyn, Llanasa	18242	Pb	SJ09908030
Bryn-yr-orsedd, Llanarmon	18017	Pb	SJ19605930
Bwlchgwyn, Brymbo	18028	Pb Ag	SJ26605340
Bwlchyddaufryn, Mold	18029	Pb	SJ20106450
Cae Tan-y-graig, Halkyn	18030	Pb Ag	SJ17207100
Caeau/Rhydfudr/Llongle/New Caeau, Holywell	104128	Pb	SJ19760729
Caemynydd/West End, Minera	12118	Pb	SJ26005200
Caepant/Lower Eisteddfod, Minera	104271	Pb Ag Zn	SJ25495245
Caerfallwch, Halkyn	103056	Pb Ag	SJ21656842
Cambrian, Holywell	18031	Pb	SJ16907570
Castell, Cilcain	18032	Au	SJ16406370
Cat Hole West/Pilkington's, Mold	18033	Pb Zn	SJ20206270
Cat Hole, Mold	10318/	Pb Zn	SJ20606270
Cefn Cilain, Mold	18231	Pb	SJ19456600
Cefn Mawr/Deborah, Mold	18057	Pb Zn	SJ20406350
Cefn Mawr/Rhydymwyn, Mold	18034	Pb Zn	SJ20906650
Cefn Spar, Mold	102898	Ca	SJ18706650
Cefn-y-gist, Esclusham Above	18035	Pb Ag	SJ24254880
Cefn-y-groes-fawr, Llanfairtalhaiarn	18036	Cu	SH91406630
Cefn-yr-Ogof, Abergele	18037	Pb	SH91507760
Cefn-yr-Ogof/Gwyrch Castle, Abergele	18038	Pb	SJ92707750
Central Minera, Minera	18122	Pb Ag	SJ25305260
Cheney Rake, Halkyn	18039	Pb Ag	SJ18957150
Chwarel Las, Halkyn	18041	Pb Ag	SJ19607150
Chwarel Wen, Halkyn	18042	Pb Ag	SJ17607388
Cilcain Hall, Halkyn	18043	Pb	SJ18606850
Clwt Militia/American, Holywell	18045	Pb Ag	SJ17307530
Coed Celyn, Cefn Meiriadog	18046	Pb	SJ01307260
Coed Du, Mold	100244	Pb	SJ19106640
Coed Mawr/Nant-y-ffrith, Bwlchgwyn	104438	Pb	SJ26505480
Coed yr Esgob/Fish, Gwaenysgor	18048	Pb	SJ06808120
Coed Ysgeirallt, Abergele	18047	Pb	SH94507550
Coed-y-fedw, Llanferres	18050	Pb	SJ19906170
Coed-y-fron, Holywell	103442	Pb	SJ18507540
Coetia Ball/St Winefred, Holywell	18051	Pb	SJ17707630
Coetia Butler/Butlersfield, Brynford	18052	Pb Ag	SJ17457545
Coetia Mawr, Holywell	18053	Pb	SJ17607522
Coetia'r Ysgall, Cilcain	18054	Pb	SJ19106660
Cornell-Llwyd, Holywell	18230	Pb	SJ18207450
Craig Boeth, Minera	18286	Pb	SJ25005220
Creigiau Eglwyseg, Llantysilio	18055	Pb	SJ21904480
Creigiog, Llanarmon	18056	Pb Ag Zn	SJ20405590
Cross Leavings/True Blue, Halkyn	18244	Pb	SJ18907300
Cwm Mawr/Gomerian Level, Esclusham Above	104224	Pb	SJ26005900
Dafern Dywyll, Holywell	18266	Pb	SJ19507275
Denbigh West/Gwaynynog, Denbigh	18058	Pb	SJ03956560
Dingle, Halkyn	18059	Pb	SJ20407150

Mine	PRN	ores	grid reference
Dog Pit, Halkyn	18060	Pb Ag	SJ19407140
Dolphin, Holywell	18061	Pb	SJ19607360
Dyffryn Aled, Llansannan	18062	Cu	SH95006690
Dyserth Castle, Dyserth	18064	Pb	SJ06017990
Dyserth, Dyserth	18063	Pb Ag	SJ05707950
Efail Parcy, Halkyn	12112	Pb	SJ18706760
Eglwyseg Extension, Penycae	18065	Pb	SJ24804750
Eglwyseg/Eglwyseagle/Craig-y-forwyn, Llangollen	18066	Pb Ag	SJ23604760
Eisteddfod Mine/Steddfod/Minera, Minera	104270	Pb Ag	SJ25305260
Erwfelin, Mold	18068	Pb	SJ20206680
Ffordd-las Bach, Abergele	18069	Pb	SH95507590
Ffos-y-Bleiddiaid, Abergele	18070	Pb Cu	SH93407699
Fron Hall United, Mold	103180	Pb	SJ22406210
Fron Ucha, Mold	18072	Pb	SJ21706150
Fron, Halkyn	18071	Pb Ag	SJ20407170
Fronfawnog, Mold	103219	Pb Ag	SJ21556385
Fronissa, Mold	102802	Pb Ag	SJ22206240
Garneddwen, Halkyn	18249	Pb	SJ17707020
Garreg, Whitford	102779	Pb	SJ13407860
Garreg-Boeth, Halkyn	18247	Pb	SJ19006720
Garth, Cilcain	18074	Pb Au	SJ14906440
Gelli Fowler, Ysceifiog	103630	Pb	SJ17637343
Gelli Loveday, Ysceifiog	18075	Pb	SJ14757380
Gilfach, Llansannan	18076	Cu	SH92106320
Gladstone, Brynford	18077	Pb Ag	SJ17057565
Glanalyn, Mold	18078	Pb Ag	SJ19606280
Glol, Whitford	18079	Pb	SJ12007850
Glyndwr/East Maeshafn, Mold	18080	Pb	SJ22106100
Golden Grove, Gwaenysgor	103302	Pb	SJ08808130
Gop Hill, Gwaeysgor	18081	Pb	SJ08308090
Gors, Ysceifiog	103649	Pb	SJ15857320
Gorsedd/Dee/Sinclair/Celyn Bog, Whitford	18082	Pb Ag	SJ15057670
Graianrhyd, Llanarmon	18083	Pb	SJ21805580
Graig Fawr, Dyserth	18084	Pb Cu	SJ06008050
Graingers, Halkyn	18246	Pb Ag	SJ19707230
Grange/Speedwell, Holywell	102918	Pb Ag	SJ17507610
Great Calcot, Holywell	18085	Pb Ag	SJ17007490
Groesffordd/Plasau, Ysceifiog	103629	Pb Ag	SJ16157126
Grosvenor, Holywell	18086	Pb Ag	SJ18607150
Gwaenysgor, Gwaenysgor	103968	Pb	SJ07308130
Gwenymynydd, Mold	103216	Pb Ag Zn	SJ21306240
Gwernymynydd Farm/St Catherine's, Mold	18237	Pb	SJ22206250
Gwter-Siani, Esclusham Above	18087	Pb	SJ24504990
Gyrn, Holywell	18088	Pb	SJ17707570
Hafod, Gwernaffield, Mold	18089	Pb	SJ21306330
Hafod-y-gog, Llanfairtalhaiarn	18090	Cu	SH90206705
Halkyn Deep Level/Pant-y-go/Pant-y-ffrith, Halkyn	18092	Pb Ag Zn	SJ20307070
Halkyn District United, Halkyn	18015	Pb Ag Zn	SJ20307070
Halkyn District United/New North Halkyn, Halkyn	103388	Pb Ag Zn	SJ20307070

Mine	PRN	ores	grid reference
Halkyn East, Halkyn	18093	Pb Ag Zn	SJ21306930
Halkyn Hall, Halkyn	103080	Pb Zn	SJ20907050
Halkyn Mines, Halkyn	18091	Pb Ag Zn	SJ21006980
Halkyn, Mount/Halkyn West, Halkyn	103419	Pb Ag Zn	SJ20106980
Halkyn, South/Rhydymwyn, Halkyn	18094	Pb Ag Zn	SJ20306780
Hazel Grove, Brynford	18095	Pb Zn	SJ17507479
Hendre Ddu, Llangernyw	18097	Pb	SH87406640
Hendre Figallt, Halkyn	18098	Pb	SJ19506790
Hendre, North, Halkyn	18099	Pb Ag	SJ19306820
Hendre, Rhydymwyn	18096	Pb Ag	SJ20206780
Hendre, South/West, Halkyn	18100	Pb	SJ18806750
Hersedd, Halkyn	18102	Pb	SJ18706910
Herward United, Holywell	104129	Pb	SJ19657415
Holway Consols/Holway United/Great Holway, Holywell	102917	Pb Ag Zn	SJ17907640
Holway District/HolwayWest/Golch Hill, Holywell	18103	Pb Ag Zn	SJ16807650
Holway Rake/Holywell Level/Great Holway, Holywell	18104	Pb	SJ17407650
Holway, Eyton's, Holywell	103435	Pb	SJ17427684
Hope Mountain, Llanfynydd	18105	Pb	SJ28505750
Hopewell, Holywell	18106	Pb Ag	SJ16207630
Hush Eisteddfod, Minera	18067	Pb Ag	SJ25605200
Jamaica, Llanferres	103186	Pb Ag	SJ21606080
Kinmel Manor, Abergele	18107	Pb	SH98007470
Lixwm/Caelanycraig, Halkyn	18108	Pb	SJ17307140
Llanarmon, Llanarmon	18109	Pb Ag	SJ21705680
Llanfair, Llanfairtalhaiarn	18111	Pb Zn Cu	SH93607030
Llewellyn, Minera	18275	Pb	SJ25105250
Lloc/Merllyn, West, Whitford	18112	Pb Ag	SJ14507670
Llwyn-y-cosyn, Halkyn	103652	Pb	SJ17907290
Llyn-y-pandy/Rhydalyn, Rhydymwyn	103158	Pb Ag	SJ19606570
Long Rake, Halkyn	18113	Pb Ag	SJ18807110
Lord Hill, Holywell	18114	Pb Ag	SJ16207620
Lower Park, Minera	104372	Pb	SJ25155138
Maenbras/Prince Patrick, Halkyn	103407	Pb Ag	SJ18707220
Maes Maelor, Llandegla	18115	Pb	SJ23105370
Maeshafn Main Site, Llanferres	18049	Pb Zn	SJ19806110
Maeshafn, Moel Findeg, Llanferres	18173	Pb Zn	SJ21206090
Maeshafn, River Alyn, Llanferres	102915	Pb Zn	SJ19306130
Maeshafn, Grosvenor Shaft, Llanferres	102803	Pb Zn	SJ20406110
Maeslygan, Halkyn	18117	Pb Ag	SJ20507220
Maesyffynnon, Minera	12117	Pb	SJ25995200
Maes-y-pwll, Llanarmon	18116	Pb	SJ20605550
Marian Ffrith, Cwm	18118	Pb Cu Fe	SJ07107800
Merllyn, Holywell	18120	Pb Ag	SJ14707690
Milwr, Holywell	103463	Pb Ag Zn	SJ19307450
Minera Union, Minera	104265	Pb	SJ25305250
Minera: Andrew's Shaft, Minera	12119	Pb Zn	SJ26755143
Minera: Boundary Shaft, Minera	104367	Pb Zn	SJ26125182
Minera: Bryn Heulwen Shaft, Minera	104262	Pb Zn	SJ26825125
Minera: Ellerton's Shaft, Minera	104260	Pb Zn	SJ26585145

Mine	PRN	ores	grid reference
Minera: Hafod-las Shaft, Minera	104268	Pb Zn	SJ26725216
Minera: Lloyd's Shaft, Minera	104261	Pb Zn	SJ26825138
Minera: Meadows Shaft, Minera	104275	Pb Ag Zn	SJ27505090
Minera: Nant, Minera	18124	Pb	SJ28405020
Minera: New, Burton's Shaft, Minera	18145	Pb Ag Zn	SJ27805080
Minera: Quarry Wood Shafts, Minera	104371	Pb	SJ26337170
Minera: Reid's Shaft, Minera	104264	Pb Zn	SJ26535168
Minera: Royle's Shaft, Minera	18241	Pb Zn	SJ26525158
Minera: Roy's Shaft, Minera	104276	Pb Zn	SJ27225105
Minera: Speedwell's Shaft, Minera	18121	Pb Zn	SJ26905133
Minera: Taylor's Shaft, Minera	100042	Pb Ag Zn	SJ27005122
Moel Arthur, Llandyrnog	18126	Pb Au	SJ14256608
Moel Dwyll, Cilcain	18127	Pb Au	SJ15306350
Moel Hiraddug, Dyserth	103489	Ni Co	SJ06307870
Moel Unben, Llanfairtalhaiarn	18128	Pb	SH90806800
Moel-y-crio, Halkyn	18130	Pb	SJ19806980
Moel y Gaer, Llangynhafal	18129	Pb	SJ14906170
Mold Mines, Cadole, Mold	18131	Pb Ag Zn	SJ21006280
Mold Mines, Pantymwyn New Shaft, Mold	18132	Pb	SJ20806520
Mostyn/Hafod, Whitford	18133	Pb	SJ12907940
Mount Pleasant, Mold	18134	Pb Ag	SJ21706140
Mwynbwll/Fagnallt, Halkyn	18135	Pb	SJ18606699
Mynydd Bodran, Llanfairtalhaiarn	18136	Pb Cu	SH94307080
Mynydd Du/Black Mountain, Llanarmon	18137	Pb	SJ21505730
Nant Uchaf, Abergele	18138	Fe Mn	SH93307570
Nant-y-Cwm Mawr/Gwter Siani, Esclusham Above	18139	Pb	SJ25404930
Nant-y-fuwch, Ysceifiog	18140	Pb	SJ18407210
Nantymwyn, Gwaenysgor	18142	Pb	SJ07708280
Nantypetre/Llangynhafal, Llangynhafal	18143	Pb Ba	SJ13706300
Nant-y-plwm, Llansannan	18141	Pb	SH92906602
North Henblas, Holywell	104137	Pb Zn	SJ19507380
Old Rake Halkyn, Halkyn	18146	Pb Ag	SJ20407060
Pant Du, East, Nercwys	18149	Pb Ag	SJ21605890
Pant Du, Llanferres	18148	Pb Ag Zn	SJ20405960
Pant Idda, Abergele	18150	Pb	SH92307580
Pant, Holywell	18147	Pb Ag	SJ19107220
Pantasaph/St David's/Lord Hill/Hopewell, Halkyn	18151	Pb	SJ16307600
Pant-y-buarth, Mold	103203	Pb Ag Zn	SJ20046410
Pant-y-ffrith, Halkyn	18152	Pb Ag	SJ20506960
Pant-y-go North/W Brynparade/Colossus, Halkyn	18153	Pb	SJ20457145
Pant-y-go, Halkyn	18073	Pb Ag	SJ20807010
Pant-y-gwlanod, Llanarmon	18154	Pb Ba	SJ20205710
Pant-y-mwyn West, Mold	18234	Pb	SJ19206450
Pantyne, New, Holywell	18155	Pb Ag	SJ17407540
Pantyne, North/South, Holywell	18156	Pb Ag	SJ17407620
Pant-y-pwll-dwr/Rowley's Rake, Halkyn	18157	Pb Ag	SJ19807220
Pant-y-pydew, Holywell	104142	Pb Ag	SJ18107350
Pant-y-rhes, Holywell	18158	Pb Ag Zn	SJ17707520
Pant-y-wacco/Rock, Whitford	18159	Pb	SJ14207650

Mine	PRN	ores	grid reference
Parc, Llanarmon	18160	Pb	SJ19805556
Park Mine: Hill Shaft, Minera	18161	Pb Zn	SJ25605210
Park Mine: New Shaft, Minera	104355	Pb Zn	SJ26105085
Park Mine: Western Shaft, Minera	104373	Pb Zn	SJ25405130
Parry's, Halkyn	103390	Pb Ag Zn	SJ19507230
Pen Bronwiski, Halkyn	103424	Pb	SJ18856885
Pengwern, Llansannan	18168	Pb Cu	SH96406820
Pen-llwyn, Llandyrnog	18162	Pb	SJ11806700
Penmachno, Cilcain	18169	Au	SJ14906445
Pennant, St Asaph	102766	Pb Ag Ba	SJ08607540
Pentre Du, Llanfairtalhaiarn	18170	Pb Cu	SH93606903
Pentre Halkyn, Halkyn	18171	Pb	SJ20007230
Pen-y-bryn/Vron, Halkyn	103462	Pb	SJ18507510
Pen-y-fron/Bryncelyn/Bryncelyn West, Mold	103159	Pb Ag Zn	SJ19806620
Pen-y-garreg Wen, Mold	18238	Pb	SJ19706296
Penygelli, Whitford	18172	Pb	SJ13707650
Pen-y-graig/Blaen-y-glyn, Llanarmon Mynydd Mawr	18110	Pb	SJ12402845
Pen-y-mynydd, Llandyrnog	18163	Au	SJ14106645
Pen-y-pylle, Holywell	18164	Pb	SJ19207430
Pen-yr-henblas, Halkyn	18165	Pb Ag	SJ19007290
Pen-yr-hwylfa, Holywell	18167	Pb	SJ19007354
Pen-yr-orsedd, Halkyn	18166	Pb Ag	SJ21106800
Picton, Holywell	18174	Pb Ag	SJ17607570
Pistyll, Tremeirchion	18175	Pb	SJ07707470
Plantation, Holywell	18176	Pb Ag	SJ15407660
Plas Captain, Ysceifiog	18177	Pb	SJ17407220
Plas Newydd/Cefn/Score, Cefn Meiriadog	18178	Pb Ag	SH99507330
Plas Winter/Plasresgob, Halkyn	103425	Pb	SJ19956915
Pool Park, Minera	104352	Pb Ag Zn	SJ24905060
Pool Park: Mary Ann/Kyrke's, Minera	18179	Pb Ag Zn	SJ25405040
Pool Park: Boundary Shaft, Minera	18144	Pb Ag Zn	SJ25155050
Portaway, Holywell	18239	Pb	SJ17007620
Priddbwll, Llansannan	18180	Cu	SH93006350
Prince Patrick North, Halkyn	18183	Pb Ag	SJ18507300
Prince Patrick South, Halkyn	18184	Pb Ag	SJ18907190
Prince Patrick, Halkyn	18182	Pb Ag	SJ19107220
Prysau, Ysceifiog	18185	Pb	SJ16307300
Pwll-clai, Holywell	18186	Pb Ag	SJ18607380
Pwllgwenllan, Halkyn	18187	Pb Ag	SJ19807080
Pwllmelyn, Halkyn	18188	Pb Ag	SJ18407150
Pwllwheal, Holywell	18189	Pb Ag	SJ18507350
Pwll-y-gaseg, Halkyn	18245	Pb	SJ18507250
Quarry, Minera	18125	Pb Zn	SJ25505200
Queen of the Mountain, Halkyn	18190	Pb Ag	SJ18907190
Ragman, Minera	104267	Pb Zn	SJ25505220
Rhewl, Holywell	18191	Pb Ag	SJ18606930
Rhosddigre, Llandegla	18192	Pb	SJ18305240
Rhosesmor/Halkyn District United, Halkyn	103055	Pb Ag Zn	SJ21306830
Rhydalyn/Llynypandy South, Mold	18223	Pb	SJ19706530

Mine	PRN	ores	grid reference
Rhydwen, Whitford	18194	Pb Ag	SJ13407670
Rhydymwyn, Cefn Mawr, Mold	18195	Pb Zn	SJ20806630
Rhyd-yr-eirin, Llanfairtalhaiarn	18193	Cu	SH94306830
Saithaelwyd, Holywell	18196	Pb	SJ16707660
Seven Stars, Holywell	12116	Pb	SJ17307532
Silver Rake, Halkyn	18197	Pb Ag	SJ18107300
Sir Edward/Frame, Holywell	18198	Pb Ag	SJ17907530
Sir George's Field, Halkyn	18233	Pb	SJ20107230
South Minera: Dixon's Shaft, Minera	104365	Pb Ag Zn	SJ25654960
South Minera: Walker's Shaft, Minera	18199	Pb Ag Zn	SJ25305010
Talacre/Gronant, Llanasa	103343	Pb Ag Zn	SJ09808290
Talacre/Kelston Farm, Llanasa	18200	Pb Ag Zn	SJ10408250
Talargoch: Central Mine Area, Dyserth	18240	Pb Ag Zn Cu	SJ05808050
Talargoch: Clive Shaft, Dyserth	102605	Pb Ag	SJ05628000
Talargoch: Coetia Llys, Dyserth	18201	Pb Ag	SJ06308085
Talargoch: Maesyrerwddu, Dyserth	18202	Pb Ag Zn	SJ05758030
Talargoch: Walker's Shaft, Dyserth	18203	Pb Ag Zn	SJ05638049
Tan-y-foel, Halkyn	18204	Pb	SJ19207010
Tan-y-graig, Llanarmon	18205	Pb	SJ19855680
Tan-yr-onen, Whitford	18217	Pb Ag	SJ14207740
Thorntree, Halkyn	103651	Pb	SJ18207280
Top Eisteddfod, Minera	104274	Pb	SJ24705250
Tre-lan, Cilcain	18206	Pb	SJ17206600
Trellynia, Holywell	18207	Pb	SJ18106940
Trelogan, Llanasa	102786	Pb	SJ12608080
Trelogan, Lower/Hannah Shaft, Llanasa	12115	Pb	SJ12588075
Trelogan, West, Llanasa	103276	Pb	SJ11108030
Trelogan/Afongoch, Llanasa	18235	Pb	SJ11508030
True Blue, Holywell	18208	Pb Ag Zn	SJ17907560
True Blue, River Alyn, Mold	18236	Pb	SJ19306320
Truro/Tir-y-Coed, Nercwys	18209	Pb	SJ21506000
Twelve Apostles, Minera	18210	Pb Ag	SJ25105250
Ty Newydd Spar, Trelawnyd	102764	Ca	SJ06907890
Ty Newydd, Trelawnyd	18211	Pb	SJ06867980
Tyddyn Morgan, Abergele	18213	Pb	SH93667650
Tyddyn Shepherd, Ysceifiog	18232	Pb	SJ16807170
Tyddyn-y-barcud, Cilcain	18248	Pb	SJ18806760
Tymaen, Holywell	18214	Pb Ag	SJ14707650
Tyntwll/Pant-y-garreg/Union, Mary Jane Shaft, Halkyn	18231	Pb	SJ19907140
Ty'n-y-celyn, Llangollen	18212	Pb	SJ23404070
Tyn-y-ddol, Llanfairtalhaiarn	18216	Pb	SH94907170
Union, Halkyn	18218	Pb	SJ19307120
Volcnant/Terfyn Hall, Gwaenysgor	18219	Pb	SJ08408300
Wacco/Bryn-y-gaseg, Whitford	18220	Pb	SJ15207620
Waen, Holywell	18221	Pb Ag Zn	SJ15407690
Waenlas, Llanferres	18222	Pb	SJ19806000
Wagstaff, Halkyn	18223	Pb Ag	SJ19707100
Wallside, Holywell	104134	Pb	SJ17307550
Wern-y-gaer/Nantfinallt, Northop	18224	Pb	SJ20506850

Mine	PRN	ores	grid reference
Westminster, Bog East, Llanarmon	18226	Pb	SJ21305689
Westminster, Bog Mary Ann, Llanarmon	18227	Pb	SJ21055685
Westminster, Bog, Llanarmon	18225	Pb	SJ20605710
Westminster, Castell Engine Shaft, Llanarmon	18228	Pb	SJ20305750
Westminster, Nant, Llanarmon	18229	Pb	SJ19775774
Westminster, New/Long Rake East, Halkyn	103386	Pb Ag	SJ19307080
Whitford, Whitford	18243	Pb	SJ13007880
Wynnstay, Esclusham Above	18230	Pb	SJ24704940
Ysgeirallt, Abergele	18144	Pb	SH94307500

GLOSSARY OF MINING TERMS

A-frame Timber frame erected over a mine shaft with a small wheel at the apex providing rope or cable haulage up and down the shaft. Also called the head-frame or shear-legs.

Air shaft Vertical shaft to the surface for ventilation.

Adit A level tunnel driven into the hillside or valley floor in order to give access to a mine, and used for drainage or the hauling of quarried ore. Deeper adits did not necessarily connect to surface, and might be used to carry water back from distant workings to a pumping shaft.

Aerial ropeway Method of transporting the ore in buckets suspended from a steel rope supported on pylons mounted on stone or concrete plinths.

Angle bob A simple lever-based device by which the direction of the reciprocal action of pump rods or flat rods, for example, could be changed from a horizontal to a vertical motion.

Balance bob A large counterweighted lever attached to the shaft pump rods and used to offset their weight and thus reduce the work of a pumping engine to lifting water alone. A surface balance bob would be mounted next to the shaft on plinths or on a masonry support at ground level (balance bob mounting); the attached counterweight (a large box filled with scrap iron or rocks) would be housed in an adjacent stone-lined pit. Other balance bobs would be installed in chambers cut into the rock next to the shaft wall as needed, to counterbalance the weight of the pump rods, especially in the case of a deep shaft.

Barrack housing Dormitory accommodation provided by a mining company for miners during the working week at remote mine sites. This form of accommodation was sometimes referred to in contemporary documents as 'lodging shops'.

Barytes Barium sulphate: a colourless or white mineral, occurring as a gangue mineral, used in chemical industries for the manufacture of paint, toothpaste etc. Considered valuable from the late 19th century, when many waste tips were reworked in search of discarded gangue.

Beam engine A type of steam-engine much favoured in Cornwall for use in pumping, winding, and providing the power to crush ores preparatory to dressing. In the case of pumping, the power from a large cylinder set vertically in an engine-house was transferred via a massive rocking beam or bob to the pumps in the shaft outside. For winding and crushing, the bob was attached to a flywheel and crank on a loading next to the bob-wall (or in the case of all indoor engines, the side wall). In most cases, the engine house formed an integral part of the framing of the engine.

Bed stone The granite or gritstone slab which formed the foundation for the cylinder of a Cornish beam engine.

Bell-pit A shallow pit or shaft, generally no more than 10–12 metres deep, broadening out towards the base. Workings of this kind were normally abandoned when they became unsafe or collapsed, and a new bell-pit was started close by. In this way, successive pits formed a run of workings along a vein.

Blende Zinc ore, bluish-brown in colour, containing sulphur and iron as impurities. Also known as sphalerite or black-jack.

Bob-pit Pit or box into which the weighted end of the balance-beam rises and falls, thus counteracting the weight of the pump rods.

Boiler house Structure, generally attached to the engine house, containing the boilers which raise steam to power the engine.

Bole furnace A primitive smelting site, using wood for fuel, generally located on top of an exposed hillside where wind could provide the blast. A basin-shaped depression contained the fire into which ore was fed. Liquid metal would run out of the bottom of the bowl and solidify when it cooled.

Bratticing Timber partition-work, such as the lagging-boards which lined the upper section of a shaft where it ran through soft ground.

Bucking The process of crushing copper and lead ore on an anvil or smooth stone surface by means of small hammers, normally down to fragments about 10mm across, following which the waste material was removed by hand. This process followed cobbing, in which it had been broken down to about 25mm across, the waste again being removed by hand. These processes, through which the majority of the highest quality ore was recovered, took place on the picking or sorting floor.

Buddle Structure used in the later stages of the separation of ore from gangue, normally after it had passed through jigs, to retrieve finer particles of ore. Early buddles took the form of inclined troughs in which the lighter waste was washed away by water as it was raked by hand, leaving the heavier ore to collect in the bottom. Circular buddles of concave and convex form developed from the mid-19th century. Crushed ore was loaded into a stream of water via a launder onto the central cone of the buddle. Rotating brushes, generally powered by a small waterwheel, swept the slurry around the buddle surface, allowing the heavier ore to collect in the middle and the lighter waste to disperse to the sides.

Calamine Zinc carbonate, resulting from the weathering of zinc blende. Used in the manufacture of cosmetics and medicines and formerly in the manufacture of brass.

Capstan A manually or steam-operated winding drum, sometimes set horizontally in capstan pit, and usually installed on a mine to raise pitwork from the shaft for maintenance or repair.

Chalcopyrite Copper ore; brassy, yellow-coloured metallic crystals, containing sulphur and iron impurities.

Chalybite Ferrous carbonate, a common iron ore.

Cobbing See description of bucking.

Coe Small shelter, usually of stone, often near a shaft, used to store the miners' tools or a change of clothing.

Costeaning pit A small pit dug in search of minerals. They are almost always found in linear groups and often at right-angles to the projected strike of known lodes. A costeaning trench was a linear excavation cut for prospecting purposes.

Country rock Local rock, solid geology.

Cross-cut Level driven to intersect a vein from a shaft, winze or other level.

Crusher house Structure housing the horizontal rollers used for crushing the ore. Widely in use from the early 19th century and powered by either water or steam.

Culvert Covered leat or tunnel carrying water.

Development rock/waste Country rock removed during the sinking of a shaft.

Dressing floor Area set aside for separating ore from the waste, generally indicated by large spoil tips of fine waste. The dressing floor might accommodate a crusher, jigs, buddles and settling tanks.

Engine bed Solid plinth on which a steam engine or heavy machinery was mounted. May be of stone, brick or concrete.

Engine house Structure housing a steam engine for pumping or winding. Vertical steam engines had been developed for mine use by Thomas Newcomen from 1712, with improved patents from Boulton and Watt from 1765. Cornish engine houses were a specific type of engine house with the chimney at one corner, developed by Richard Trevithick in about 1811, though the term is often used as a general descriptive term for vertical steam engine houses. Water heated in large boilers produced steam which was fed into a cylinder within the engine house. A piston within the cylinder was connected to a balance-beam, causing it to move when steam was injected or released. The balance-beam was connected to pump rods, or via a crankshaft to a winding drum. The size of the cylinder bore determined the power of the engine, so that an engine accompanied by an 80-inch cylinder would be known as an 80-inch pumping or winding engine.

Engine shaft Usually the main working shaft of the mine, powered for pumping and/or winding by a horse whim, waterwheel or steam engine.

Fathom A distance of 6 feet, commonly used in measuring the depth of mine workings.

'Finger' spoil heaps Linear tips of waste material from a mine or quarry, flat-topped to allow material to be barrowed or trammed along it, and often equipped with a temporary tramway track.

Firesetting An ancient technique which prepares the ore-bearing rock for extraction. Wood was piled against a rock face and burnt, causing the rock to expand and weaken. Dousing the rock with water caused it to shatter. The weakened rock was then broken up using bone or stone tools. Firesetting leaves characteristic concave surfaces in the rock face and the shattered rock and charcoal is often found in adjacent tips. The technique is known to have been used on Bronze Age mining sites throughout Britain.

Flat-rods Reciprocating iron rods used to transfer power from a steam engine or waterwheel to the pump rods, which may be some distance away. The track-bed on which the flat-rods ran is generally all that survives, appearing as a linear gully earthwork.

Flywheel A heavy wheel, often attached to the drive shaft of an engine, used to increase momentum and thereby improve stability and a reserve of power.

Fault Geological displacement of rock.

Galena Lead ore. Characteristically high density, with a silvery, metallic colour.

Gangue The mineral deposit accompanying the primary ore being mined; initially considered to be less commercially valuable and commonly including quartz, calcite or barytes.

Halvans Low-grade lead or zinc waste tips, reprocessed in the later 19th century in a mechanised halvans plant. The word is a 19th-century term derived from 'half/halve'.

Headframe Tall structure set over a winding shaft which carried the sheave wheels over which the winding ropes ran. Headframes usually contained ore bins or ore chutes to allow the broken rock in the skips or kibbles to be tipped into trams at the surface.

Horizontal engine A steam engine with the cylinders sited on horizontal beds; the piston rods attached to a crank and flywheel used for winding.

Horse whim or **horse gin** Similar to a capstan, but in this case power is supplied by a horse walking around a circular platform or whim circle and linked to an overhead winding drum. They were frequently used for winding from small shafts, especially during exploratory work and shaft sinking. The smaller under-gear whims found in some 19th-century farms were little used on mines.

Hotching tubs See description of jigs.

Hushing Method of exposing veins by releasing a torrent of water, the force of which removed topsoil and exposed mineral bearing rocks. Reservoirs gathered large supplies of water, which were regularly released down the hillside, via hushing channels, ultimately resulting in a substantial open scar with a fan of waste material at the bottom. The technique may have been used initially as a means of prospecting, or on some sites as a means of extracting the ore.

Incline A track or a tramway constructed on a gradient to transport ore in skips.

Jigs/jiggers Water-filled wooden tubs into which a mesh-bottomed box containing ore-bearing material is raised and lowered by means of a lever. Agitation caused the heavier ore to settle in the bottom of the box, making the separation of waste easier. The invention is attributed to Captain Barrett of Grassinton Moor Mine, who in 1810 hung a sieve on the end of a lever which supported it in a tub to make it easier to operate. From the mid 19th century processing mills were constructed to house mechanised jigs powered by steam engines or waterwheels, some to the design patented by George Green of Aberystwyth and produced at his Cambrian Foundry. Hand-operated jigs were also known as hotching tubs.

Kibble A large, strongly-constructed, egg-shaped iron container used for ore and rock haulage in earlier shafts, superseded by skips.

Lagging boards Timber boards lining the upper section of a shaft where it passed through unstable ground.

Launder Wooden trough carrying a flow of water.

Leaching tanks Stone tanks, generally square and lead-lined, used for treating copper-rich ground water from waste tips with sulphuric acid to produce copper sulphate. The copper was precipitated from the solution with scrap iron.

Leat An artificial watercourse or channel, sometimes stone-lined.

Level Tunnel driven into the hillside or leading off from a shaft, giving access to a mineral vein or providing ventilation and access for haulage or machinery.

Loading The masonry platform, often in front of an engine-house, on which machinery such as cranks, flywheels or winding drums were mounted and on which the reciprocal motion of the sweep rod attached to the beam was converted into a rotative motion.

Lode See vein.

Magazine See description of powder magazine.

Opencast Exposed quarry-like surface workings.

Open-cut Generally an elongated and steep-sided cut, where mining has progressed down from the surface to the level of the water-table. A similar feature might be created where underground stopes emerged at the surface.

Ore-bin A stone-built hopper, often built in groups, into which gangue raised from the shaft was temporarily stored before being sorted or taken to the crusher. Ore was loaded into the top of the hopper and raked out through an opening at the bottom for sorting. The level areas in front of the ore-bins, sometimes referred to as picking floors, was where the preliminary manual separation of ore from waste rock was often carried out.

Ore-slide Chute, usually made of wood, which carried ore downslope. Undressed ore was often first loaded into an ore-bin which formed the head of the ore-slide.

Overburden The topsoil and subsoil removed in the process of opening or extending a mine.

Pelton-wheel High-pressure waterwheel developed during the late 19th century.

Picking floor See description of ore-bin.

Pitwork The term used to describe the pump rods, rising main, shaft guides within a shaft.

Portal The entrance to an adit. Often timbered or stone vaulted.

Powder magazine Building, often of substantial proportions and sometimes double-walled, used to store the explosives, also referred to as powder houses. For reasons of safety they were generally sited some distance from the mine workings. Gunpowder had been in use for blasting from the 17th century, but its use remained highly dangerous until the invention of the safety fuse by William Bickford in 1831.

Pumping rods Linked iron rods that descended the shaft in the rising main and were pulled up and down by the engine house beam. They were connected to a valve at the base of the shaft which sucked water into the rising main and drew it to the top of the shaft. See also flat-rods.

Rose The cast-iron strainer attached to the bottom lift of pumps.

Rotative beam engine Beam engine used for winding, developed from the 1870s in Cornwall. Also referred to as a whim engine. The reciprocating movement of the beam was transferred to rotary motion by a sweep rod, crank and flywheel.

Sett A mining area owned or leased to a mine company and sometimes defined by boundary banks or stones.

Settling pits Rectangular tanks or reservoirs, often laid out in series, where waste slurry or slimes was collected after undergoing jigging and buddling processes. The waste was allowed to settle before the final stage of ore recovery was attempted. Also referred to as slime pits.

Shaft Vertical or near-vertical mine working, sunk to extract ore, or for drainage or ventilation.

Shears or **Shear legs** A tall timber frame carrying a

pulley or sheave wheel erected in front of an engine house over a shaft and used for the installation and maintenance of pitwork.

Skip An iron or steel container, generally elongated, equipped with small wheels or brackets running on the shaft guides (buntings) and used for rock and ore haulage in later mines.

Slag Residue of impurities in the ore produced from roasting, smithing and smelting operations.

Slimes Slurry formed by fine waste and water from the buddling process. See also settling pits.

Sluice Wooden gate that can be opened and closed to control the flow of water on a leat or launder.

Smelter A furnace where metals were extracted from the ore by heating to high temperatures, driving off impurities which were collected as slag. Early smelters took the form of primitive bole furnaces. Sophisticated smelt mills were in operation by the 19th century which housed the smelting furnaces and were usually accompanied by long flues which carried the fumes to a distant chimney.

Sphalerite Zinc sulphite, also known as blende or black jack. A shiny mineral, characteristically yellow, brown, or black in colour.

Spoil tip A general term used for discarded waste material, consisting of development rock from sinking a shaft, waste material from underground workings, or the processing waste from jigs or buddles.

Stamps A mechanical device for crushing ore-bearing rock to a fine sand or grit usually driven by a waterwheel or rotative steam engine. Heavy, vertically-mounted beams (or later iron rods) carrying cast or forged iron heads were lifted and dropped onto the prepared ore beneath them by a series of cams mounted on a rotating drum.

Stone-crusher Portable belt-driven machinery for breaking up rock and ore.

Stope Underground chamber excavated during the extraction of ore, often either above or below a level or cross-cut. They occasionally reached the surface.

String Veins branching off the main vein also referred to as flyer or scrin.

Tailings Finely-ground particles of waste material resulting from processing the ore, particularly after jigging.

Tailrace The channel along which water flows after having passed over or under a waterwheel.

Tramway Narrow-gauge railway, with trucks or skips

sometimes drawn by horses, but often pushed by hand.

Trommel Cylindrical sieve, usually sited beneath the crusher rolls in a crusher house. Generally, several trommels were mounted on a central rotating axle powered by water and set at an angle so that the ore would move downwards.

Vein Mineralised material within the local country rock, often referred to as the lode, and generally associated with faults.

Waterwheel Wheel fitted with buckets or paddles around its periphery, and driven by the weight or force of a stream of water directed onto them.

Wheelpit A structure built to house a waterwheel, either set in a pit dug into the ground or as a free-standing structure above ground level.

Winze Shaft sunk underground to connect working levels, not exposed to the surface.

Whim circle Usually, a level, circular platform on which a horse whim was sited. Their surfaces are generally composed of gravel or finely crushed stone and their edges are sometimes defined by upright stones. There is often a small pit at the centre where the vertical post supporting the winding-drum was set.

Witherite Native barium carbonate.

BIBLIOGRAPHY

Adams, D R, 1992 The Mines of Llanymynech Hill, *Shropshire Caving and Mining Club, Account No 14*

Annels, A E and Burnham, B C, 1983 *The Dolaucothi Gold Mines*. National Trust

ArchaeoPhysica, 2002 Geophysical Survey at Clive Engine House, Talargoch Mine, Dyserth, Denbighshire. Unpubl rep for Clwyd-Powys Archaeological Trust

Atkinson, D and Taylor, M V, 1924 Flint excavation report, *Flintshire Hist Soc J* **10**, 1, 5–23

Bennett, J, (ed) 1995 *Minera: Lead Mines and Quarries*. Wrexham: Wrexham Maelor Borough Council

Bevan-Evans, M, 1960 Gadlys and Flintshire lead mining in the eighteenth century, Part 1, *Flintshire Hist Soc J*, **18**, 75–130

Bevan-Evans, M, 1961 Gadlys and Flintshire lead mining in the eighteenth century, Part 2, *Flintshire Hist Soc J*, **19**, 32–60

Bevan-Evans, M, 1962 Gadlys and Flintshire lead mining in the eighteenth century, Part 3, *Flintshire Hist Soc J*, **20**, 58–89

Bick, D, 1985 *Dylife A famous Welsh lead mine*, revised edn. Newent

Bick, D, 1990 *The Old Metal Mines of Mid Wales*, Parts 4 and 5, 2nd edn. Newent

Bick, D, 1991 *The Old Metal Mines of Mid Wales*, Part 6. Newent

Bird, D, 2001 Aspects of Roman gold mining: Dolaucothi, Asturias and Pliny, in N J Higham (ed) *Archaeology of the Roman Empire: a Tribute to the Life and Works of Professor Barri Jones*, 265–75, BAR Int Ser 940. Oxford: British Archaeological Reports

Blockley, K, 1989a Excavations at the Romano-British settlement at Ffrith, Clwyd 1967–9, *Flintshire Hist Soc J*, **32**, 135–65

Blockley, K, 1989b *Excavations at Prestatyn 1984–5*, BAR Brit Ser 210. Oxford: British Archaeological Reports

Briggs, C S, The conservation of non-ferrous mines, in Briggs (ed) 1992 *Welsh Industrial Heritage: A Review*, 32–41, CBA Res Rep 79. London: Council for British Archaeology

Britnell, W J, 2004 Elan Valley Historic Landscape: Historic Landscape Characterization, Unpubl rep, Clwyd-Powys Archaeological Trust Rep 613.

Available: http://www.cpat.org.uk/projects/longer/histland/histland.htm

Britnell, W J and Martin, C H R, 1999 Dyffryn Tanat Historic Landscape: Historic Landscape Characterization, Unpubl rep, Clwyd-Powys Archaeological Trust Rep 319. Available: http://www.cpat.org.uk/projects/longer/histland/histland.htm

Britnell, W J, Martin, C H R, & Hankinson, R, 2000 Holywell Common and Halkyn Mountain Historic Landscape: Historic Landscape Characterization, Unpubl rep, Clwyd-Powys Archaeological Trust Rep 357. Available: http://www.cpat.org.uk/projects/longer/histland/histland.htm

Burnham, B C, 1997 Roman mining at Dolaucothi: the implications of the 1991–3 excavations near the Carreg Pumsaint, *Britannia* **28**, 325–36

Burt, R, Waite, P and Burnley, R, 1992 *The Mines of Flintshire and Denbighshire*. Exeter

Cadw 1998 *Landscapes of Historic Interest in Wales, Part 2 of the Register of Landscapes, Parks and Gardens of Special Historic Interest in Wales: Part 2.1 Landscapes of Outstanding Historic Interest*. Cardiff: Cadw Welsh Historic Monuments. Available: http://www.ccw.gov.uk

Cadw 2001 *Landscapes of Historic Interest in Wales, Part 2 of the Register of Landscapes, Parks and Gardens of Special Historic Interest in Wales: Part 2.2 Landscapes of Special Historic Interest*. Cardiff: Cadw Welsh Historic Monuments. Available: http://www.ccw.gov.uk

Cadw 2003. *Guide to good practice on using the Register of Historic Landscapes of Historic Interest in Wales in the planning and development process*. Cardiff: Cadw

Campbell, S D G and Hains, B A, 1988 *Deeside (North Wales) Thematic Geological Mapping. British Geological Survey Onshore Geology Series*, Technical Report WA/88/2. Nottingham: Brit Geological Survey

Craddock, P and Lang, J (eds) 2003 *Mining and Metal Production through the Ages*. London: British Museum Press

Crew, P, and Crew, S, (eds) 1990 *Early Mining in the British Isles*, Plas Tan y Bwlch Occasional Paper 1. Maentwrog.

Davies, E, 1949 *Prehistoric and Roman Remains of Flintshire.* Cardiff

Davies, O, 1935 *Roman Mines in Europe.* Oxford

Davies, O, 1938 Ancient mines in Montgomeryshire ' Part 4, *Montgomeryshire Collect,* 44, 55–60

Davies, W, 1810 A General View of the Agriculture and Domestic Economy of North Wales. London

Down, C G, 1980 *Manganese Mines of North Wales.* Sheffield: Northern Mines Research Society

Earp, J, 1958 *Mineral Veins in the Minera-Maeshafn District of North Wales,* Bulletin of the Geological Survey of Great Britain 14, 44–69

Ebbs, C, 1993 *The Milwr Tunnel. Bagillt to Loggerheads 1897–1987.* Llanferres

Ellis, B, 1995 Quarrying and limeburning, in Bennett (ed) 1995

Ellis, B, 1998 *The History of Halkyn Mountain.* Wrexham

Evans, D L, 1929 *Flintshire Ministers' Accounts 1328–53,* Flintshire Hist Soc Rec Ser 2

Ford, T D and Willies, L (eds) 1994 *Mining Before Powder: Papers presented at the Georgius Agricola 500th Anniversary Conference, Ambleside, Cumbria, March 1994,* Bulletin of the Peak District Mines Historical Soc, 12, No 3

Foster-Smith, J R, 1972 *The Non-ferrous Mines of Denbighshire,* British Mining 5. Billingham: Northern Cavern and Mine Research Society

Foster-Smith, J R, 1974 *The Non-ferrous Mines of Flintshire,* British Mining 7. Billingham: Northern Cavern and Mines Research Society

Frere, S S, 1989 Roman Britain in 1988, *Britannia,* 20, 258–326

Frost, P, 1994 Clwyd Metal Mines Survey 1993: Consultation Draft, Unpubl rep, Clwyd-Powys Archaeological Trust Rep 88

Hall, G W, 1993 *Metal Mines of Southern Wales.* Kington

Hesketh, G E, 1955 An account of excavations in the cave in Big Covert, Maeshafn, Llanferres, *Flintshire Hist Soc J,* 15, 141–8

Hawkins, D, 1985 The Groves of Cwm Elan, *Trans Radnorshire Soc* 60, 45–9

Hoover, H and L (trans) 1912 *De re metallica / Georgius Agricola; translated from the first Latin ed. of 1556.* London

Hughes, S, 1988 *The Archaeology of the Montgomeryshire Canal.* Royal Commission on the Ancient and Historical Monuments of Wales

Hughes, S J S and Mason, J 1992 Results of Investigations at Van Mine near Llanidloes, July 1992, Unpubl rep, S J S Hughes Mining Reports

Jones, G D B, 1961 Montgomeryshire. Caersws: the Roman road system, *Bull Board Celtic Stud* 19, 177–92

Jones, N W, 2002 Clive Engine House, Talargoch Mine, Dyserth, Denbighshire, Unpubl rep, Clwyd-Powys Archaeological Trust Rep 472

Jones, N W and Frost, P, 1995 Powys Metal Mines Ground Survey 1995, Unpubl rep, Clwyd-Powys Archaeological Trust Rep 111

Jones, N W and Frost, P, 1996 Clwyd Metal Mines Ground Survey 1995, Unpubl rep, Clwyd-Powys Archaeological Trust Rep 165

Jones, N W and Frost, P, 1997 Nantygarw Lead Mines, Powys: archaeological ground survey, Unpubl rep, Clwyd-Powys Archaeological Trust Rep 248

Jones, O T, 1922 *Lead and Zinc. The Mining District of North Cardiganshire and West Montgomeryshire,* Memoirs of the Geological Survey Special Reports on the Mineral Resources of Great Britain 20

Judge, C W, 1997 *The Elan Valley Railway: The Railway of the Birmingham Corporation Waterworks.* Usk

Kidner, R W, 2003 *The Mid-Wales Railway.* Usk

Lewis, A, 1994 Bronze Age mines of the Great Orme: interim report, in Ford and Willies (eds) 1994, 31–6

Lewis, P R and Jones, G D B, 1969 The Dolaucothi gold mines I: the surface evidence, *Archaeol J,* 49, 244–72

Lewis, W J, 1966 Lead Mining in eastern Montgomeryshire in 1751, *Montgomeryshire Collect,* 58, 114–24

Lewis, W J, 1967 *Lead Mining in Wales.* Cardiff: University of Wales Press

Lewis, W J, 2000 James Baker and the Pool Quay Smelthouse, *Montgomeryshire Collect,* 88, 25–35

Linnard, W, 2000 *Welsh Woods and Forests. A History.* Llandysul

Lowe, J, 1985 *Welsh Country Workers Housing 1775–1875.* Cardiff: National Museum of Wales

Mansergh, J, 1894. The Birmingham water scheme, in R E Tickell (ed), *The Vale of Nantgwilt: A Submerged Valley,* 11–17. London

Moore-Colyer, R, 2002 *Welsh Cattle Drovers.* Ashbourne

Morgan, D, 1994 Archaeological Investigation at the Gowdal Lead Mine, Holywell, Unpubl rep, Greenfield Heritage Park, Flintshire County Council

Murphy, M, 1997 Maria's Dreams: Lady Mary Herbert, 1685–1775, *Montgomeryshire Collect* 85, 87–100

Murphy, M, 1998 Maria's Dreams: the reckoning, *Montgomeryshire Collect* 86, 65–80

Musson, C R and Northover, J P, 1989 Llanymynech hillfort, Powys and Shropshire: observations on construction work, 1981, *Montgomeryshire Collect,* 77, 15–26

North, F J, 1962 *Mining for Metals in Wales.* Cardiff: National Museum of Wales

O'Leary, T J, Blockley, K and Musson, C R, 1989 *Pentre Farm, Flint 1976–81: an official building in the Roman lead mining district,* BAR Brit Ser 207. Oxford: British Archaeological Reports

Palmer, M and Neaverson, P, 1989 Nineteenth-century

tin and lead dressing: a comparative study of the field evidence, *Industrial Archaeol Rev*, **12**, No 1, 20–39

Pratt, D, 1962 The lead mining community at Minera in the 14th century, *Denbighshire Hist Soc Trans*, **11**, 28–36

Pratt, D, 1976 Minera: township of mines, *Denbighshire Hist Soc Trans*, **25**, 114–54

Putnam, W G, 1962 Excavations at Pen-y-crocbren, *Montgomeryshire Collect*, **57**, 34–41

Rees, D M, 1968 Copper mining in north Wales, *Archaeol Cambrensis*, **117**, 172–97

Rogers, I, 1995 An Archaeological Survey of Pennant Lead Mine, Rhuallt, Denbighshire, Unpubl rep, Gifford and Partners Project Rep 6421

Sharpe, A, 1992 *St Just – An Archaeological Survey of the Mining District.* Cornwall Archaeological Unit

Sharpe, A, 1993 *Minions – An Archaeological Survey of the Caradon Mining District.* Cornwall Archaeological Unit

Silvester, R J, 1993 The Minera Halvans Site, *Industrial Archaeology Review*, **15**, 208–10

Smith, B, 1921 *Lead and Zinc Ores in the Carboniferous Rocks of North Wales*, Memoirs of the Geol Survey 19, HMSO, Sheffield

Smith, L T, (ed), 1907–10. *The Itinerary of John Leland the Antiquary, in or about the years 1535–45*, 5 vols. London.

Thomas, G C G, (ed) 1997 *The Charters of the Abbey of Ystrad Marchell.* Aberystwyth: National Library of Wales

Thorburn, J A, 1986 *Talargoch Mine (Clwyd).* Sheffield: Northern Mines Research Society

Timberlake, S, 1990 Excavations at Parys Mountain and Nantyreira, in Crew and Crew (eds) 1990, 15–21

Timberlake, S, 1996 Llanymynech-Ogof copper mine, *Archaeology in Wales*, **36**, 68–70

Timberlake, S, 1998 Survey of early metal mines within the Welsh uplands, *Archaeology in Wales*, **38**, 79–81

Timberlake, S and Mason, J, 1997 Ogof Wyddon, Machynlleth, *Archaeology in Wales*, **37**, 62–5

Tomlin, R S O, Frere, S and Roxan, M (eds) 1990 *The Roman inscriptions of Britain. Vol 2 – Instrumentum domesticum (Personal belongings and the like)*, fasc 1. Gloucester

Walters, M 1994 Powys Metal Mines Survey 1993, Unpubl rep, Clwyd-Powys Archaeological Trust Rep 89

Webster, G, 1952–3 The lead-mining industry in North Wales in Roman times, *Flintshire Hist Soc J*, **13**, 5–33

White, R, 1995 *A Landscape of the Lead Mining Industry: the Yorkshire Dales*, in M Palmer and P Neaverson (eds) *Managing the Industrial Landscape*, 61–6, Leicester University Mongraphs 2

Whittick, G C, 1982 The earliest Roman lead-mining on Mendip and in north Wales: a reappraisal, *Britannia*, **13**, 113–23

Williams, C J, 1980 *Metal Mines of North Wales.* Rhuddlan

Williams, C J, 1987 *The Lead Mines of the Alyn Valley.* Hawarden: Flintshire Hist Soc

Williams, C J, 1994 The mining laws in Flintshire and Denbighshire, *Bulletin of the Peak District Mines Historical Soc*, **12**, No 3, 62–8

Williams, D H, 1997 Book review, *Montgomeryshire Collect*, **85**, 128–30

Williams, D N, 1993 Archaeological Field Evaluation, Van Lead Mines, Llanidloes, Unpubl rep, Glamorgan Gwent Archaeological Trust Rep 93/076

Williams, J, 1905 *A General History of the County of Radnor.* Brecon

Williams, R A, 1985 *The Old Mines of the Llangynog District*, British Mining 26. Sheffield: Northern Mines Research Society

INDEX

Illustrations are denoted by page numbers in *italics*. Principal descriptions are indicated by page numbers in **bold**. For individual mines see also the gazetteer (166–75)